DREAMS OF A WOMAN

GOD'S PLAN FOR FULFILLING YOUR DREAMS

DREAMS OF A WOMAN

GOD'S PLAN FOR FULFILLING YOUR DREAMS

SHARON JAYNES

TYNDALE

Tyndale House Publishers, Inc.
Wheaton, Illinois

ISBN: 1-58997-156-6

A Focus on the Family book published by
Tyndale House Publishers, Wheaton, Illinois 60189

"I Dreamed A Dream"
From the musical *Les Miserables*
By Alain Boublil and Claude-Michel Schonberg
Music by Claude-Michel Schonberg
Lyrics by Alain Boublil, Herbert Kretzmer and Jean-Marc Natel

All Scripture quotations, unless otherwise indicated, are taken from the *Holy Bible, New International Version*®. NIV®. Copyright © 1973, 1978, 1984 by International Bible Society. Used by permission of Zondervan Publishing House. All rights reserved. Scripture quotations marked (NKJV) are taken from the *New King James Version*. Copyright © 1982 by Thomas Nelson, Inc. Used by permission. All rights reserved. Scripture quotations marked (NASB) are taken from the *New American Standard Bible* ®. Copyright The Lockman Foundation 1960, 1962, 1963, 1968, 1971, 1972, 1973, 1975, 1977, 1995. Used by permission (www.Lockman.org).

Focus on the Family books are available at special quantity discounts when purchased in bulk by corporations, organizations, churches, or groups. Special imprints, messages, and excerpts can be produced to meet your needs. For more information, contact: Focus on the Family Sales Department, 8605 Explorer Drive, Colorado Springs, CO 80920; or phone (800) 932-9123.

Editors: Kathy Davis and Jean Stephens
Cover Design: Sally Leatherman
Cover Photo: Russ Miller Studio

Library of Congress Cataloging-in-Publication Data
Jaynes, Sharon.
    Dreams of a woman : God's plan for fulfilling your dreams / by Sharon Jaynes.—1st ed.
        p. cm.
    Includes bibliographical references.
    ISBN 1-58997-156-6
    1. Christian women—Religious life. I. Title.
    BV4527 .J385 2004
    248.8'43—dc22   2003017589

Printed in the United States of America
1 2 3 4 5 6 7 8 9 / 10 09 08 07 06 05 04

To my husband, Steve—the man of my dreams.
The moment I met you I felt as though I had known you all my life,
for I had dreamed of you from my earliest remembrance.

Contents

Acknowledgments

I am deeply indebted to the many women who have shared their dreams with me: Gayle Montgomery, Anabel Gillham, Madeline Rives, Louise Wright (my mother), Genia Rogers, Suzi Kallam, Cynthia Price, Luanne Johnson, Patricia Dilling, Amanda Bailey, and Wendy Ellis—just to name a few. I have been blessed by your transparency and willingness to share your heart with so many others.

A special thanks to:

Judie Lawson for sharing her gifts and talents in the words of "Wedding Feast of the Lamb."

Barbara Givens and Linda Eppley for being mighty prayer warriors on my behalf.

Mark Maddox, Stacey Herebic, and Edie Hutchinson of Focus on the Family for believing in this project and the work of Proverbs 31 Ministries.

Kathy Davis for her editing expertise and sweet spirit.

Yvette Maher for her passion to encourage and equip women.

Joe and Barb Spencer, my Shanghai pals, for their enduring friendship and comic relief after arduous days of writing.

My husband, Steve, and son, Steven, for enduring stacks of papers on the kitchen table and listening to me read and reread parts of the manuscript.

The incredible staff of Proverbs 31 Ministries: Lysa TerKeurst, Bonnie

Schulte, Marie Ogram, Shelly Chen, Glynnis Whitwer, Laurie Webster, Scott Ogram, Sherri Killion, Van Walton, Renee Swope, Mary Southerland, and Sharon Hodde. I am constantly in awe of your gifts, talents, and obedience to God's call to minister to women.

My *tas philos* Bible study. What a blessing each of you have been in my life.

Introduction

I sat in the darkened opera hall and watched as Fantine, the leading lady in the musical *Les Miserables,* sang a lament about her life. She clutched her chest and spilled her heart to the invisible audience peering from the darkness.

> I dreamed a dream in days gone by
> when hope was high and life worth living.
> I dreamed that love would never die.
> I dreamed that God would be forgiving.
>
> Then I was young and unafraid
> and dreams were made and used and wasted.
> There was no ransom to be paid,
> no song unsung, no wine untasted.
>
> But the tigers come at night
> with their voices soft as thunder.
> As they tear your hope apart,
> as they turn your dream to shame.
>
> He slept a summer by my side.
> He filled my days with endless wonder.

He took my childhood in his stride.
But he was gone when autumn came.

And still I dreamed he'd come to me,
that we would live the years together.
But there are dreams that cannot be,
and there are storms we cannot weather.

I had a dream my life would be
so diff'rent from this hell I'm living,
so diff'rent now from what it seemed.
Now life has killed the dream I dreamed.[1]

When she finished singing and the house lights went up, I noticed many people, both men and women, sat with tears trickling down their cheeks. I don't believe the tears were solely in sympathy for the character on stage. They were also for the disappointments in the lives of those in the audience: for misspent years, for the broken promises, for the unattained goals, for the life that killed the dreams they dreamed.

This was not simply the song of a character in a play. It was the song of many women around the world. Perhaps their dreams were not shattered in the same way as Fantine's, but many were forlorn because life simply hadn't turned out as they had hoped it would.

As a little girl, I read the story of Cinderella time and time again. I wanted so much to be a beautiful princess and be carried away by a handsome prince. Cinderella was doomed to scrubbing floors, but then she received a beautiful dress and finally met her handsome prince. However, in real life we are more likely to meet our handsome prince, get the beautiful dress, and then live the rest of life scrubbing floors! Author and Bible teacher Beth Moore said it this way:

The enemy is an expert archer with lots of practice aiming fiery darts. When women are the targets, often the bull's-eye is childhood dreams or expectations. We grew up believing in Cinderella, yet some of us feel as if our palace turned out to be a duplex, our prince turned out to be a frog, and the wicked stepmother turned out to be our mother-in-law. Our fairy godmother apparently lost our addresses.[2]

When I was a little girl, I had many dreams, but five are prominent pictures in my mind. Now that I am in my forties, I realize that most women I meet had similar longings. I dreamed I would have a daddy who loved me like the ones I saw walking through the park with their little girls hand-in-hand; that one day I would be a bride in a flowing satin gown waltzing down a long, red-carpeted church aisle; that I would be a mommy with a houseful of children to adore and be adored by; that I would be beautiful like a princess in a fairy tale; and that I would have a lifelong best friend.

I asked my friend Linda what she dreamed of being when she was a little girl. She answered, "I wanted to be a princess." Then she quickly tried to correct herself through her giggles. "No, I'm just kidding. Let me think a minute." But she wasn't kidding. It was a moment of truth, and she felt embarrassed to admit it. Our childhood dreams linger long after the gray hairs and wrinkles replace our youthful glow.

As this idea of the dreams of a woman unfolded in my heart, I began to survey women across the country about their childhood dreams. The list reads like a stroll down the Barbie aisle in the toy store: gymnast, astronaut, teacher, nurse, nun, career woman, TV anchor, veterinarian, missionary, dancer, flight attendant, singer, and so on. But the five most common dreams of women were the same as mine: to have a daddy who loved them, to be a bride, to be a mommy, to be beautiful, and to have a best friend.

In *Dreams of a Woman* we will take a look at those five childhood dreams. We will study women in the Bible: Sarah, who interfered with God's plan and made her dream come to pass on her own; Naomi, who forgot her dream but watched God restore it through Ruth; and Esther, who fulfilled God's dream for her life even though it was very different from her own.

We will also look at shattered dreams, which are inevitable; restored dreams, which are sometimes inconceivable; and interrupted dreams, which can be for our instruction.

You'll meet many women along the way who will share their dreams, their personal struggles, and victories. Don't be surprised if you see your heart's desires, disappointments, and daring hopes for the future penned in the words of a woman you haven't met. Whether I spoke with a woman with a six-figure income or a woman in a homeless shelter, the dreams of women are much the same.

So far, life may not have turned out as you had hoped or expected, but it can be even better than you imagined. You may even discover that God indeed fulfilled your dreams, but you didn't recognize them because He did not fulfill them in the way you anticipated.

Some of us need to learn how to dream again, discover God's dreams for our lives, and then begin the exciting journey that God planned all along. He can surpass our dreams when we place our hand in His.

PART ONE

Little Girls' Dreams

1

To Have a Daddy Who Loves Me

Once upon a time, not so very long ago or far away, a baby girl was born to parents who could not keep her. Neither parent was willing to release her for adoption, but neither was able to care for her. So while the legal system shuffled her case back and forth, the baby girl grew into a toddler in a foster home.

Her care was certainly adequate, her physical needs were met, and she never went hungry. Her clothes, though not new, were never dirty. Her toys, though not her own, were always sufficient. This little girl was not mistreated or abused, and yet, in her heart was a hollow space. She desperately wanted what she had never had—a mommy and a daddy of her own.

Only a few doors from the foster home lived a kind couple with a teenage son. The family wanted a little girl, the little girl needed a family, and the details of a trying and lengthy adoption were worked out. And while this little girl received a wonderful mommy and an adoring big brother, her relationship with her daddy was extra special.

Ashley was two years old when she entered his life. She was thin, pale, and clingy. By the time the adoption was finally complete, she was almost three. Ashley had never seen the ocean, eaten a Happy Meal, or slept in a bed in a room of her own.

"I never knew my dad cared about me, let alone loved me. I grew up with abuse and being shipped back and forth from parent to parent. No roots, no identity, no love, no security."—*Debbie*

A few months after the adoption, Ashley traveled to the beach for her first family reunion. She was overwhelmed with excitement and pride. She had received so much so fast, and it was hard to take it all in. Ashley asked everyone she met if they were part of her family. "Are you my aunt?" "Are you my uncle?" "Are you my cousin?" She ran from person to person showering hugs and kisses on her newly acquired family. "I love you!" she told them. "I love you all!"

When her new daddy took her to McDonald's for the first time, Ashley didn't join the other children on the playground equipment. She was too busy asking important questions: "Do you have a daddy? I have a daddy! See, that's my daddy over there," she exclaimed with excitement and wonder. "Isn't he wonderful?"

"What's your name?" she asked. "My name is Ashley Jordan *Ambrose,* just like my daddy. I'm named after my daddy!"

Five years later, tanned, transformed, and confident, Ashley returned to the annual family reunion. This time she brought a scrapbook of pictures to share with anyone who would sit still long enough to look and listen. "This is my story," she would say. "See, this is where I lived before Mommy and Daddy adopted me. They picked me out special. See, this is my room now. It's all my own. And these are my toys and my own clothes, and here's a picture of my kitty and one of my dog and . . . "

Ashley has love overflowing for everyone, but no one is higher on her list than her daddy. He knows how to polish toenails, drip sand castles, tie hair ribbons, hold her in the night—and he calls her his little princess. [1]

My Dream

When I was a little girl, my father spent most of his waking hours working at his building supply company, observing construction sites, and socializing with his colleagues and associates. Even though his place of business was only a few blocks from our home, his heart was miles away in a place I could not find.

My father didn't drink alcohol every day, but when he did, it consumed him. Dad was filled with a rage that always seemed to be hiding just beneath the surface of his tough skin. And when he drank, that rage spewed out like hot lava onto those around him. Unfortunately, my mother was the most common target.

As a child, many nights I crawled into bed, pulled the covers tightly under my chin or even over my head, and prayed that I would quickly fall asleep to shut out the noise of my parents yelling, fighting, and hitting. Occasionally I'd tiptoe over to my pink ballerina jewelry box, wind up the music key in the back, and try to focus on the tinkling sound as the ballerina twirled with her hands overhead.

I was afraid of my father. Even when he was sober, I kept my distance. At the same time, I observed how other daddies cherished their little girls.

I saw them cuddle them in their laps, hold their hands while walking in the park, or kiss their cheeks as they dropped their daughters off at school in the mornings.

Deep in my heart, a dream was birthed. I dreamed that one day, I would have a daddy who loved me—not because I was pretty or made good grades or could play the piano well, but just because I was his. I dreamed that one day I would be a cherished daughter.

A Common Dream

In speaking to women across the country, I have seen eyes fill with tears when I talk about my dream of having a daddy who loved me. But the tears are not for me. Rather, they reveal the longing in the hearts of these women.

"Butterfly Kisses," a song by Bob Carlisle that climbed the charts in 2000, received international recognition in both the Christian and secular music industries. The song was about the tender love between a father and his daughter, starting from her birth to her wedding day. Mr. Carlisle said, "I get a lot of mail from young girls who try to get me to marry their moms. That used to be a real chuckle because it's so cute, but then I realized they didn't want romance for mom. They want the father that is in that song, and that just kills me."[2]

Our modern society has downplayed the importance of fathers over the past 40 years. Television programs such as *Leave It to Beaver, Father Knows Best,* and *Make Room for Daddy* portrayed dads as a wellspring of wisdom, compassion, and guidance.

By the end of the sixties, that began to change. In 1971, *All in the Family* featured Archie Bunker, a bigoted, bungling oppressor. Then came Tim Taylor of *Home Improvement* with the recurring theme of Tim messing something up and his wife, Jill, straightening it out. I could go on with *The Simpsons, Roseanne,* and even the *Berenstain Bears* cartoons. In the nineties, Murphy Brown (played by Candace Bergen) announced to the world that children really didn't need a father at all. Suffice it to say that now fathers on television are more likely to be portrayed as obstacles than as overcomers of obstacles.

"I dreamed I would have a daddy who spent time with me, loved me, and defended me."—*Lisa*

In 1995, about 40 percent of American children went to sleep in homes in which their fathers did not live.[3] The 2000 census showed that 84 percent of children in America who live in single-parent families live with their mothers.[4] The feminist movement has tried to teach women that they do not need men—fathers or husbands. In 2000, an article in *Time* magazine suggested that remaining unmarried can be "incredibly empowering for women," even when the choice involves raising children without the presence of a father.[5] "Who needs men?" some women taunt.

I'll tell you who—children. All the feminist rhetoric has not erased the deep-seated need that women have tucked in the recesses of their hearts—to be fathered by the father of their dreams. Little girls want a daddy to protect them, help them, guide them, nurture them, and cheer them on through the struggles of life. That relationship changes when a father takes his daughter's hand and places it into the hand of her husband on her wedding day. But she still longs to know that she has a special, treasured place in her daddy's heart.

The Invitation

In the Old Testament, God has many names. He is Elohim, the Creator; El Elyon, God Most High; El Roi, the God who sees; El Shaddai, the

All-Sufficient One; Adonai, the Lord; Jehovah, the Self-Existent One; Jehovah-Jireh, the Lord Will Provide; Jehovah-Rapha, the Lord that heals; Jehovah-Shalom, the Lord is peace; Jehovah-Raah, the Lord my Shepherd; and many more. His covenant name with the people of Israel was I AM. In *Knowing God,* J. I. Packer states, "He is: and it is because He is what He is that everything else is as it is."[6]

In the New Testament, Jesus introduced a new name for God: Father. It is the name that Jesus referred to more than any other and the name that He invites us to use to address the creator of the universe. Think about that for a moment. The God of the universe who created the heavens and the earth; who always has been and always will be; who is all-knowing, all-powerful, and present everywhere at once—that same God invites you to call Him Daddy!

When the disciples asked Jesus to teach them how to pray, He said:

"But when you pray, go into your room, close the door and pray to your *Father,* who is unseen. Then your *Father,* who sees what is done in secret, will reward you. And when you pray, do not keep on babbling like pagans, for they think they will be heard because of their many words. Do not be like them, for your *Father* knows what you need before you ask him. This, then, is how you should pray: Our *Father* in heaven, hallowed be your name. . . ." (Matthew 6:6-9, italics added)

J. I. Packer wrote, "For everything that Christ taught, everything that makes the New Testament new and better than the Old, everything that is distinctly Christian as opposed to merely Jewish, is summed up in the knowledge of the fatherhood of God."[7] All other religions demand followers to worship created beings such as Mohammad or Buddha. But Jehovah the Creator, the great I AM, invites us to crawl up in His lap, become His child, and call Him Abba, Daddy. He said, "I will be a Father to you, and you will be my sons and daughters" (2 Corinthians 6:18).

The Only Perfect Parent

For many women, the idea of God being their father may not be a pleasant one. We have a human tendency to project our perception of fatherhood, based on our experiences with our earthly fathers, onto our idea of the fatherhood of God. Some of us never knew our earthly fathers, some had abusive fathers, some of us were deserted by our fathers, some of us lost our fathers to sickness or catastrophe, and some had loving, endearing fathers.

When I was growing up, I never had lengthy conversations with my father. Therefore, when I became a Christian it was very difficult for me to have lengthy conversations with my heavenly Father. Prayer was difficult. We need to remove the mask of our earthly fathers from the face of God. Even the best earthly fathers have feet of clay and will disappoint their children.

"I was never a daddy's girl in real life, but I always dreamt I was."
—*Loretta*

No matter what your past experience with your earthly father has been, your heavenly Father is the perfect Parent. He loves you, cares for your every need, is interested in all you do, skillfully guides you, wisely trains you, never deserts you, is always available to you, and cherishes you as His precious child.

God has made a way for us to clearly understand what He is like. If we want to know the Father, the only perfect Parent, we have but to look at the life of His Son. Jesus said, "Anyone who has seen me has seen the Father. . . . The words I say to you are not just my own. Rather, it is the Father, living in me, who is doing his work" (John 14:9-10). The writer of Hebrews explained, "The Son is the radiance of God's glory and the exact representation of his being, sustaining all things by his powerful word" (Hebrews 1:3). If you understand what Jesus is like, you understand what God is like. And the more intimately you know the Son, the more clearly you understand the character of the Father.

Adoption

One reason Ashley's story at the beginning of this chapter is so precious to me is because she was adopted. The Bible says that you and I have also been adopted (Ephesians 1:5) and made God's heirs (Galatians 4:7). Let's look at how adoption was carried out in Jesus' day.

In ancient Rome, fathers chose a child for adoption when they weren't able to have children of their own. They adopted a son in order to have someone to carry on the family name and inherit their property. It was a legal relationship: All ties to the child's natural family were severed, and the child was placed in a new family with the same prestige and privileges of a natural child, including becoming an heir. If the child had any debt, it was immediately cancelled. The adoption was a sealed process with many witnesses making it official.[8]

In modern times, we tend to think of adopting a baby. However, in biblical times adoption usually took place after the child was older and had proved to be fit to carry on the family name in a worthy manner.[9] How incredible that our heavenly Father chose us, not because of any merit of our own, but before the beginning of time. He chose us, not because we were worthy, but in spite of the fact that we were not:

For he chose us in him *before the creation of the world* to be holy and blameless in his sight. In love he predestined us to be adopted as his sons through Jesus Christ, in accordance with his pleasure and will—to the praise of his glorious grace, which he has freely given us in the One he loves. (Ephesians 1:4-6, italics added)

Our adoption takes place the moment we accept Jesus Christ as our Lord and Savior. Our debt is canceled (paid in full), and we are placed in God's family to carry on His name and become an heir: "And you also were included in Christ [in His family] when you heard the word of truth, the gospel of your salvation. Having believed, you were marked in him with a seal, the promised Holy Spirit, who is a deposit guaranteeing our inheritance until the redemption of those who are God's possession—to the praise of his glory" (Ephesians 1:13-14). "He anointed us, set his seal of ownership on us, and put his spirit in our hearts as a deposit, guaranteeing what is to come" (2 Corinthians 1:21-22).

Many verses refer to God's children as sons. This does not mean that God has only male children or that only male children inherit the kingdom of God. In her book *In My Father's House,* Mary Kassian explains:

In the Hebrew language the word *son* can be used figuratively to characterize people as to their **origin** and **nature.** Hence, we see such expressions as "sons of the prophets" (Acts 3:25, NKJV), "sons of the resurrection" (Luke 20:36, NKJV), "a son of peace" (Luke 10:6) . . . Thus, the biblical term *sons of men* means "humans," people of mortal origin and character . . . Understanding the biblical term *son* helps clarify that the term *sons of God* does not mean "male offspring." In calling believers His sons, God is communicating that believers find their origin in Him and bear the same nature He does.[10]

The apostle Paul wrote to the Galatians, "You are all sons of God through faith in Christ Jesus, for all of you who were baptized into Christ have clothed yourselves with Christ. There is neither Jew nor Greek, slave nor free, male nor female, for you are all one in Christ Jesus" (Galatians 3:26-28).

"I was a daddy's girl. When I entered a room, my daddy's eyes would sparkle and a big smile would spread over his face. He always would take me places with him and show me off. We were inseparable."—Karen

In J. I. Packer's words, "Adoption is a family idea, conceived in terms of love, and viewing God as father. In adoption, God takes us into His family and fellowship, and establishes us as His children and heirs. Closeness, affection and generosity are at the heart of the relationship. To be right with God the judge is a great thing, but to be loved and cared for by God the father is greater."[11]

A Daddy Who Protects Me

One of the wonderful benefits of embracing the truth that we are children of God is the removal of fear: "For you did not receive a spirit that makes you a slave again to fear, but you received the Spirit of sonship. And by him we cry, 'Abba, Father.' The Spirit himself testifies with our spirit that we are God's children. Now if we are children, then we are heirs—heirs of God and co-heirs with Christ" (Romans 8:15-17). When we understand that God our Father is in total control of our lives, what is there to fear? Also, when we understand His fatherly concern and care, we do not need to be afraid of approaching Him with the burdens and worries of our everyday lives.

The first thing I needed to learn about my new Father was that He loves me. I grew up singing, "Jesus loves me! This I know, for the Bible tells me so," but I really didn't believe He did. It wasn't until I was much older that I learned about His unconditional love, His unfailing love, His unlimited love, and His undeniable access.

Unconditional Love

Anabel Gillham was a woman who loved God but had trouble accepting that God could love her. Sure, she knew the Bible verses that talked of God's unconditional love for her. Yet she knew herself and doubted that a God who knew her innermost thoughts would approve of her.

The root of her problem was how she saw God and how she believed God saw her. She knew what kind of God He was, but she believed she had to earn His love. Then God used a very special person to help Anabel understand the depths of God's love for her—her second child, Mason David Gillham, who was profoundly retarded. Anabel relates her story in her book, *The Confident Woman*.

Mace could sing one song with great gusto, just one: "Jesus Loves Me." He would throw his head back and hold on to the first "Yes" in the chorus just as long as he could, and then he would get tickled and almost fall out of his chair. I can still hear him giggle when I think back on those days that seem so distant and so far-away. How poignant that memory is to me.

I never doubted for a moment that Jesus loved that profoundly retarded little boy. It didn't matter that he would never sit with the kids in the back of the church and on a certain special night walk

17

down the aisle, take the pastor by the hand, and invite Jesus into his heart. It was entirely irrelevant that he could not quote a single verse of Scripture, that he would never go to high school, or that he would never be a dad. I knew that Jesus loved Mason.

What I could not comprehend, what I could not accept, was that Jesus could love Mason's mother, Anabel. You see, I believed that in order for a person to accept me, to love me, I had to perform for him. My standard for getting love was performance-based, so I "performed" constantly, perfectly. In fact, I did not allow anyone to see me when I was not performing perfectly. I never had any close friends because I was convinced that if a person ever really got to know me, he wouldn't like me.[12]

Anabel carried that belief into her relationship with God and was horrified to learn that He knew her every thought, let alone everything she said or did (Psalm 139:1-4). She realized that God knew her completely and saw when she wasn't "performing well." Because of her perception of performance-based acceptance, she concluded without a doubt that God could not possibly love her, that He could never like what He saw in her.

Mace could never have performed for his parents' love, or for anyone's love, but oh, how they loved him. His condition deteriorated to such a degree—and so rapidly—that they had to place him in an institution when he was very young. His parents enrolled him in the Enid State School for Mentally Handicapped Children. They drove regularly 120 miles to see him but occasionally also brought him home for a visit.

On one particular visit, Mace had been with them since Thursday evening. On the following Saturday afternoon God painted a vivid picture of His great love for Anabel through her mentally retarded son. She was standing at the kitchen sink, dreading what lay ahead. In just a few moments, she would be gathering Mace's things together and taking him back to his "house." She had done this many times before—and it was never easy—but today God had something in mind that would change her life forever.

As she was washing the dishes, Mason was sitting in his chair watching her, or at least he was looking at her. That's when it began. Her emotions were spinning, her stomach started tumbling with the familiar sickening thoughts of packing Mason's toys and his clothes and taking him away again. She stopped washing the dishes and got down on her knees in front of Mace. Anabel took his dirty little hands in hers and tried desperately to reach him.

"Mason, I love you. I love you. If only you could understand how much I love you," she cried.

He just stared. He couldn't understand; he didn't comprehend. She stood up and started on the dishes again, but that didn't last long. This sense of urgency—almost a panic—came over her. Once more she dried her hands and knelt in front of her precious little boy.

"My dear Mason, if only you could say to me, 'I love you, Mother.' I need that, Mace."

Nothing.

I stood up to the sink again. More dishes, more washing, more crying—and thoughts, foreign to my way of thinking, began filtering into my conscious awareness. I believe God spoke to me that day, and this is what He said: "Anabel, you don't look at your son and turn away in disgust because he's sitting there with saliva drooling out of his mouth; you don't shake your head, repulsed because he has dinner all over his shirt or because he's sitting in a dirty, smelly diaper when he ought to be able to take care of himself. Anabel, you don't reject Mason because all of the dreams you had for him have been destroyed. You don't reject him because he doesn't perform for you. You love him, Anabel, just because he is yours. Mason doesn't willfully reject your love, but you willfully reject Mine. I love you, Anabel, not because you're neat or attractive, or because you do things well, not because you perform for Me, but just because you're Mine."[13]

Hearing Anabel's story transformed my thinking about God's love for me. We have a heavenly Father who adores us, warts and all, just because we're His! It was what I had always dreamed of: a daddy who loved me as I was, not because I was pretty or made good grades or behaved like a little lady in public or could play the piano well or hit a baseball out of the park.

The New Testament word for the type of love that God has for us is *agape*.[14] This is unconditional, unchanging, unfathomable, immeasurable love. Like Anabel, my dreams have come true. I have a heavenly Father who loves me—just because I am His.

Unfailing Love

The year 2002 brought transition for me. I changed positions at the ministry where I work, my son packed up to go away to college, my thyroid went out of control and had to be purposely destroyed with radioactive iodine, my first book went out of print, the grocery store quit carrying my favorite coffee, and Revlon discontinued the eyeliner that I'd been using for 10 years. Like a little girl who had lost her best friend, I whined, "Doesn't anything ever stay the same? Isn't there one thing I can count on being the same tomorrow as it is today?"

Then I heard that gentle whisper I've grown to love: "'Though the mountains be shaken and the hills be removed, yet my unfailing love for you will not be shaken nor my covenant of peace be removed,' says the LORD, who has compassion on you" (Isaiah 54:10).

Yes, there is one thing that will never change—God's unfailing love for His children. The word *compassion* in Isaiah 54:10 is the Hebrew word *racham,* which means "to soothe; to cherish; to love deeply like parents; to be compassionate, be tender . . . This verb usually refers to a strong love which is rooted in some kind of natural bond, often from a superior one to an inferior. [Now here's the best part.] Small babies evoke this feeling."[15]

When my son, Steven, came into the world, a love was birthed in my heart that I never thought possible. Elizabeth Stone said it well: "To make a decision to have a child, it's momentous. It is to decide to have your heart go walking around outside of your body for the rest of your life."[16] That is how our heavenly Father feels about His children!

"When I think about my dreams of being a bride and even my relationship with my dad, I see how much impact he had on my life. He allowed me to be a kid and just have fun like kids should. When I was looking for a husband, I looked for someone just like my dad."—*Geneva*

The beautiful Hebrew word *hesed* is translated "unfailing love" in Isaiah 54:10. It is also often translated "loving-kindness," "steadfast love," "grace," "mercy," "faithfulness," "goodness," and "devotion." This word is used 240 times in the Old Testament and is considered one of the most important in the vocabulary of the Old Testament.[17] Why? Because God's unfailing love is one of the most important themes of the entire Bible. It is who He is and what He does (1 John 4:8).

Would you like to memorize half of a psalm in 10 seconds? Turn to Psalm 136. After each sentence, there is an echo: "His love endures forever." Say that sentence 26 times and you've quoted half of the psalm!

David begins by reminding us that God created the world, led the captives out of Egypt and through the desert, and conquered the enemies of the Israelites so they could move into the Promised Land. While God works in many varied ways and with many different people, one thing remains the same: "His love endures forever!"

Paul echoes David's words in his letter to the Romans: "For I am convinced that neither death nor life, neither angels nor demons, neither the present nor the future nor any powers, neither height nor depth, nor anything else in all creation, will be able to separate us from the love of God that is in Christ Jesus our Lord" (Romans 8:38). "His love endures forever!"

Unlimited Love

Cary and Madeline Rivers read about the overcrowded orphanages in Eastern Europe, and God stirred their hearts to look into adoption. Foreign adoptions are very costly, but God had blessed the couple financially, and the cost was not prohibitive. They decided to adopt not one, two, or three, but four children! After eight months and miles of red tape, the adoption process was complete, and the couple traveled across the ocean to gather their new family.

The arduous journey was 22 hours, so when they arrived at the Atlanta airport for a two-hour layover on the trip home, the parents decided to let the rambunctious boys run around the terminal to work off some of their energy. Of course, they never let their new sons out of their sight. After a short while, Madeline noticed one of the boys watching a man drinking at a water fountain. Because the child could not speak English, he was making hand motions and using body language to communicate. To Madeline's horror, the man reached in his pocket and handed her new son a dollar bill.

The little boy had learned how to beg by using his eyes, hands, and facial expressions. He had no idea of the riches that came with his adoption. His every need would be met by his new daddy. And even though he was now part of a family with great wealth, he continued to beg for what was freely his.

Oh, dear sister, do you see yourself in the little boy? Are you begging for handouts when your daddy owns "the cattle on a thousand hills"? Are you scavenging for crumbs when your heavenly Father has provided everything you need "for life and godliness through our knowledge of him who called us by his own glory and goodness" (2 Peter 1:3)?

"How great is the love the Father has lavished on us, that we should be called children of God!" (1 John 3:1). To lavish is to give freely, profusely, extravagantly, and abundantly. He doesn't give us everything we want when we want it. No father wants spoiled children. Rather, He gives us everything we need to become well-behaved children who bear His name well.

Undeniable Access

One of my favorite people is author and speaker Patsy Clairmont. We were discussing my first book on the telephone one day and trying to set up a time to meet face to face when she came to speak at a Women of Faith conference in my hometown.

I said, "Patsy, I'd love to spend some time with you before the conference, but I don't have a backstage pass. I won't have access to the part of the building where you will be."

"No problem," Patsy answered. "Just go to my book table and tell my son who you are. He'll bring you to me."

The day of the conference arrived, and I swam through a sea of women to reach Patsy's crowded book table. It wasn't hard to spot her son—a male version of Patsy herself. After proper introductions, Jason and I were off to find his mom. First we passed through heavy mahogany double doors that led to an area called The Crown Room, for the VIPs who attended professional basketball games and other events.

Then we stepped into an elevator that took us to the location where the speakers were tucked away. A stern-faced security guard pointed his finger in my face and announced, "You're not supposed to be here, young lady. Where's your backstage pass? You're going to be in a lot of trouble."

He whipped out his walkie-talkie and was about to use it. Before I could force one word out of my dry mouth, Patsy's son stepped forward, showed the guard his credentials, and gallantly stated, "She's with me."

"There is a lot of hurt when I think about having a daddy who loves me. I dreamed of long walks, talks, cuddles, and strong arms that would always be there to protect me. I dreamed of daddy's tears when his little girl got married, when he held my babies as they were born, and falling asleep in my rocking chair."—*Laura*

"That's right," I agreed when I once again found my tongue. "He's Patsy Clairmont's son, and I'm with him."

"Oh, okay then," the guard said, and he was off to seek other dangerous Christian women like me who were attending the conference.

I had a wonderful visit with Patsy and left the conference inspired by each one of the speakers. But perhaps the best lesson I learned was on that elevator ride. Revelation 12:10 says that Satan, "the accuser," stands before God accusing me day and night. He calls me "unworthy" and questions my credentials as he points his gnarly finger in my face and tells me I'm not good enough to pass through heaven's doors. But just when I begin to feel unworthy to approach the throne room, God's Son, like Patsy's son, steps forward and says, "Leave her alone. She's with me, and I'm all the credentials she needs."

In the Old Testament, there is a sense that God was unapproachable because of His holiness. In the temple, a veil separated the Holy of Holies where God resided from the other areas of the temple where the priests attended daily. The high priest entered the Holy of Holies only once a year, on the Day of Atonement. Before he could enter, the priest went through a rigorous ceremonial cleansing process. Bells were hemmed to the bottom of his robe and a rope was tied around his foot. The people outside listened for the tinkling bells to make sure the priest was still alive. If the sound ceased, they pulled the dead priest out by the rope.

But in the New Testament things changed. God was and is still the great and holy I AM. But He invites us to enter the Holy of Holies with the confidence of a child approaching her daddy. When Jesus died on the cross of Calvary, God tore the veil of the Holy of Holies from top to bottom, inviting all those who believe in Christ to enter with assurance and confidence (Mark 15:38). "Let us then approach the throne of grace with confidence, so that we may receive mercy and find grace to help us in our time of need" (Hebrews 4:16).

No longer do we have to offer blood sacrifices as they did in the Old Testament. Jesus Christ is our perfect High Priest who offered the perfect sacrifice—Himself.

> Therefore, brothers, since we have confidence to enter the Most Holy Place by the blood of Jesus, by a new and living way opened for us through the curtain, that is, his body, and since we have a great priest over the house of God, let us draw near to God with a sincere heart in full assurance of faith, having our hearts sprinkled to cleanse us from a guilty conscience and having our bodies washed with pure water. (Hebrews 10:19-22)

Just as the security guard pointed his gnarly finger in my face and told me I didn't have the right credentials to enter the secured area, Satan will tell us that we don't deserve access to the Father. Never fear, my friend. Just as Patsy's son showed his pass to allow me to enter the secured room, Jesus Christ will show His credentials that allow us to enter the throne room of God. As a child of God, you have undeniable access because God's Son is with you and in you—and He's all the credentials you need.

He Calls You by Name

Several people in my life never seem to remember my correct name. A few of my more popular aliases are Sarah James, Susan James, Shannon James, and Jane Jaynes. Then there are the people who can't remember me at all and don't even try to fish a name from their memory pool. To tell you the truth, it has never really bothered me. After all, I'm not very good with names either.

But names are very important to God. In the Bible, a person's name revealed a unique quality of his or her character. Moses meant "drawn out of water." Ruth meant "woman friend." Naomi meant "pleasant," but she changed it to Mara, which meant "bitter." Her two sons' names meant "puny" and "piney." Needless to say, these two fellows weren't strapping young he-men, and both died at an early age. If a person had an encounter with the living God, many times God changed his or her name to better fit the experiences He had planned for that person's future. Abram was changed to Abraham. Sarai was changed to Sarah. Saul was changed to Paul.

Yes, names are very important. When someone very dear to me forgot mine, it broke my heart. My father accepted Jesus as his Savior when I was 21 years old. The transformation I saw in him was nothing short of miraculous. One benefit I received was that he did learn to love me. In my father's later years, we had a very tender and dear relationship. But it was short-lived.

A few years after Dad committed his life to Christ, I noticed him becoming very forgetful. At first it was small matters: forgetting an order at work, misplacing his shoes or keys, not remembering what day it was, drawing a blank on a close friend's name. Then it progressed to more serious absentminded behavior: forgetting where he parked in a parking deck (and even which parking deck); coming home to take my mother to the market, forgetting he had already taken her an hour before; and becoming confused when taking measurements for cabinets, which he had been doing for over 40 years. In 1987, our greatest fears were confirmed. Dad had Alzheimer's disease. He was 55 years old.

My dad had been a tough guy as a young man. From the time he was 55 to 65, I watched a strapping, quick-witted entrepreneur reduced to a man who could not remember how to speak, button his shirt, or move a spoon from his plate to his mouth. But what pained me the most was the day he forgot my name. I still remember holding his face in my hands and saying, "Daddy, it's me. Do you know who I am?" But I was met only by a childish grin and eyes that seemed to look straight through me.

Names. They are important. In Isaiah 43:1, God says, "Do not fear, for I have redeemed you; I have called you by name; you are Mine!" (NASB). In Isaiah 49:1, the prophet announces, "Before I was born, the LORD called me; from my birth he has made mention of my name." Because you are God's child, He has called you by name, and the Bible promises He will never forget it. Your name is engraved on the palm of His hand (Isaiah 49:16).

On a Friday morning in May of 1996, the Lord graciously came and took my earthly father to his new home in glory. He's probably up there right now measuring for cabinets and working on all those mansions we've read so much about. His memory has been restored, and I look forward to the day when my earthly father and my heavenly Father welcome me with open arms and say, "Welcome, Sharon, my daughter, my child."

What a joy to have a Daddy who loves me.

2

To Be a Bride

When I was five years old, I remember wrapping a long white sheet around my slender body and a bath-sized towel around my head. Then I clutched a bouquet of plastic flowers to my chest and stood at the end of the long hallway of my parents' home. Suddenly, in my imagination, the sheet became a pearl-studded wedding gown with a satin train, and the towel became my lace veil. I could almost hear the trumpets sounding and the organ filling the air with the wedding march as I proceeded to waltz down the hall. Yes, all eyes were on me as the guests stood to honor the bride.

I had seen *The Sound of Music* and I wanted to have a wedding in a great cathedral as Sister Maria (played by Julie Andrews) did. Oddly enough, I never did make it to the end of the hallway to see who the groom would be. That didn't really matter. This was my dream about becoming a beautiful bride—not about becoming a wife. (Several years later, it did matter who would be at the end of that hallway!)

Little girls (and big girls) love to dream about becoming a bride. One of the most popular Barbie dolls is the Bride Barbie, and the women reading

29

Bride magazine are not necessarily engaged. Yes, most little girls dream of one day wearing the long satin dress with lacy trailing veil and walking down the aisle to meet the man of their dreams.

After the Wedding Comes the Marriage

Have you studied the face of a bride as she glides down the aisle? I don't think a woman ever looks lovelier—so full of hope and promise. But for many, what occurs after the couple says "I do" is not what they expected. As they light the unity candle and snuff out their individual candles, many begin snuffing out each other. They remember that the pastor said, "And the two shall become one," but they just aren't sure which one.

No matter what your marital state—married, divorced, single or widowed—most women dream of having the ideal union with a man to love, cherish, honor, and protect them. Most women dream of the day when they can walk down the red-carpeted aisle of a church, dressed in a flowing white gown, with misty-eyed friends and family standing in their honor.

Glancing through the magazine racks in the bookstore, I noticed several bride magazines, but when I asked where the groom magazines were located, the clerk just grinned. Of course there were none. The dream of having a wonderful wedding is strictly a female phenomenon. Most little boys do not dream of the day they will become a groom.

Samuel Gets a Bride

Various cultures have differing wedding customs. Let's take a journey back to the days of the Old Testament to discover the Hebrew traditions of selecting and preparing a bride for a groom. Instead of telling you the particulars, imagine with me for a moment. Think about an imaginary family living during the time of Jesus, somewhere in the Middle East.

Samuel was finally approaching the age of maturity. His father knew the day was coming as he saw the boy's beard thicken and his shoulders broaden. Yes, it was time for Abram to begin searching for a bride for his firstborn son.

On a warm summer morning, Abram set out to visit some of his friends from days gone by. He had made a mental list of the ones who had daughters within a few years of his son's age and plotted his course.

"Goodbye," Abram called to his son as Samuel worked diligently in the carpentry shop. "I may be gone for several days."

"I dreamed of being a bride with lots of beautiful lace,
roses, and a flowing gown."—*Yvonne*

"Where are you going?" Samuel asked.

"You'll find out soon enough," Abram replied. "You just take care of your mother, brothers, and sisters while I am away."

Stopping at many small villages along the way, Abram visited the homes of friends with prospective brides for his son. There were young girls of every shape, size, and stature, but when he saw Miriam, his spirit sang a victor's song. Her form was lovely, her eyes were like a dove's, and her silky black hair glistened in the sunlight as she played and cared for her younger brothers and sisters. Yes, she would be a lovely wife for his son.

After a dinner of roast lamb, fresh baked bread, and aged wine, Abram revealed the reason for his visit to Miriam's father. "I have come to seek a wife for my son Samuel," he explained. "I have watched your daughter, Miriam; how she serves others, cares for her younger siblings, and honors the God of Abraham, Isaac, and Jacob. Would you consider giving your daughter in marriage to my son?"

"It would be an honor for our families to join by such a union," Mathias agreed. "Please, send the boy to our home and we will make the necessary arrangements."

Abram rode his donkey home as quickly as the old animal could go. "Momma, Momma!" he exclaimed as he burst through the door of their home. "I've found the perfect wife for our son!"

"I don't think I even considered the possibility I would not get married. I dreamed I would marry a young, charming man like the ones I saw on TV. I did marry a charming young man, but things are not always as easy as they are for the fairy tale princesses. Funny how we never see Cinderella or Snow White thinking about paying bills or towing cars."—*Kristi*

"Was anyone going to tell me about this?" Samuel asked as he peeked his head through the door of his room.

"Son, you know it is tradition for your father to find your bride," his mother chided. "Now that he has, you are the first to know."

"Well, actually the second," Abram corrected.

"Tell me, Father, what is she like?"

"Why don't you find out for yourself? I've arranged for us to return to the house of Mathias tomorrow!"

That night, Samuel took a long bath, trimmed his beard, and chose a clean tunic for the next day's journey. His mother packed gifts for Miriam's family, the gold and silver for the price of the bride, and a scarlet tunic she had crafted several years ago for her future daughter-in-law. Of course there was no sleep in the house of Abram that night. Soon Samuel would meet his bride!

The following day, father and son set out for the house of Mathias. All the while, Samuel wondered what he would find at the end of their journey. When they arrived, a servant led their donkeys to the stable, and then the duo made their way to the front door. After they knocked only once, it slowly creaked open, and a set of onyx eyes like Samuel had never seen before met his gaze.

"Samuel," his father said, "I'd like you to meet Miriam."

The two nodded a greeting. Samuel was grateful for the thickness of the tunic that hid the pounding of his heart.

After dinner, Samuel followed the procedure he had practiced with his parents many times before.

"Mathias, son of Seth, I would like to ask permission to marry your daughter, Miriam."

"And what is your *mohar*, the price you are willing to pay for my daughter?" Mathias asked.

Samuel brought forth the box of gold and silver coins he had been saving since boyhood and handed it to Mathias.

"I dreamed about being a bride and played
dress-up bride all the time."—*Cathy*

"Miriam," her father asked, "are you willing to go with this man?"

"I am," she replied.

"Very well, then. Rachel," Mathias called to his wife, "bring out the wine."

Mathias then poured a goblet of wine. "Now we shall drink of the wine to signify the acceptance of the marriage contract." He first passed the wine to Miriam. Then he held the cup for Samuel, who placed his lips on the very spot where his bride's had been.

Looking at first one and then the other, Mathias continued the wine ceremony. "This wine that you drink today signifies the acceptance of the wedding contract. As Miriam has drunk from the cup, this signifies her acceptance of your proposal. As you, Samuel, have drunk from the cup, this signifies your promise to care for her. This *ketubah* is an unbreakable covenant that is legally binding.

"You will not drink of a second cup until the day you take your bride to her new home and consummate your vows. As you know, the *erusin,* or time of engagement, is more important than the wedding itself. From this time forward, you are legally married, though not living together."

"I always dreamed about being a radiant bride. I had my wedding planned out my entire life. It was a huge affair filled with flowers and white dresses, just like a fairy tale."—*Lindsey*

Then Miriam's father placed a veil over his daughter's face just below her eyes, which would not be removed until her groom lifted it on their wedding day.

That night, there was a grand celebration as Rachel invited her neighbors and friends to join in the family's happiness and meet their future son-in-law. During the festivities, Samuel and his father crept up onto the roof to catch a breath of fresh air and gather their thoughts about what had just happened in the past few hours. After many minutes of silence, Samuel spoke. "Father, you did well."

Both men let out a hearty laugh, embraced, and slapped each other on the back. Their laughter slowly turned to tears of joy as father and son realized the magnitude of what had just taken place. Yesterday Samuel had been a boy. Today he was a man.

Before Samuel and his father departed for home the next day, they left gifts for Miriam to remind her of her groom until he returned. Samuel also left gifts for her family.

For the next 12 months, Samuel worked diligently on a home for his bride. The *huppah,* as it was called, was a room or a bridal chamber built onto his father's house. Samuel could not return for his bride until his father said the house was constructed to his satisfaction.

While Samuel was building the new home for his bride, Miriam had preparations of her own. The time of separation was called *kiddushin.* It was a time of sanctification or consecration, which means she was "set apart" or "holy." Before the ceremony, she would take a special bath called a *mikveh* in a pool of water used for ritual purification. It was a part of a ceremonial cleansing that prepared her for the days ahead. This bath represented a separation from her old life and prepared her for the new one to come. It also represented a change in authority—coming out from the authority of her father and going under the authority of her husband.

During their engagement period, Samuel continued to build his new house. When Abram was satisfied with the construction, he gave his approval. Then Samuel, along with several of his friends, traveled to her hometown to get his bride. In the middle of the night they ran down the street to her home with blazing torches lighting the night sky and a blaring ram's horn breaking the silence. The ruckus was to let Miriam know the groom and his groomsmen were on their way. When she heard the noise, her bags were packed and she was ready!

After Samuel kidnapped his bride, he whisked her off to the bridal chamber he had prepared to consummate their marriage. Afterward, their family and friends joined them for a grand reception that lasted for seven days. When the marriage ceremony was over, Samuel lifted Miriam's veil and kissed his bride. It was then they drank from a second cup of wine.

Our Love Story

What a romantic scenario! Can't you see the oil lamps springing to life along the darkened street as the groom made his way to capture his bride in the middle of the night! Imagine the excitement of the bride as she waited to be whisked away and taken to her new home prepared just for her!

Friends, this is no fairy tale. It is my story and your story as well. Whether you are married, single, divorced, or widowed, I have good news for you. Your dream of becoming a bride came true the moment you accepted Jesus Christ as your Savior. In Revelation 19:7 God refers to Christians as the bride of Christ, and He left no detail unchecked. Let's go back and see how the Hebrew tradition was a foreshadowing of our becoming the bride of Christ.

Just as Abram sought out and chose a bride for his son, Samuel, God sought out and chose you to be the bride for His Son, Jesus: "You did not choose me, but I chose you," Jesus said to His disciples (John 15:16). He never did anything except what the Father told Him to do. In other words, Jesus chose you in obedience to His Father's command, because you were His choice: "The LORD your God has chosen you out of all the peoples on the face of the earth to be his people, his treasured possession" (Deuteronomy 7:6). He sought far and wide and decided that you were a perfect match for His Son. You might say you were made for each other.

Even though the Father chose you, He still waited for you to accept the invitation, just as Miriam had a choice to accept or reject Samuel's proposal. "For God so loved the world that he gave his one and only Son, that whoever *believes in* Him shall not perish but have eternal life" (John 3:16, italics added).

Samuel paid a *mohar,* or price, for his bride, and Jesus paid a price for you. He gave something much more valuable than silver and gold— He gave His life (1 Peter 1:18-19). You were bought at a very high price

36

(1 Corinthians 6:20). Paul encourages earthly husbands to "love your wives, just as Christ loved the church and *gave himself up for her* to make her holy, cleansing her by the washing with water through the word, and to present her to himself as a radiant church, without stain or wrinkle or any other blemish, but holy and blameless" (Ephesians 5:25, italics added).

As Samuel and Miriam drank from the cup of wine to seal their marriage covenant, Jesus drank from a cup of wine to seal His marriage covenant with the church. He also said He would not drink of that same cup until He comes to take her home. In the Upper Room at the Last Supper before His crucifixion, Luke records, "And he took bread, gave thanks and broke it, and gave it to them, saying, 'This is my body given for you; do this in remembrance of me.' In the same way, after the supper he took the cup, saying, 'This cup is the new covenant in my blood, which is poured out for you'" (Luke 22:19-20). "I will not drink of this fruit of the vine from now on until that day when I drink it anew with you in my Father's kingdom" (Matthew 26:29).

"I wanted to be a bride and a mother, but most
of all have someone who cherished me."—*Janet*

Even though Christ's bride is not living with Jesus yet, our marriage contract is legally binding and nothing can break that covenant. He said, "No one can snatch them out of my hand" (John 10:28). Jesus has left gifts for the bride so she will not forget Him while He is away. One of those gifts is the Holy Spirit. Paul calls the Holy Spirit a down payment for all the riches that are still to come (Ephesians 1:13).

Where is our groom and when will He return? Jesus has gone back to His Father's house and is preparing our new home. He said, "In my

Father's house are many rooms; if it were not so, I would have told you. I am going there to prepare a place for you. And if I go and prepare a place for you, I will come back and take you to be with me that you also may be where I am" (John 14:2-3). Even Jesus doesn't know when He will return. He is waiting for the Father to tell Him the bridal chamber is completed to His satisfaction (Matthew 24:36). But when He gets His Father's approval, Jesus will come and get His bride. Even though we cannot know the exact time of Christ's return, He assures us we will have plenty of warning to let us know the time is drawing near (Acts 2:19).

In the meantime, we are to prepare for His return. We are in a time of sanctification, and our ritual bath is the Word of God. Every time we read God's Word, He uses it to cleanse and purify us. Our job is to get ready!

No matter what your marital status, God has chosen you to be the bride of Christ. Do you know the old saying "Always a bridesmaid, never a bride"? When you know Christ, you are always a bride and never a bridesmaid. There are no runners-up in the kingdom of God. He chose you and longs to see your face. He loves you and is working as we speak to complete your bridal chamber. Oh how I long for the day when I can sing, "Let us rejoice and be glad and give him glory! For the wedding of the Lamb has come, and his bride has made herself ready" (Revelation 19:7).

An Unlikely Bride

The story of the Jewish wedding ceremony is a lovely foreshadowing of Jesus and the bride of Christ. But His encounter with a Samaritan woman shows the great lengths He will go to pursue and capture the heart of His beloved. In the gospel of John, we find a story of a woman looking for Mr. Right in all the wrong places. Then one day, Mr. Right came to her.

After Jesus had spent some time ministering in Judea, He decided to go back to His hometown of Galilee. Most respectable Jews would cross the Jordan River and travel along the east side of the banks to avoid the despicable country of Samaria. The Samaritans were half-breeds who had intermarried with Gentiles, and the Jews didn't want anything to do with them. However, Jesus "had to go" through Samaria because His Father had sent Him on a divine appointment.

"When I was a little girl, I dreamed of being a beautiful bride.
My girlfriends and neighbors and I used to play 'getting married.'
It was a dream I have yet to fulfill. I'm leaving it in God's
hands to pick me a husband, if that is His will. For now,
I am His bride and that's all I need."—*Karen*

Jesus traveled ahead of His disciples and reached Jacob's well while the others went into town to purchase some food. He was exhausted and sat down by the well's edge. After a few moments, a Samaritan woman came to draw her water for the day. Traditionally, the village women came to draw water early in the morning or at the end of the day to avoid the heat of the sun. However, this particular woman did not want to associate with the other women, or at least they did not want to associate with her. She was tired of the piercing stares, the hissing whispers, and the cutting sideways glances cast her way. For her, the scorching sun was easier to endure than the scorn of the villagers. So she came to the well at noon.

As she prepared to dip her bucket into the well, Jesus asked, "Will you give me a drink?" (John 4:7).

The woman was shocked that Jesus would make such a request. She replied, "You are a Jew and I am a Samaritan woman. How can you ask me for a drink?" (John 4:9).

It wasn't unusual for a thirsty traveler to ask for a cool drink of water, but it was scandalous for a Jewish man to carry on a public conversation with a woman, especially a Samaritan woman. And it was unheard of for a Jewish rabbi to drink from the same cup as a Samaritan, male or female.

Her reply to Jesus had been given with a hint of sarcasm, but Jesus did not let that deter His mission. He was more interested in winning the woman than winning the argument. "Jesus answered her, 'If you knew the gift of God and who it is that asks you for a drink, you would have asked him and he would have given you living water. . . . Everyone who drinks this water will be thirsty again, but whoever drinks the water I give him will never thirst. Indeed, the water I give him will become in him a spring of water welling up to eternal life'" (John 7:10-14).

Living water. Never thirsty again. Just the thought of not having to come to the well and face the townspeople again was enough to pique her interest. But Jesus had more for this woman than water for her parched body—He had satisfaction for her parched soul.

If ever there was a woman who wanted to be a bride, it was this woman. Yes, she had tried to satisfy the longing in her heart, but each marriage proved to be less than what she had hoped, leaving her feeling empty and disappointed. Five times she had been a bride, and five times divorce had shattered her dreams. When Jesus met her at the well, she was living with potential husband number six. Jesus knew all of this before she even spoke a word.

"The woman said to him, 'Sir, give me this water so that I won't get thirsty and have to keep coming here to draw water.'

"He told her, 'Go, call your husband and come back.'

"'I have no husband,' she replied.

"Jesus said to her, 'You are right when you say you have no husband. The fact is you have had five husbands, and the man you now have is not your husband. What you have just said is quite true'" (John 4:15-18).

The Light of the World had revealed her innermost darkness. She was amazed that Jesus saw right through her as if He had seen every day of her life. She believed Him when He said He was the Messiah. All her life she had been seeking fulfillment. She had gone from one man to the next, but her heart had remained as empty as the water pot she carried to the well. However, on this day, she met the only One who could satisfy her every dream. On this day, she became the bride she had always wanted to be. No longer did she need her water pot, but left it by the well as she ran into town to tell the villagers about the Restorer and Fulfiller of dreams.

I'm glad the woman in this story remained nameless, for she could be any one of us who has ever searched for our deepest longings to be fulfilled in another person but come up empty time and time again. Jesus "had to go" to Samaria to see this nameless woman, just as He "had to go" to the Cross to seek you—His bride.

"I had many dreams that came and went through the years, but being a wife and mother always stayed."—*Vickey*

Does that cause stirrings in your heart? Do you have an overwhelming sense of His fathomless love for you? Does your heart quicken thinking of His pursuit? Another woman in the Bible was overwhelmed by Jesus' love. In the seventh chapter of Luke, we see her pushing her way through a crowd and intruding on a dinner party given by a Pharisee. This woman had lived a very sinful life and was no doubt well-known among the party goers, some by personal experience and some by reputation. She had heard Jesus was dining at the Pharisee's home and searched through the dusty streets to find Him. The scorn and jeers she would surely receive were worth enduring to catch a glimpse of her Lord.

At last, she saw Him reclining at the table. The woman was so moved by love for Love Incarnate who forgave sinners that she wept, not at His feet, but on His feet. An overflow of salty tears left tiny streamlets on Jesus' dusty feet. In those days, it was scandalous for a woman to let down her hair in public. That was a pleasure reserved only for a husband. But she did it. She let down her hair and wiped Jesus' tear-streaked feet with her hair.

Then she broke her alabaster vase filled with perfume and anointed His feet. No doubt, as was also the custom, this perfume was the woman's dowry reserved for her husband-to-be. Ah, it was not wasted. She had used the treasured dowry for her husband after all.

Cinderella

In the introduction, I mentioned the beloved childhood fairy tale of Cinderella. Let's go back for a few moments and visit with this soot-covered beauty and see how she moves from the furnace room to the ballroom with the help of her fairy godmother.

You recall the story. This one so fair lives in a house with her evil stepmother and two wicked stepsisters. Her lot in life is to clean the house, wait on the terrible trio hand and foot, and live in seclusion from the outside world. She is relegated to the furnace room with her only true friends, the mice who love her.

It doesn't matter that she wears a tattered dress and dingy apron. She is beautiful. But Cinderella doesn't think she is beautiful at all. She believes her jealous, wicked stepmother and stepsisters, who tell her she's ugly. *Why doesn't Cinderella look into the mirror and see that she is much more beautiful than they are?* I muse. *Look at their crooked noses stuck up in the air and their mean, sour faces.*

Not only is Cinderella beautiful on the outside, her sweet disposition makes her lovely on the inside as well. If it is obvious to me, surely she can see the truth. But her stepsisters' voices are loud and convincing. She believes them.

One day an invitation comes from the king asking all the young women in the village to a ball at which his son will select a bride. The stepsisters laugh when Cinderella shyly asks if she might attend. After all, the invitation is extended to all the young, unmarried ladies in the kingdom. She has just as much right to attend as her stepsisters do. But Cinderella listens to their accusations and scorn, and her tiny flicker of hope is extinguished.

Then, as John Eldredge and Brent Curtis write in *The Sacred Romance*, "When God's grace comes in the form of Cinderella's fairy godmother and dresses her in a beautiful gown, she does finally look in the mirror and sees clearly her great beauty, but she believes it is all due to magic."[1] Her rags are transformed into a shimmering ball gown, the mice that served as her friends in the furnace room are changed into coachmen and prancing horses, and a pumpkin becomes transport fit for a queen. Of course, when the prince sees Cinderella, he realizes she is the woman of his dreams. He immediately recognizes her inner and outer beauty and knows that he has found his maiden so fair.

The one stipulation of the fairy godmother's spell is that Cinderella's good fortune ends at the stroke of midnight. She barely makes it out of the palace doors before the magical spell is lost, her gown changes back to rags, her coachmen back to mice, and the coach back to a pumpkin. However, in her race to beat the final stroke of midnight and keep her secret, she loses one of her tiny glass slippers on the palace steps.

With this one clue, the prince is determined to find the true love of his life. He searches the kingdom, and when he slides the glass slipper on Cinderella's slender foot, he knows he has found his bride. As the final page is turned, they live happily ever after.

Cinderella was doomed to a life in the ashes until her fairy godmother showed up! Ah, there's the gospel. "But God demonstrates his own love for us in this: While we were still sinners, [covered in ashes of shame, destined to spend all of eternity in the furnace of hell], Christ died for us" (Romans 5:8). However, God is no fairy godmother; He's our heavenly Father. And Jesus is more than a handsome prince; He's the Prince of the Ages.

"When I was a little girl, I dreamed about being married.
I loved romance books and movies where the girl is chosen.
I recently saw *The Princess Diaries* and cried as I watched the
timeless story of love and beauty unfold. I turned to my friend Mike,
who is 46 and also single, and gushed, 'Wasn't that just great?'
He shrugged and said, 'Yeah, I liked it all right.'"—*Mariana*

Reading this story as an adult, I see the claw marks of Satan running throughout. He bears a striking resemblance to the stepfamily that oppressed Cinderella and convinced her that she would never be anything but a homely house servant. Likewise, Satan tells us that we are worthless paupers; in reality, we are children of the King. Satan tells us we are not worthy of going to the ball, when in reality we have a personal invitation signed in Christ's blood and sealed by the Holy Spirit. Satan tells us that we are slaves to sin who deserve a life groveling in the soot by the furnace of hell, but in reality we are children of the Most High God who have been washed white as snow.

Satan tells us our place is one of shame, dressed in rags, while in reality God has given us a garment of righteousness and clothed us in Christ Himself. Satan tells us we are filled with darkness, when in reality God has delivered us from the domain of darkness, transferred us to the kingdom of Christ, and filled us with light. Satan tells us no one could possibly love us, when in reality God loved us so much He gave His only Son so that we could live in eternity with Him. Satan tells us we are not beautiful enough to be a bride, when in reality God chose us from all others for that very purpose. Now that's a happy-ever-after story worth savoring!

Mrs. Edwards Finds Mr. Right

Let me tell you another Cinderella story that is dear to my heart. It is about my mother, Louise Edwards. She married my father a few weeks after she graduated from high school. From the very beginning they had a rocky marriage. My father had a drinking problem, and my mother became a very bitter and angry person. Nothing was ever right, life was terrible, and marriage was something to be endured. For years, I thought of my mother as a person who was surviving life, not living life. She was a very attractive woman who had plenty of material possessions but felt destitute in her soul.

Both of my parents became Christians later in life, but they didn't experience the joyful marriage that comes with that relationship. As I mentioned in chapter one, when my dad was 55 he developed Alzheimer's disease, and I watched a strong, vibrant man turn into a person who was unable to feed himself, bathe himself, or walk by himself. As I watched my mother care for him, I noticed what little light she had in her eyes almost completely dim. Ten years after the initial diagnosis, my father died.

Not too long after my dad passed away, my mother met a wonderful man, Pete Wright. Pete said he had never seen someone as pretty as my mom with so much sadness in her eyes. He decided he would make it his mission to pursue my mom, win her affection, and rekindle the light that had gone dim.

Mr. Wright did pursue my mother. He is one of the sweetest, kindest, gentlest men I have ever known. For the first time in my life, I saw my mother truly happy. She had met "Mr. Right" and was transformed before my very eyes. The sun shone brighter, her steps were lighter, and her eyes danced with excitement and joy. For the first time in her life, she felt completely and totally loved, cherished, and adored. Pete and my mother became husband and wife on December 21, 2001. She is still glowing as a result.

Oh dear sisters, I want you to experience that same joy, that same zest for life, that same transformation that comes when you accept the proposal of "Mr. Right." Jesus Christ has chosen you, He is wooing you, and He wants to take care of you as His precious bride. He's standing at the altar, just waiting for you to say "I do."

Whether you are divorced with a heart broken by betrayal, widowed with a bed chilled and lonely, single with still no promise of a ring on your finger, or happily joined to the man of your dreams, Jesus longs to take you in His arms, not "for as long as you both shall live," but for all eternity. "'In that day,' declares the LORD, 'you will call me "my husband"; . . . I will betroth you [with a binding agreement] to me forever'" (Hosea 2:16-19).

An Easter Bride

It was a beautiful day for a wedding. The sun shone brightly as the daffodils danced in the gentle breeze, nodding their happy faces in conversation. A choir of robins, cardinals, and finches sang rounds of cheerful melodies, which floated through a clear blue sky that was a reflection of the bride's sparkling eyes. The air had that unusual crisp quality of spring, reminding us of the chill from winters past and the warmth of summer's promise.

The day was Easter Sunday of 1997, the day the Groom chose to be joined to His beloved. As in the Jewish custom of old, He proposed to His young maiden, and then promptly went away to prepare a home for her. On this day, His Father signaled the home was ready, and the Son could claim His bride

Iris had been waiting for her Husband to come and take her to the wonderful home He had prepared for her. *How like Him to pick Easter,* she thought to herself, *my favorite day of the year.* She smiled as she heard Him coming, and her heart fluttered with the anticipation of seeing His face.

She wore a white dress with flecks of blue and carried a bouquet of pink carnations and white mums with a spray of asparagus fern as wispy as her baby-fine hair. A sweet smile spread across her face as she saw her beloved Jesus hold out His strong hand to help her cross the threshold of the temporal and into the hall of eternity. She walked into His loving embrace and drank in the loveliness of her surroundings, which He had perfectly described in His many letters.

On Easter Day in 1997, my husband's dear, sweet, 74-year-old Aunt Iris went home to be with the Lord. As we all gathered around to say our last goodbyes, I could not manage to be mournful. Yes, I was going to miss her. But Iris had never been married on this side of eternity, and the vision I had in my mind was of her joining the Lord as the bride of Christ. For me, it was not a funeral. It was a wedding.

In Isaiah 61:3, the prophet describes what God will do for the bride of Christ. He will bestow on her a crown of beauty instead of ashes, anoint her with the oil of gladness instead of mourning, and place on her shoulders a garment of praise instead of a spirit of despair. Are you feeling brokenhearted because of broken dreams? Have you been in mourning because your dream of being a bride has not turned out as you had hoped? God desires to blow away the ashes and place the crown of a royal bride on your head. So lift your head, dear one, and accept your crown from the King of Kings.

"I delight greatly in the LORD; my soul rejoices in my God. For He has clothed me with garments of salvation and arrayed me in a robe of righteousness, as a bridegroom adorns his head like a priest, and as a bride adorns herself with her jewels" (Isaiah 61:10).

Wedding Feast of the Lamb

There is a place prepared for me
A table by the crystal sea
Where my Beloved bids me rest
And gently lean upon His breast
He dries my tears, He breaks my chains
He binds my wounds, He heals my pain
He soothes my tired and troubled soul
He fills my cup, it overflows
The finest wine, the choicest bread
By His own nail-scarred hands I am fed
He hides my shame in holy dress
He clothes me with His righteousness
He lifts my veil, He draws me close
Proclaims me His to the heavenly host
While angels sing His reverence
He leads me in a sacred dance
There is a place by the crystal sea
Where my Beloved waits for me
He bids me come just as I am
To the wedding feast of the Lamb.[2]

by Judie Lawson

3

To Be a Mother

I can still remember cuddling, rocking, and singing to my favorite baby dolls when I was a little girl. I'd love them until their hair was matted together, their clothes were tattered and torn, and their painted cheeks were marred. I even enjoyed changing their diapers. Yes, one particular dolly had a tiny hole between her pink cherub lips. When I fed her a bottle of water, it promptly exited through a tiny hole in her bottom!

Most little girls dream of one day being a mommy. In the hundreds of surveys I collected for this book, to be a mommy was the number one dream. And of all the dreams of a woman, this one can cause the most pain. Not being able to have children; not being able to control the children that we have; or losing a child due to miscarriage, stillbirth, or untimely death can be the most heart-wrenching experiences of a woman's life. These losses hit at the very core of womanhood.

After I was married, my dream to be a mother began to grow. It seemed my arms ached to have a child to nurture, love, and pour my life into. When I was 26, Steve and I decided it was time to increase our family of two. We conceived on our first attempt, and nine months later, Steven Hugh Jaynes, Jr. came screaming into the world. As I nestled that baby boy with thick black hair and long Bambi-like eyelashes against my breast, I knew I was holding God's first deposit in His great plan for my life—to be a mother. I had never felt more fulfilled in my life and was certain I was born to bear children. When Steven was about two years old, we began praying for baby number two.

"I dreamed I would be a mother who rocked her children to sleep, read them stories, and cooked them meals and treats."—*Cindy*

"Steven," we explained to our son, "God is the one who gives babies to mommies and daddies, so we are going to pray that He will send us another Jaynes baby so you can have a little brother or sister." This sounded like a good idea to him, so he added that request at the end of our family prayers each night. Conception happened so easily the first time, we thought this would be a wonderful opportunity to show Steven how God answers prayer.

Six months passed, and there was no news of another Jaynes baby on the way. Then one year passed with no news. And one year became two years. During that time, we began traveling down the frustrating road of doctor visits, infertility treatments, and timed intimacy (which is anything but intimate.) We also began building our dream home with bedrooms for four children and a children's bathroom with two sinks so the brood wouldn't argue about whose turn it was. When the house was near completion, I walked from room to room: "Please Lord," I prayed, "don't let us move into this house without the hope of children to fill it." My heart felt as empty as those bedrooms that seemingly would have no children occupying them.

God did not answer my prayer as I hoped. After many years of infertility treatment and hormone (and mood) altering drugs, the children's bedrooms lay empty, the blankets unruffled, and the dream unfulfilled. It appeared there would be no more children. While Steven, Jr. was everything I could have ever hoped for wrapped up in one package, my desire to have a houseful of little progeny was not God's will. Was I thankful for the child I did have? Absolutely, but that did not negate the desire in my heart to be a mother of many.

The inner turmoil that is associated with infertility is a raw wound that many women avoid discussing. Each month, the hopeful mother experiences a mini-death, grieves her loss, and then by day 14 of the following month, begins to hope once again. My friend Amanda Bailey wrote the following piece, which compares an actual hurricane and an emotional hurricane, trying to explain her personal struggle.

It was eerily silent, this patch of ground in the eye of the storm that was raging only a half-mile away from our home. The sound of the wind had been unimaginable, with its roar like a plane engine and the occasional screech of splitting wood like a myriad of axes hammering in unison. My heart still vibrated and the stench of burning plastic from overhead telephone wires set afire by lightning burned in my nostrils. The sparks had preceded the electricity outage only by seconds.

But here in the eye of the storm, the grass was bright green with water droplets glistening in the rays. The sun was peeking through the dark clouds, and the fallen trees lay as still as soldiers on the battlefield, with the standing ones keeping watch. Sensing a momentary peace, I expected the return of the storm, but my mind screamed for it to delay. "Not now! Not yet!" I cried. "It's too soon."

As I turned to face the storm, I was startled by a small swatch of color moving over the bushes. The butterfly flitted up and off into the horizon where the orange sun set on the storm's dark horizon.

My experience with infertility has been much like living through that hurricane so many years ago. The storm rages when the test proves negative. Then the eye of the storm comes around day 14 with renewed hope and a sense of calm. The calm continues as I think, *Perhaps this will be the month when my cycle will be interrupted and a baby will be conceived.* But when my period announces otherwise, I once again hear the roar of the storm approaching and I wonder why others around me can't hear it as well. The winds blow, the lights go out, and life around me seems to fall apart.

But then there's the butterfly that says, "Hope again." And the eye of the storm returns.

I understand the storm and the hope that Amanda described. Weary from the ups and downs, I was relieved when Steve and I decided to stop trying to conceive and be content with our family of three.

When God Says No

My son, Steven, continued to pray that God would give us another Jaynes baby. He prayed it every night. When he was about four-and-a-half years old, I thought it was time to tell him to stop. But how do you tell a child to stop praying a prayer? This was something God was going to have to do because I did not know how.

One day, Steven and I were sitting at his miniature table eating our lunches when he looked up at me and said, "Mommy, have you ever thought maybe God wants you to have only one child?"

You can imagine my shock at this statement coming out of the blue from an almost-five-year-old. Once I regained my composure, I answered. "Well, yes, I have thought maybe that's the plan. If it is, I am so thankful, because He gave me all I ever hoped for in a child wrapped up in one package—YOU!"

Then Steven cocked his little head and continued. "Well, what I think we ought to do is to keep praying until you're too old to have one. Then we'll know that was His answer."

What a great idea. Steven had no idea how old "too old" was, but he did know that God could do anything. If His answer was no, he didn't have a problem with that. I told Steven no many times, and he knew it did not mean, "I don't love you." Saying no meant I was his parent and knew what was best for him. I was the one having trouble with God telling me no.

Steven used to sing this song by Ruth Harms Calkin:

My God is so big, so strong and so mighty
There's nothing my God cannot do.
The mountains are His,
The valleys are His,
The stars are His handiwork too.
My God is so big, so strong and so mighty
There's nothing my God cannot do.

The Lord taught me a great lesson that day. Through Steven's child-like faith, I saw an example of the attitude of trust that I should have toward my heavenly Father who loves me and knows what's best.

Trusting God in the Dark

Those years of infertility were a stormy time in my life, but then a tidal wave hit.

"Steve, can you meet me for lunch? I have a little surprise for you."

I was so excited to tell Steve this unexpected news that I called him at the office and asked him to meet me for lunch. After five years of infertility treatment, we had become content with our family, but now it seemed Steven was going to have a little brother or sister after all. I handed my husband a tiny wrapped package. He gingerly pulled back the paper and opened the lid to discover a baby pillow nestled in soft white tissue paper.

"Does this mean what I think it means?"

"Yes," I replied, with tears filling my eyes.

My dream was coming true! There would be more children—or so I thought. While the baby was growing well inside my womb and the nursery was being planned, the dream came to a screeching halt. I lost the child due to a miscarriage. For me, it was not the loss of a child that was to be. It was the loss of a child that was very real, and for months I grieved. There are still times today when I look at the portraits of our family of three and I can almost see a shadow of a fourth. But there will come a time when my little one will not be a mere shadow. I will hold her in my arms. Until then, it gives me great comfort to picture her healthy and whole and playing at the feet of Jesus.

During those summer months following our loss, a friend sang the song "Trust His Heart" for me.

> God is too wise to be mistaken.
> God is too good to be unkind.
> So when you can't understand,
> When you don't see His plan,

When you can't trace His hand,
Trust His heart. [1]

I have learned much along this journey of trying to conceive and then losing a child. One thing I've learned is that I am not alone. In 1995, the National Center for Health Statistics estimated that 6.1 million women between the ages of 15 and 44 experienced an impaired ability to have children and 9.3 million were using infertility services.[2] Also, approximately 25 percent of pregnancies end in miscarriage.[3] It is a common problem, but there is nothing common about the pain. Because of my journey with infertility and miscarriage, God has allowed me to minister to many women who suffer the pain of empty arms through miscarriage, infertility, or the untimely death of a child. Perhaps there is no other life laboratory that affects the heart of women more than having or not having children, for God has placed a desire in the hearts of most of us to mother.

God's Punishment or God's Plan

In the Old Testament, women were shamed who did not bear children. They saw it as a curse from God. However, barrenness, or infertility, has been a part of God's plan for many women. Sarah was barren for 90 years before she miraculously gave birth to Isaac. She was called the "mother of many" even though she gave birth to only one child. In the New Testament, Elizabeth, the mother of John the Baptist, was barren for many years until God spoke to Zechariah in the temple.

However, when someone experiences infertility, loss of a child by miscarriage, birth of a child with congenital defects, or the death of a child shortly after birth, many questions flood her mind: *Is God punishing me? Why do women who abuse their children conceive, but I am not able to? Does*

God think I would be a bad mother? Is God punishing me for sin in my life? Is He punishing me for the abortion I had several years ago? How could God really love me if He is withholding such a desire of my heart?

To add to the pain of a woman's fears and doubts, many times well-meaning friends come along with a plethora of advice that only accentuates the feelings of inadequacy: "Try to conceive every other day." "I think you exercise too much." "I think you don't exercise enough." "You're not conceiving because you are too thin." "Infertility treatment is not of God. If He wanted you to conceive, He would do it without medical intervention." "Try infertility treatment. If it's not God's will for you to conceive, it won't work anyway." "You just need to relax and not think about it!"

"I dreamed about being a mommy. I was the oldest of five children and just loved mothering my younger siblings. My mother made being a mom look like the most rewarding job in the world."—*Cathy*

Confused? Imagine how the wounded woman feels as she tries to assimilate the bombardment of wise counsel. This "helpful advice" only adds fuel to the fire of a woman's feelings that her infertility is her own fault; she thinks she's just not doing something right.

Perhaps one of the most common misconceptions is when a woman feels she is being punished by her barrenness. In Luke 1:5-7, the writer describes the barren couple Zechariah and Elizabeth as "upright in the sight of God, observing all the Lord's commandments and regulations blamelessly." The *New American Standard Bible* describes them as "righteous." And yet, they were without children. They were not being punished, but rather God had a specific plan for their lives.

I truly believe that if God calls us to be childless, He has a different but wonderful plan in mind. However, many times barrenness, as with all seemingly unfulfilled dreams, can so overshadow our lives that we are unable to see what God's dreams for us really are.

In John 9:2, Jesus' disciples asked Him about the correlation between a certain lost dream and sin: "As he went along, he saw a man blind from birth. His disciples asked him, 'Rabbi, who sinned, this man or his parents, that he was born blind?'"

"Neither this man nor his parents sinned," said Jesus, "but this happened so that the work of God might be displayed in his life" (John 9:2-3).

Jesus basically told the disciples that they were asking the wrong question. They were looking for someone to blame instead of looking for what God could do. When our dreams of becoming a mother don't turn out as we had hoped, perhaps we need to make sure we are asking the right questions. Instead of, "Why me?" perhaps we should ask, "What now?"

Be Fruitful and Multiply

God fashioned women to be childbearers. Our wombs, breasts, hips, and hormones were uniquely designed for conceiving and giving life. There is an inborn nature to nurture, and while we may not give birth to our own flesh and blood in a delivery room, we can still—must still—bear and nurture, labor over and love, those in our sphere of influence.

When God created Adam and Eve, He commanded them to "be fruitful and multiply, and fill the earth, and subdue it" (Genesis 1:28, NASB). In the New Testament, we see another kind of fruitfulness as Jesus sent out the disciples: "Therefore go and make disciples of all nations" (Matthew 28:18). He could have said, "Be fruitful and multiply," which is exactly what they did.

In the last chapter, we met the Samaritan woman at the well. After she realized that Jesus was the Messiah, she left her water pot, ran back to town, and brought an entire village to meet the man who told her every-thing she had ever done. As the mass of humanity came pouring over the hill to meet Jesus, He turned to His disciples and said, "I tell you, open your eyes and look at the fields! They are ripe for harvest" (John 4:35). As a result of this woman's testimony, many Samaritans came to believe in Jesus as God's Son. The Samaritan woman was fruitful and multiplied, bringing many spiritual children into God's kingdom.

The prophet Isaiah wrote, "'Sing, O barren woman, you who never bore a child; burst into song, shout for joy, you who were never in labor; because more are the children of the desolate woman than of her who has a husband,' says the LORD" (Isaiah 54:1). The woman at the well was a personification of Isaiah's prophecy of the desolate woman who had many children.

"I wanted to have a huge family. The children I could not give birth to in the natural, God has given me by letting me 'mother' other people's kids. My husband and I have conflicting blood types that makes it difficult for me to carry babies to term. We lost five children, have two biological children and one adopted child."—*Rebekah*

Think for a moment about why little girls want to grow up and become mommies. We want to cuddle and care for, rear and raise, mold and shape, teach and train. We want to pour our love into another human being in the hopes that person will give that same love in return. Recently, I asked over 200 elementary-school-age children to tell me why they thought their moms were great and why they thought their dads were great. My favorite response was, "My mom is a great mom because she takes care of me. My dad is a great dad because he lets me do things my mom won't let me do!" The bottom-line response was, "Moms nurture and dads are fun!"

God has created women with a desire to nurture, but I think it goes much deeper than just having children. Most long to invest their lives in something that matters. Most of the time that something is other people. The Bible calls that being fruitful. Jesus said, "I am the vine; you are the branches. If a man remains in me and I in him, he will bear much fruit" (John 15:5). He also tells us that the true sign of a Christian is that he or she will bear fruit (John 15:8).

"I dreamed about having twelve children—that was until I had four!"—*Cathy*

After Henrietta Szold's love of her life died, she wrote, "Today it is four weeks since my only real happiness was killed." In her mind, her dream of happiness was lost. However, she went on to found Hadassah and in the 1930s, involved the organization in a program that rescued 22,000 Jewish children from Hitler's concentration camps. Henrietta, who mourned her disappointment in never marrying and having children, became the mother of thousands.[4]

Sometimes when our dream of motherhood is shattered, we have to let it die and allow God to bring forth what He wills. It is as if He is saying to us, "When you are letting go, remember that I am planting seeds of new life in you. Your grief is only for a season. My end is not death. It is always life. I am the author of life."[5] Whether it is the dream of having one child, the dream of having seven children, or the dream that a child will turn out a particular way, we must all eventually give that dream to God.

In my own life, I think of the woman who led me to Christ when I was 14. She was a mother in my neighborhood who took me under her wing, nurtured, mentored, and discipled me. God used her to be my spiritual mother. If it wasn't for her obedience to Him, I'm not sure where I would be today.

My heart broke one day when I read about the pop star Madonna. She's known as the bad girl of MTV, Sean Penn's ex-wife, Dennis Rodman's born-to-be-wild girlfriend, and David Letterman's foulmouthed guest. She's a movie star, the author of a sex book, and a woman who talked her personal trainer into inseminating her.

"Because I was adopted, I always dreamed about having babies that looked like me. I've never had anyone in my life resemble me so I'd try to picture someone who had characteristics like mine."—Annette

A television interviewer asked Madonna the usual shocking questions, to which she gave the regular shocking answers. The two of them were sitting there bantering questions and answers until the interviewer prefaced her next question something like this: "You're a woman who has it all. You're a singer, actress, and author. You've got money, fame, and a place in American pop culture. You've been on the cover of almost every magazine. You're not just a global figure, you're a global force."

Madonna sat there, taking all this in and nodding her head—until the last question: "Is there anything you would give it all up for?"

Suddenly Madonna's face froze. Her eyes filled with tears. Her lip quivered. She took a deep breath and answered.

"To have a mom."[6]

I never knew until I read that account that Madonna's mother died when she was five years old. I wonder what she would be like today had someone come along and been a mother to her. It could have made all the difference in the world.

Being a spiritual mother isn't limited to the spiritual birthing process but extends to nurturing a baby Christian as well. Karen said, "I am a first-generation Christian and I don't know what a Christian woman is supposed to look like or be like. I don't know how to be a wife or a mother and I'm feeling my way in the dark. I watch the women around me at church, but I need a mentor to show me how to follow Christ in my day-to-day living." She needs a woman who is brave enough to be a spiritual mother.

Birth Pains

Let me share Beverly's story of her dream to become a mother and how God fulfilled it. For many years, Beverly worked at Bank of America in the corporate lending group and was the personification of a young professional on the move up the corporate ladder. She was beautiful, intelligent, articulate, and had the reputation for accomplishing her well-thought-out goals. She married at 26 and the dream of having children began to bloom in both her and her husband's hearts. However, Beverly was born with only half a uterus and one functioning ovary. While the doctors said conception would not be impossible, they warned the couple it could be difficult. The doctors' prediction proved to be true, and years of infertility treatment ensued.

One night at dinner, Beverly mentioned to a lawyer friend, "Dana, if you ever have the opportunity to place a child for adoption, I'd love to be considered."

"How serious are you?" Dana inquired.

"Very serious," Beverly assured her.

The next day, Dana called with the news of a baby being released for adoption. With tears in her eyes, she described the birth parents to Beverly. "The mother is 5 feet 8 inches tall with a medium build and brown hair. The father is 6 feet tall with red hair, blue eyes, and fair skin."

Dana could have been describing Beverly and Todd. Four weeks later, little Todd, Jr. was placed in the loving arms of his adoptive parents. Three weeks later, Beverly's dearly beloved father died of a massive heart attack at 55 years of age. With that loss, she lost a large piece of her heart, which little Todd grew to fill.

"I dreamed of having a family and a white picket fence.
And I imagined a boy and girl dressed in matching outfits
playing on the white sandy beaches of Florida."—*Sue*

Beverly still had a deep longing to bear a child of her own. The couple went through various infertility treatments, but each hopeful month ended in a mini-death of that hope. Finally, after several years of trying to conceive, the stick turned blue to show a positive pregnancy. However, a few months later, that dream was lost when Beverly had a miscarriage.

"Oh, Bev," one of her friends consoled, "I feel that God has other plans for you. Maybe He is calling you to birth children in another way."

Beverly was angered at the comment. *I'm not sure what God's idea of birth is,* she thought to herself, *but mine involves a slap on a tiny bottom and the first breath of air from a new baby.*

In the previous months, she had developed a relationship with a woman named Carol at the gym where they both taught aerobics. Carol was not a Christian and was very curious to see how Bev handled this loss in her life. She saw Bev's pain, but she also saw her heart soften toward God and His will for her life.

"I'm amazed at how you've handled this loss in your life," Carol commented.

"It's only because of Jesus Christ and the support of my friends that I have gotten through this at all," Beverly replied.

Over the next weeks and months, Beverly began to share Christ with Carol by bringing her tapes, suggesting various books, and taking her along to women's events at her church. Even though Carol appeared to be confident and content, the gaping hole that can be filled only by Jesus Christ became evident. Such a spiritual hunger Bev had never seen before. Almost a year later, in a Wednesday night prayer service, Carol accepted Jesus as her Savior.

"I am so thankful for Beverly Spencer," Carol told the congregation. "For many months she shared Christ with me and allowed me to be a part of her life. She was willing to climb into the 'mud' with me and help me work through all the dirt in my life. I never really understood the role that Jesus Christ plays in our lives until I saw Him guiding hers. I realize that Beverly has placed many parts of her life on hold in order to help me understand the eternal life that could be mine."

With tears in her eyes, Beverly felt God whisper in her ear, "Carol is my child that you have birthed."

One year after Beverly's miscarriage, she and her husband decided to adopt again. After much prayer, a birth mother chose Beverly and Todd. Shortly after the adoption coordinator told them the good news, she called back again.

"Oh, I forgot to tell you the birth mother's name," she said. "It's Carol."

Beverly hung up the phone and fell on her knees thanking God for His presence in and providential plan for her life. In spite of her seemingly dashed dreams of bearing a child of her own, she had remained available to God to fulfill His dreams for her life. She allowed His truths to flow through her to one of His precious hurting children. As she was acting as a spiritual mother to birth His child, Carol, He was forming her precious daughter in the womb of another by the same name. The story of two births will forever be woven together with the two precious Carols.

Arriving at a Different Destination

The dream of being a mother and what that particular dream looks like in your mind's eye can be like planning a trip to one place but finding you've landed in another. I love this piece Emily Pearl Kingley wrote. It's about how she did not get what she expected after her child was born with Down syndrome. She said it was like planning a fabulous trip to Italy, boarding the plane, but then hearing a disturbing welcome from the flight attendant as the plane touches down.

"Welcome to Holland!"

"Holland!" you exclaim. "What do you mean, Holland? I signed up for Italy! I'm supposed to be in Italy. All my life I've dreamed of going to Italy."

But there's been a change in the flight plan. You've landed in Holland and there you must stay. The important thing is that they haven't taken you to a horrible, disgusting, filthy place, full of pestilence, famine, and disease. It's just a different place.

So you must go out and buy new guidebooks. And you must learn a new language. And you will meet a new group of people you would never have met.

It's just a different place. It's slower paced than Italy, less flashy than Italy. But after you've been there awhile and you catch your breath, you look around. You begin to notice that Holland has windmills. Holland has tulips. Holland even has Rembrandts.

But everyone you know is busy coming and going from Italy,

and they're all bragging about what a wonderful time they had there. And for the rest of your life, you will say, "Yes, that's where I was supposed to go. That's what I had planned."

And the pain of that will never, ever, ever go away, because the loss of that dream is a very significant loss. But if you spend your life mourning the fact that you didn't get to Italy, you may never be free to enjoy the special and very lovely things about Holland.[7]

No matter where your journey has taken you, or where it will take you in the future, I pray that you will begin to enjoy where you've landed. No, it might not be what you dreamed of, but it might have many wonderful features yet to be explored.

The Rose of Sharon

In closing, I want to take you back to where we began with my story. As you recall, I do have one incredible blessing in my son, Steven. But my dream to have a house full of children did not materialize as I had hoped. During one of my times with the Lord, I was studying in the Song of Songs about being the bride of Christ. This is a very romantic book of the Bible about the courtship, engagement, and eventual marriage between a man and a woman. Many compare it to the relationship of Jesus with His bride, the church.

I read Song of Songs 2:1 and God stopped me.

"I am a rose of Sharon," the woman said to her beloved.

What was her name? God seemed to say.

"Sharon," I answered.

What is your name? He again seemed to ask.

"Lord, my name is Sharon," I whispered aloud.

Look it up, He prompted my heart.

I went to my Bible dictionary and looked up *Sharon.* It meant "a fertile valley near Mount Carmel." God was telling me that while my medical chart had "INFERTILE" stamped across the front, He made sure that my name meant "fertile" before I was born. No, I do not have a house full of children, but He has caused me to be fertile in many other ways. Why, I have spiritual children all around the world! Through the privilege of writing, speaking, radio, and simply obeying God when He nudges me to reach out to one of His own, He has allowed me to birth children and nurture them to maturity.

"I wanted to be a different sort of mom than I had as a child. I would not work and I'd be home when my children came home from school, volunteer in their classrooms, and attend their extracurricular activities without complaining. They would always know by my words and deeds that they were loved and special."—*Mary*

Someone asked me recently, "Would you rather have the house full of children, or the ministry opportunities you have today?"

"I want exactly what God wants for my life—nothing more and nothing less," I answered, "because I know that whatever He has planned for my life is much greater than anything I could ever imagine or conceive."

4

To Be Beautiful

I was sitting in a crowded restaurant with my family when she walked by in her full-length white satin dress delicately trimmed in lace and studded with tiny "jewels," a crinoline that swished as she moved across the room, a rhinestone tiara upon her head, and pearl-studded slippers on her feet. Golden ringlets framed her rosy cheeks, and puckered lips glistened with a hint of gloss. She knew she was beautiful and glanced around at the admiring smiles of onlookers as she walked through the crowd. She was three years old.

I'm not sure when the dream to be beautiful enters a little girl's mind, but I do know when the dream ends—when the preacher says, "May she rest in peace." In my book *Ultimate Makeover: Becoming Spiritually Beautiful in Christ*, I told about my shenanigans as a little girl who wanted to be a grown-up beauty.

I remember as a little girl sneaking into my mother's closet and slipping my child-size feet into her size-seven high heels. I'd also stand on my tiptoes on a chair, pull a hat off the top shelf, and plop it on my head like an oversized lampshade. Her satin evening jacket with sleeves that hung eight inches below my fingertips gave a nice elegant touch to my outfit. A lady going to a party would never be caught without "putting on her face," so I crept into the bathroom, opened the forbidden drawer, and created a clownish work of art on the palette of my face. Red rouge circles on my cheeks, heaps of blue eye shadow on my munchkin lids, and smeared orange lipstick far exceeding the proper border were finished off with a dusting of facial powder with an oversized brush.

From the time a little girl stretches on her tiptoes to get a peek in the mirror, she desires to be beautiful—perhaps like her mommy. As the girl moves into the teen years, she experiments with makeup, delves into fashion, and attempts various hairstyles. Then it's on to makeover ideas in magazines and on talk shows. If one idea doesn't work—well there's always next month.[1]

I believe the dream to be beautiful is not cultural, but at the very core of womanhood. John Eldredge, in his book *Wild at Heart,* describes three longings that lie at the heart of every man: a battle to fight, a beauty to rescue, an adventure to live. He also ventures to say that a woman has three longings of the heart as well: to be fought for, to share in an adventure, and to have her beauty unveiled. "Not to conjure," Eldredge explains, "but to unveil."

Most women feel the pressure to be beautiful from very young, but that is not what I speak of. There is also a deep desire to simply and truly be the beauty and be delighted in. Most little girls will remember playing dress up, or wedding day, or "twirling skirts," those flowing dresses that were perfect for spinning around in. She'll put her pretty dress on, come into the living room and twirl. What she longs for is to capture her daddy's delight.[2]

I'd say Mr. Eldredge, father of two rambunctious boys, understands the feminine heart very well.

Created for Beauty

We should never be ashamed of our dream to be beautiful. One travesty of the feminist movement is that it has tried to strip women of their femininity and make them more male. It is as if those in the movement were saying that being a woman wasn't good enough. They tried to turn us into men by making women tough, independent, and rugged individuals who didn't need anyone or anything. But those who were banking on the tenets of feminism were left spiritually and emotionally bankrupt.

Studies now show a correlation between taking care of one's appearance and being happy or content. One of the signs of depression is a lack of desire to take care of one's personal appearance. Many times a depressed or emotionally numb woman will give up and think, *Why bother?*

One of my friends, Patty, sank into a severe clinical depression and had to be hospitalized. For seven days, she refused to eat, shower, or comb her hair. But on the eighth day when she took her heavenly Father's hand and began to emerge from the deep dark hole of depression, she showered, fixed her hair, and even put on a smattering of makeup.

A woman was and is one of God's most magnificent creations. As a matter of fact, she was His grand finale. After He fashioned Eve, creation was complete and He took a rest! God has placed in our hearts a love for beauty and a desire to be beautiful. Let's go back to the beginning of time and reflect on our magnificent beginnings.

After God created the sun, moon, stars, earth, waters, creeping and flying animals, He created man. But something was missing. There was no creature suitable for Adam. This was the only time God said an aspect of His creation was not good: "It is not good for the man to be alone" (Genesis 2:18).

"So the Lord God caused a deep sleep to fall upon the man, and he slept; then He took one of his ribs and closed up the flesh at that place. The Lord God *fashioned* into a woman the rib which He had taken from the man, and brought her to the man" (Genesis 2:21-22, NASB, italics added).

While God created the world and all it contains, He did something a little special when He made woman: He *fashioned* Eve. He didn't simply make you; He fashioned you with extra care and meticulous detail. You are a thing of beauty, a sight to behold, and one of His most spectacular masterpieces.

Up to this point in the creation story, Adam remained silent. But when he saw Eve, I imagine he said, "Whoa! Now this is good!" We don't know for sure, but we do know his first recorded words upon seeing the lovely Eve: "This is now bone of my bones and flesh of my flesh; she shall be called 'woman', for she was taken out of man" (Genesis 2:23).

In the New Testament, Paul writes, "For we are God's workmanship" (Ephesians 2:10). The Greek word for *workmanship* means "a work of art." Listen to these words as David describes the Creator at work:

For you created my inmost being;
you knit me together in my mother's womb.
I praise you because I am fearfully
and wonderfully made;
Your works are wonderful,
I know that full well.
My frame was not hidden from you
when I was made in the secret place.
When I was woven together
in the depths of the earth,
your eyes saw my unformed body.
(Psalm 139:13-16)

Like an artist who sees the finished work in his mind's eye, God saw your unformed substance and then began to fashion you from head to toe. He made no mistakes but planned each detail of your being.

The Barbie Syndrome

Did you ever wonder what Eve looked like? I must admit, I've always pictured her looking a bit like Barbie. After all, isn't that what the artists always depict? Waist-length, flowing tresses, hour-glass figure, creamy smooth complexion, delicate feet begging for high heels—a perfect 10. Unfortunately, Barbie is the standard that much of our society has adopted as ideal beauty. But is that realistic? If you blew Barbie up to life-size proportions, her measurement would be 38-18-33, and she would be six feet tall.[3] The only blemish I can find on Barbie is "Made in Japan" stamped on the bottom of her otherwise perfect foot. Maybe I don't travel in the right circles, but I don't know anyone who fits that description. But I do know many who try.

"I wanted to be beautiful, and when I was in school, that's all I ever thought about."—*Jean*

Americans spend over seven billion dollars a year on cosmetics.[4] Magazine racks bulge each month with periodicals promising dramatic makeovers for women of every shape, color, and size. They tell us how to thin thighs, firm flab, tuck in tummies, build biceps, tighten tushes, lengthen lashes, whiten teeth, and plump lips. We can learn the proper way to apply makeup, choose the best hairstyles to frame and flatter facial shapes, and determine what color wardrobe is best for our particular skin tone. Cosmetic surgery procedures among women have increased by a dramatic 165 percent since 1992.[5] A recent study showed American women spent a half-billion dollars on shape-enhancing garments.[6]

The obsession with outward appearance isn't limited to older women who have expendable income for fighting the effects of aging and gravity. In the year 2000, American youths spent $155 billion on beauty products and trips to salons and spas—financed by willing parents.[7] In Mexico, nose jobs are the status gift for girls celebrating their *quinceañero,* the traditional coming-of-age fifteenth birthday party. In California, young girls are getting breast implants as high school graduation gifts.[8]

But when is all the manipulation enough? When are we ever satisfied? I think of Eve. She was absolutely a perfect 10, and still, it wasn't enough. She wanted more. It was the same with Satan. Ezekiel describes him as once being "full of wisdom and perfect in beauty," with every precious stone as his covering (Ezekiel 28:12). But that wasn't enough. He wanted more. As a result, he was cast out of heaven with a third of the angels following him.

"My princess dream started very young. Like most little girls, I played dress-up, putting on long dresses and high-heeled shoes. My house was my castle, and I dreamed of being rescued by a handsome prince who would love me and take away all my hurts."—*Mary*

Today, more than ever before, women have unreal expectations placed on them by a society that glorifies youth and beauty. A few hundred years ago, women compared themselves to other women in their small villages. Today, women compare themselves to airbrushed models in magazines, on billboards, and on the silver screen. Most models admit that even they don't measure up to the pictures of themselves. Before a photo shoot, a model's hair is arranged by a professional stylist, her face made over by a professional makeup artist (they don't call them artists for nothing), and her image is captured under just the right lighting to make her eyes and lips sparkle. Then, if she still isn't perfect, the photographer touches up the picture with digital manipulation to remove any flaws.

Another symptom that reveals how unsatisfied women are with their appearance is talk shows that feature makeovers. Viewers love to watch an artist transform a frumpy, middle-aged housewife into a sophisticated cosmopolitan with just a snip of the scissors, stroke of blush, and updated wardrobe. Silently we wonder, *Could that ever be me?*

I'm not saying I've never read the makeover articles in the magazines or tried a few of their suggestions. But I do know this: No skin creams, makeup, designer clothes, or exercise regimens will make a woman truly beautiful, for true beauty is an outward reflection of an inward glow.

The Most Beautiful Woman

I love this story by Carla Muir found in my book *Ultimate Makeover: Becoming Spiritually Beautiful in Christ.*

A successful beauty product company asked the people in a large city to send pictures along with brief letters about the most beautiful women they knew. Within a few weeks, thousands of letters were delivered to the company.

One letter in particular caught the attention of the employees, and soon it was handed to the company president. The letter was written by a young boy who was obviously from a broken home and living in a run-down neighborhood. With spelling corrections, an excerpt from his letter read: "Beautiful woman lives down the street from me. I visit her every day. She makes me feel like the most important kid in the world. We play checkers, and she listens to my problems. She understands me and when I leave, she always yells out the door that she's proud of me."

The boy ended his letter saying, "This picture shows you that she is the most beautiful woman. I hope I have a wife as pretty as her."

Intrigued by the letter, the president asked to see this woman's picture. His secretary handed him a photograph of a smiling, toothless woman, well advanced in years, sitting in a wheelchair. Sparse gray hair was pulled back in a bun and wrinkles that formed deep furrows on her face were somehow diminished by the twinkle in her eyes.

"We can't use this woman," explained the president, smiling. "She would show the world that our products aren't necessary to be beautiful."[9]

This little boy had discovered a valuable truth. Beauty—true beauty—begins on the inside and works its way out.

True Beauty

So where does real beauty come from? It comes from the heart. Rosalind Russell said, "Taking joy in life is a woman's best cosmetic." While joy in life is a good cosmetic, the peace that comes through a relationship with Jesus Christ is the *best*.

Peter wrote this about beauty: "Your adornment must not be *merely* external—braiding the hair, and wearing gold jewelry, or putting on dresses; but *let it be* the hidden person of the heart, with the imperishable quality of a gentle and quiet spirit, which is precious in the sight of God" (1 Peter 3:3-5, NASB).

I think the key word is *merely,* which is used in the *New American Standard Bible* but omitted in the *New International Version.* We can't depend on the outward, because the inward will inevitably seep through. There's nothing wrong with buying nice clothes, or wearing jewelry or makeup, but we must not depend on those coverings to mask what lies beneath. This verse does not mean that we should not wear jewelry. If it did, it would also mean that we are not to wear clothes! The Proverbs 31 woman wore purple and scarlet clothes, which were very expensive in her day. She did give attention to her appearance, but what made her truly beautiful was her love for the Lord.

"I wanted to be a teacher so I could wear pretty dresses.
I haven't gotten a degree or the chance to wear pretty
dresses or stand behind a podium."—*Tansy*

The Bible has some pretty harsh words to describe our inward ugliness before we accepted Jesus Christ as our Savior and Lord. For example, Paul said we were "dead in [our] transgressions" (Ephesians 2:1). A mortician can put makeup on a corpse, but the corpse is still dead. Likewise, we can dress up a dead spirit, but it is still dead—like a whitewashed tomb. Before Christ, we weren't only in darkness (1 Thessalonians 5:4); we *were* darkness (Ephesians 5:8).

But God didn't leave us that way. While we were yet sinners in darkness with ugly dead spirits, Christ gave His life so that we might gain ours (Romans 5:8). When we confess with our mouth that Jesus is Lord and believe in our hearts that God raised Him from the dead, He makes our dead spirits come alive, and we are spiritually born again to live in heaven with Him for all eternity (John 3:3). Our spiritual makeover takes place in the twinkling of an eye, in the time it takes us to say, "I believe." However, being conformed to the image of Christ, or the ultimate makeover, as I call it in my book by the same title, takes the rest of our lives. After we come to Christ, we are no longer darkness; God uses words such as the following to describe us: *light of the world* (Matthew 5:14), *holy* (Ephesians 4:24), *righteous* (Romans 6:18), *new* (2 Corinthians 5:17), and *dearly loved* (Colossians 3:12).

"I dreamed about being a ballerina and twirling my way through theaters all over the world. I dreamed about living in the jungle with Tarzan. Looking back, they appear quite the opposite, but actually they were quite similar. Both involved excitement and a physical rush of flying through the air and falling into the arms of a handsome man. One wore tights and the other a loin cloth. What could get any better!"—*Christie*

Doris Mortman said, "Until you make peace with who you are, you'll never be content with what you have."[10] Until you understand that you are God's workmanship, a child of God who resembles her Daddy, you'll never be content with the features He gave you. Do you believe you are a happenstance mixture of your parents' genes, or do you believe that you were intentionally woven and knitted together by God with a specific design in mind? What we believe about our origin greatly affects what we believe about our destiny.

And even though we become a new, righteous, and holy creation in Christ the moment we believe, we become more beautiful each time we spend time in God's presence. We become truly beautiful, not by adding layers on the outside, but by removing layers on the inside.

Moses had to cover his face to mask the glow emanating from it after spending 40 days in God's presence. Our faces will radiate the love of Christ when we spend time with Him. King Solomon wrote, "Wisdom brightens a man's face and changes its hard appearance" (Ecclesiastes 8:1).

God even gives us a new wardrobe: "For all of you who were baptized into Christ have clothed yourselves with Christ" (Galatians 3:27). "I delight greatly in the LORD; my soul rejoices in my God. For he has clothed me with garments of salvation and arrayed me in a robe of righteousness" (Isaiah 61:10).

Most women love the idea of spending a day at the spa and coming out a brand-new person. Queen Esther in the Bible spent an entire year at the spa before she claimed her title of Mrs. Xerxes. Her beauty regimen included six months with oils of myrrh and six months with perfumes and cosmetics (Esther 2:12). Now there's a spa package worth looking into!

One of the best presents my husband ever gave me was a day at the spa. My back was massaged, hands dipped in paraffin, face sloughed, feet kneaded, nails painted, makeup applied, and hair poofed. My makeover was on Friday, but by Monday the visit seemed like a distant memory. The dry flakes returned to my face, the tension knots developed in my neck again, the red polish chipped off my big toes, and the bleach bathroom cleaner caused my white French manicure to turn a pale shade of yellow. And my hair refused to submit to my commands; I unwillingly exchanged my trendy new look for early American housewife frump.[11]

Yes, a day at the spa can be fun, but there is only one beauty treatment that has lasting results. You won't find it in a spa, at the cosmetic counter at the mall, or in a makeover article in a magazine. You will find it only in the Word of God. We become more and more beautiful every time we sit as Jesus' feet. "And we, who with unveiled faces all reflect the Lord's glory, are being transformed into his likeness with ever-increasing glory, which comes from the Lord, who is the Spirit" (2 Corinthians 3:18). As my country grandmother used to say, we just keep "gettin' purdier and purdier."

Beauty That's Only Skin-Deep

There is nothing worse than purchasing a beautiful, highly polished Red Delicious apple and biting into it only to find it mealy and mushy on the inside. Well, maybe there is something worse—a beautiful woman who opens her mouth to reveal a harsh, cruel, cold soul on the inside. Solomon says that's "like a gold ring in a pig's snout" (Proverbs 11:22). What a waste.

Becky experienced this firsthand when she was 19 years old. She was performing as a runway model at her hometown department store. She was 5 feet 2 inches and 100 pounds, just the perfect size to model apparel from the petite department. But she had always longed to be tall and slender like the runway models from the big cities. On one occasion, the management of the store where Becky worked flew in a New York model to add to the excitement of a fashion show. Becky was thrilled to watch a professional parade up and down the runway with poise and elegance.

Becky explained, "I can remember standing behind a rack of clothes and peering admiringly as the 5-feet-8-inch, sleek blond glided up and down the runway with the grace and poise of a queen. 'Oh God,' I prayed, 'how I wish I could be like her.'"

After the fashion show was over, Becky was gathering her belongings when she overheard the model in a fit of rage. "I don't even know what happened," Becky said. "All I know is that this beautiful woman who I had so admired, almost worshipped, was spewing the filthiest language I had ever heard and slinging clothes and shoes all around the room. I ran out of the store and cried all the way home. Disappointment and disillusionment filled my heart. 'Oh God,' I prayed once again, 'please don't ever let me be like her.'" Becky learned at an early age that outer beauty is only as attractive as the heart that lies beneath. "Oftentimes under silken apparel, there is a threadbare soul."[12]

Many men have married what they thought was a beautiful woman only to discover a contentious nagger when the honeymoon was over. King Solomon likens that to a constant dripping (Proverbs 19:13). Outer beauty has a way of diminishing in importance when a woman's true self comes out. In *Beauty by the Book,* Nancy Stafford writes, "Beauty of form affects the mind, but then it must not be the mere shell that we admire, but the thought that this shell is only the beautiful case adjusted to the shape and value of a still more beautiful pearl within."[13]

"I dreamed I'd be beautiful, confident, and loved."—*Denise*

I do want to add something important here. I am not saying that a woman should ignore her appearance. God created men to be visual creatures. When a wife disregards her appearance and doesn't care how she looks, it is an affront to her husband and shows a lack of concern and respect for his feelings. In Willard Harley's book *His Needs, Her Needs,* he lists "To have an attractive spouse" as one of a man's five basic needs.[14] This does not mean he needs to have a beauty queen for a wife, but he does need a wife who takes care of her appearance, who doesn't let herself go, and whom he is proud to take out in public.

I hear many women who ignore their appearance say, "He should love me for who I am on the inside." He probably does. But would you put a diamond in a brown paper bag? No, you'd put it in a velvet case! If we truly love our husband, we will give him the gift of a wife he can be proud of. Don't be angry that your husband is a visual creature. God made him that way. It is most likely what drew him to you in the first place. Instead of resenting his God-given nature, seek to please him.

Many times I've spent all day writing in my workout clothes, hair tied back in a ponytail, with no makeup on. I'm sure I've scared the UPS man half to death by my ghastly appearance. However, at 4:30, I run upstairs, put on something presentable, comb my hair, and apply a bit of makeup. Why do I do this so late in the day? Because I know that in a few moments, one of my greatest gifts from God is going to walk through my door, and I want him to be glad to be home.

A Princess Defiled

Let's visit Cinderella once again. She went from being a slave held captive to being a captivating belle of the ball, from being covered with ashes to being crowned with jewels, from being despised by her wicked stepfamily to being adored by her entire village. We all love "And they lived happily ever after" endings.

In 2 Samuel 13 there is a story that reminds me of Cinderella's story somewhat, but with two major differences: It is no fairy tale, and the events occur in reverse. Tamar was a lovely princess, the daughter of King David. She was one of the most beautiful young ladies in the entire kingdom. Her name meant "palm tree," a symbol of victory and honor. Tamar had several brothers, half brothers, sisters, and half sisters. It was a royal blended mess.

One of her half brothers, Amnon, lusted after his beautiful sister to the point he couldn't sleep at night. On the advice of a wicked friend, Amnon plotted to lure Tamar into his bedroom with the help of their unsuspecting father. Amnon pretended to be sick and requested some of Tamar's special baked bread. He also requested that she feed it to him with her own hands. Tamar obeyed her father's request to tend to her brother. After she entered his bedroom, the supposedly sick Amnon commanded the servants to leave the room and lock the door behind them. He grabbed Tamar, threw her on his bed, and even though she begged and pleaded for him to stop, he stole her most treasured possession, her virginity. After he had his way with her and his lust was satisfied, Amnon told his servant to get Tamar out of the room and bolt the door.

The distraught, devastated, and demeaned Tamar tore her royal robes and put ashes on her head. When her brother Absalom came to her rescue, he surmised what had happened and had her come to his house to live.

And even though Tamar was still a royal princess, she spent the rest of her days secluded in a darkened room, wearing sackcloth as if in mourning, and placing ashes on her head in shame. Never again did she place the royal robe, which was rightfully hers, on her shoulders or live as the princess she truly was. She lived the rest of her life believing she could never be restored.

"I never dreamed about being beautiful because I had too many brothers who assured me I wasn't."—*Carmen*

This is not just the story of Tamar, but the story of many women I meet every day—hiding because of shame, feeling ugly and unworthy to accomplish God's dreams. Paul reminds us that we are a new creation in Christ (2 Corinthians 5:17), but many women conceal or cover up that beauty with shame from past mistakes or abuse. It is as if they rise each morning and put a fresh dusting of ashes on their souls, the very ashes that Jesus came to wash away. And dear sister, it is Satan who holds the box of ashes in his hand with the lid open ready for us to take some of the contents.

Oh, we may not be walking around with ashes on our heads or dressed in burlap sacks, but we wear the mantle of shame that Satan has placed on our shoulders and secured with guilt-inducing deception and lies. I meet many women who have children, a husband, a successful career, and appear beautiful on the outside. But they are spending their days in desolation of the soul because Satan has convinced them that's where they belong. They are wearing the cloak of shame because of past abuse, misuse, or mistakes. They don't realize that Jesus Christ has washed them clean, purchased a robe of righteousness made just for them, and He is eager to place it on their shoulders.

Please don't let Satan deceive you into believing that you are anything less than a beautiful princess. Do not allow him to convince you your dignity cannot be restored because the truth is, it already has been. We simply need to start believing the truth. "All glorious is the king's daughter [you] within her chamber; her gown is interwoven with gold. In embroidered garments she is led to the king" (Psalm 45:13-15).

The prophet Isaiah spoke of Jesus in these verses:

He has sent me to bind up the brokenhearted, to proclaim freedom for the captives and release from darkness for the prisoners . . . to comfort all who mourn, and provide for those who grieve in Zion—to bestow on them a crown of beauty instead of ashes, the oil of gladness instead of mourning, and a garment of praise instead of a spirit of despair. (Isaiah 61:1-3)

Jesus has the glass slipper in His hand. He's looking for the princess's foot to place it on. It is your foot, my friend. Don't let Satan tell you it doesn't fit. The One who made your foot has already decreed that it does. You are the belle of the ball.

The Beautiful Beloved

In the Song of Songs, the bridegroom or lover drenched his beloved with words of admiration for her many physical attributes. For centuries, commentators have noted a parallel between the lover and the beloved and Jesus and His bride. You may blush a bit, but listen to a few of the lover's observations.

Your cheeks are beautiful with earrings, your neck with strings of jewels. (1:10)

How beautiful you are, my darling! Oh, how beautiful! Your eyes are doves. (1:15)

Like a lily among thorns is my darling among the maidens. (2:2)

Your hair is like a flock of goats descending from Mount Gilead. (4:1)

Your teeth are like a flock of sheep just shorn, coming up from the washing. Each has its twin; not one of them is alone. (4:2)

Your lips are like a scarlet ribbon; your mouth is lovely. Your temples behind your veil are like the halves of a pomegranate. (4:3)

Your neck is like the tower of David, built with elegance. (4:4)

Your two breasts are like two fawns, like twin fawns of a gazelle that browse among the lilies. (4:5)

Your lips drop sweetness as the honeycomb, my bride; milk and honey are under your tongue. (4:11)

How beautiful your sandaled feet. (7:1)

Your graceful legs are like jewels, the work of a craftsman's hands. (7:1)

Your waist is a mound of wheat encircled by lilies. (7:2) [This is my favorite verse. A mound of wheat, mind you, not a flat plain!]

All beautiful you are, my darling; there is no flaw in you. (4:7)

This woman's betrothed adored her rosy cheeks, her long neck, her black, flowing hair, and her ruby lips. He adored the fact that she had all of her teeth and shapely legs and small breasts. He even thought her poochy tummy was adorable.

But what did she think of herself? Not very much: "Do not stare at me because I am dark, because I am darkened by the sun. My mother's sons were angry with me and made me take care of the vineyards; my own vineyard I have neglected" (Song of Songs 1:6).

She felt inferior to others because she was darkened by the sun. To be tan in those days was not desirable. Women went to great lengths to shade their skin from the scorching sun. This woman, however, was very dark. Because she was forced to take care of her brothers' vineyards, she had neglected to take care of herself. But amazingly, in the end, she began to see herself as her bridegroom saw her. Oh, that we would do the same.

"I was the beautiful princess in my family, but the other siblings came along, and I had to share my crown."—*Christie*

Is the Song of Songs our song? I think so. Jesus, the Lover of our soul, looks at us and thinks we are absolutely beautiful. However, we tend to look in the mirror and see our flaws. I read once that when a man looks in the mirror, he focuses on his best features. But when a woman looks in the mirror, she focuses on her worst. I don't know how men see themselves, but I do know that most women focus on their negative features instead of their positive ones. Perhaps Satan is pointing out our flaws to distract us from the beauty of Jesus Christ, who lives in each of us. But we need to look into the only mirror that matters, the Word of God, which tells us we are beautiful.

I promise you this: Nothing can convince a woman of her beauty more than being admired by her husband. While that may not be the case every day in our lives, we can be assured that as the bride of Christ, He sees us as altogether lovely. What is He saying even now? "My dove in the clefts of the rock, in the hiding places on the mountainside, show me your face, let me hear your voice; for your voice is sweet, and your face is lovely" (Song of Songs 2:14).

Jesus desires to hear our voice and see our face. Both are a delight. "The fruit of our love affair is our beauty; it is not something we can manufacture, manipulate, or control. Beauty springs entirely from the One who lavishes jewels and finery within our hearts. He sees our clamoring, hears our rage, knows our fear, and yet He runs to lift the veil from our face with His blood-stained hands. We are beautiful to Him."[15]

Mona Lisa

Last summer I visited the Louvre art museum in Paris. At the end of a long corridor lined with famous paintings, a crowd gathered to capture a glimpse of the famous *Mona Lisa*. Honestly, to me she looked rather plain. What was the draw? I didn't understand until I heard the tour guide explain her history.

No one is really sure of Mona Lisa's true identity, but many think her to be Francesco di Bartolommeo di Zanobi del Giocondo's third wife, Lisa di Antonio Maria di Naldo Gherardini. (Try remembering those names! No wonder most people just say, "We don't know who it is.") She was painted by Leonardo da Vinci between 1503 and 1507. The painting moved from King Francis I's castle, to Fontainebleau, to Paris, to Versailles, to Napoleon's estate, and ended up in the Louvre.

However, on August 21, 1911, Mona Lisa was stolen by an Italian thief. During that time, the Parisians placed another painting in Mona Lisa's spot, but the citizens missed her terribly. Two years later, she emerged in Florence and was returned to Paris. Today, she remains in the Louvre behind a bullet-proof glass.

Why is she loved today? Because once she was lost, but now she is found. She was stolen from her place of honor, but someone found her, paid the price for her, and put her back in her rightful place. No wonder she's smiling.

So it is with us, dear friends. Once we were lost but now we've been found and, as we have already established, we are in our rightful place as a child of the King. That makes each of us a princess. We're not in a museum; our rightful position is in the King's eternal heavenly castle.

David wrote, "The king is enthralled by your beauty" (Psalm 45:11). That means He is captivated, fascinated, enraptured, smitten, spellbound, and taken with you. He has given you "a crown of beauty instead of ashes, the oil of gladness instead of mourning, and a garment of praise instead of a spirit of despair" (Isaiah 61:3).

Mirror, Mirror, on the Wall

We've talked about Cinderella, but now let's turn our attention to another childhood favorite—Snow White. Long long ago, in a land far away, there lived a lovely young princess named Snow White. Her stepmother, the queen, was very cruel and jealous of Snow White's beauty. Every day, the vain queen approached her magic mirror and asked, "Mirror, mirror on the wall, who's the fairest of them all?" For many years, the mirror answered, "You are fairest of all, O Queen." All the while, Snow White grew from a little girl into a fair young maiden, and as the saying goes, "The mirror doesn't lie."

One day, the queen approached her magic mirror and asked, "Mirror, mirror on the wall, who's the fairest of them all?" Much to her regret, the queen heard the answer she knew would inevitably come.

"Fair is thy beauty, Majesty, but behold: A lovely maid I see, one who is more fair than thee. Lips red as a rose, hair black as ebony, skin white as snow."

The queen shrieked in anger, knowing that the mirror spoke of none other than Snow White, her beautiful stepdaughter. At once the queen decided to eliminate her competition. She ordered one of her huntsmen to kill the fair princess in yonder woods.

The next day, the huntsman took the princess to the woods but could not bring himself to end the life of one so lovely. Thus, he left her in the forest, hoping the queen would think he had accomplished his mission. Snow White stumbled across seven adorable dwarfs with giant hearts who loved and cared for her.

The next day, the evil queen asked the mirror once again, "Mirror, mirror on the wall, who's the fairest of them all?"

Once again, the mirror answered, "Snow White."

"Did I dream of becoming a beautiful princess?
Well, I am a girl, aren't I?"—*Vickey*

Realizing her competition was not dead, the queen transformed herself into a witch (which did not take much effort, I might add) and went to find the girl. When she did, she devised a foolproof plan to offer Snow White a poisoned apple that would kill her.

The dwarfs warned Snow White not to talk to any strangers while they were away doing their chores in the forest. But when the witch came bringing the tempting apple, Snow White took a bite and fell into a deep sleep.

As a child, I remember reading the story of Snow White and almost crying at the fate of one so lovely. As an adult, I read the story and realized it is more than a fairy tale; it is our story as well.

Satan was once a lovely prince. Ezekiel describes him as once being "full of wisdom and perfect in beauty," with every precious stone as his covering. He was the anointed cherub who was on the mountain of God (Ezekiel 28:12-14). But pride was his downfall, and he wanted to be like God. As a result, God cast Satan from heaven with one-third of all the angels (Isaiah 14:12-23). After his downfall, he was no longer the "fairest of them all." Satan, like the cruel and wicked queen, then came after us with poisoned fruit of disobedience.

But the story of Snow White didn't end with her caught in the evil spell. One day a handsome prince came riding through the forest on his white horse. When he saw Snow White deep in sleep, he fell in love with her and placed a kiss upon her lips. When he did, she sat up, blinked her eyes, and sprang to life. The prince scooped Snow White into his arms and took her off to his castle, where they lived happily ever after.

Oh dear sisters, a handsome Prince has come into our lives as well. His name is Jesus. Our Prince has placed a kiss upon our lips, taken us in His strong arms, and lifted the evil curse. Now when we look into the mirror of God's Word and ask, "Who's the fairest of them all?" God answers, "You are, my child," for He sees the reflection of His Son in our eyes.

> As a child of God
> Looks daily into the Word of God
> And beholds intently the glory of God
> As manifested in the Son of God,
> She shall, by the will of God,
> Be transformed into the image of God.
>
> Harry Reeder[16]

5

To Have a Best Friend

Anne tipped the vase of apple blossoms near enough to bestow a soft kiss on a pink-cupped bud, and then studied diligently for some moments longer.

"Marilla," she demanded presently, "do you think that I shall ever have a bosom friend in Avonlea?"

"A—a what kind of friend?"

"A bosom friend—an intimate friend, you know—a really kindred spirit to whom I can confide my inmost soul. I've dreamed of meeting her all my life. I never really supposed I would, but so many of my loveliest dreams have come true all at once that perhaps this one will, too. Do you think it's possible?"

"Diana Barry lives over at the Orchard Slope and she's about your age. She's a very nice little girl, and perhaps she will be a playmate for you when she comes home. She's visiting her aunt over at

Carmody just now. You'll have to be careful how you behave your-self, though. Mrs. Barry is a very particular woman. She won't let Diana play with any little girl who isn't nice and good."

Anne looked at Marilla through the apple blossoms, her eyes aglow with interest.

"What is Diana like? Her hair isn't red, is it? Oh, I hope not. It's bad enough to have red hair myself, but I positively couldn't endure it in a bosom friend."

"Diana is a very pretty little girl. She has black eyes and hair and rosy cheeks. And she is good and smart, which is better than being pretty."

"Oh, I'm so glad she's pretty. Next to being beautiful oneself—and that's impossible in my case—it would be best to have a beautiful bosom friend. When I lived with Mrs. Thomas, she had a bookcase in her sitting room with glass doors. There weren't any books in it. Mrs. Thomas kept her best china and her preserves there—when she had any preserves to keep. One of the doors was broken. Mr. Thomas smashed it one night when he was slightly intoxicated.

"But the other was whole, and I used to pretend that my reflec-tion in it was another little girl who lived in it. I called her Katie Maurice, and we were very intimate. I used to talk to her by the hour, especially on Sunday, and tell her everything. Katie was the comfort and consolation of my life. We used to pretend that the bookcase was enchanted and that if I only knew the spell, I could open the door and step right into the room where Katie Maurice lived, instead of into Mrs. Thomas's shelves of preserves and china. And then Katie Maurice would have taken me by the hand and led me out into a wonderful place, all flowers and sunshine and fairies, and we would have lived there happy forever after.

"When I went to live with Mrs. Hammond, it just broke my

heart to leave Katie Maurice. She felt it dreadfully, too. I know she did, for she was crying when she kissed me good-bye through the bookcase door."[1]

Anne of Green Gables is one of my favorite childhood stories. In the above scene, Anne shares her dream of having a lifelong bosom friend and echoes the hopes and dreams of most little girls, still—to have a best friend, someone who understands your past, believes in your future, and accepts you just the way you are, warts and all.

When I was a little girl, I had the dream to have a bosom buddy or best friend. In the first grade, my best friend was Kim. In the second, third, and fourth, it was Pam. In the fifth, it was another Kim. And in the sixth grade, it varied from week to week as competition and coyness crept in to create havoc on the friendships of budding young adolescents.

Then there was Liz. From the seventh grade until the day we both walked across the stage to receive our high school diplomas, we were "bosom friends." But sometimes the flow of life has a strange way of causing friends to drift apart. Liz and I went away to different colleges and found our own circle of friends that did not include each other. Interests, life choices, future goals, and personal passions grew in opposite directions like divergent streams, and a love that once flooded the banks evaporated to a mere trickle. Currents of thought shift, rivers of choices diverge, and hundred of tributaries of other acquaintances form anew.

Even though I am in my 40s and have been married for over 20 years, I still feel the tug to have a best girlfriend.

Little Girls' Friendships Are Different from Little Boys'

I have a teenage son, and it has been interesting over the years to watch how little boys' relationships and little girls' relationships differ. Little girls are more likely to be drawn to one or two best friends, and boys tend to be a part of a team or group. Little girls huddle to tell secrets, giggle, and chat about this or that, while boys huddle in dugouts and on sidelines, participating in group activities such as baseball, basketball, or football.

Sociologist Janet Lever notes the differences in the relationships between girls and boys: "There is usually an open show of affection between little girls, both physically in the form of hand-holding and verbally through 'love notes' that reaffirm how special each is to the other. Although boys are likely to have best friends as well, their friendships tend to be less intimate and expressive than girls'. Hand-holding and love notes are virtually unknown among boys, and the confidences that boys share are more likely to be group 'secrets' than expressions of private thoughts and feelings."[2]

In second grade, our principal (a woman) visited our classroom to have a heart-to-heart with the girls: "You girls need to stop walking down the hall with your arms around each other. Think how silly it would look if Mrs. Macon and I walked down the hall hand in hand or with our arms on each other's shoulders." At that point she and Mrs. Macon put their arms over each other's shoulders. We snickered. They did indeed look strange. But we were little girls, not old ladies (which is how we viewed the two of them). How sad I felt for them not to have a good friend like I did.

Big Girls' Friendships Are Different from Big Boys'

Elliot Engel observed a female phenomenon in the relationships his wife had with other women. When he watched his wife and her best friend say good-bye before a cross-country move, he found their last hugs were so painful to witness that he finally had to leave the room. He said, "I've always been amazed at the nurturing emotional support my wife can seek and return with her close female friends. . . . Her three-hour talks with friends refresh and renew her far more than my three-mile jogs restore me. In our society it seems as if you've got to have a bosom to be a buddy."[3]

Just as our bodies were crafted to bear children, our hearts were crafted to "bear" friends. This is even evident in the cradle. Studies show that girl babies are more likely than boy babies to cry (as if in sympathy) when they hear other babies crying.[4]

"I have dreamed of having a best friend of my very own my whole life. I dreamed we'd grow old together after sharing our lives, our kids would grow up together and we'd live close by."—*Colette*

For most women, talking with friends is more than a pastime; it is essential to our well-being and a major way to connect on an intimate level. In fact, research has shown that women who enjoy close friendships are more likely to live longer and have fewer incidents of depression.[5] Another interesting study showed the following: "Friendships between women are special. They shape who we are and who we are yet to be. They soothe our tumultuous inner world, fill the emotional gaps in our marriage, and help us remember who we really are. But they may do even more. Scientists now suspect that hanging out with our friends can actually counteract the kind of stomach-quivering stress most of us experience on a daily basis."[6]

"Until this study was published, scientists generally believed that when people experience stress, they trigger a hormonal cascade that revs the body to either stand and fight or flee as fast as possible," explains Laura Cousino Klein, Ph.D., now an assistant professor of biobehavioral health at Pennsylvania State University in State College and one of the study's authors. "It seems that when the hormone oxytocin is released as part of the stress response in a woman, it buffers the 'fight or flight' response and encourages her to tend children and gather with other women instead. When she actually engages in this tending or befriending, studies suggest that more oxytocin is released, which rather counters stress and produces a calming effect. . . . In fact, the results were so significant, the researchers concluded, that not having a close friend or confidante was as detrimental to your health as smoking or carrying extra weight."[7]

I just knew those Frappuccinos I have with my friends were good for me!

"When I was little, I always had a best friend. As we got older, my best friend and I went separate ways and lost contact. There are times now I dream of having a best friend again."—*Tammy*

After a draining week of ministry, I am refreshed by two hours of conversation with a girlfriend at a coffee shop. On the other hand, after a hard week at work, my husband is refreshed by four hours of golf and swing analysis with a foursome on the greens. When he comes home, I always ask, "What did you guys talk about?" He looks at me with a strange expression and replies, "We talked about our game." You'd think I'd stop asking after a while.

Big Girls Need Friends Too

At almost every retreat or conference where I speak, a woman shares her hidden pain of not being able to develop deep, enduring friendships. "I have been at this church for three years," Nancy shared. "I see women all around me who have best friends. I've tried everything I know, inviting others to lunch, offering my house as the place for Sunday school socials, and sending people cards from time to time. But it just seems like the women in the church already have established friendships and there's no room for me."

After two years, Camma dropped out of her Bible study. "I've tried to be their friend, but not one of them called me to go to lunch or included me in their weekend activities. I hear them talk about their fun times shopping or going to the movies and I feel so left out."

Wherever I go, women echo Nancy and Camma's lament. We long to be in relationship with one another. We thirst for a friend who knows what we need without even asking, who picks us up when we are down, who doesn't criticize our husband or children but encourages us to love them well, who is eager to hear our dreams for the future, and is willing to help us make those dreams come true.

"I dreamed about having a best friend who would be a
loving, unconditional person that lends me her ear at any
given moment, holds me when I hurt, laughs with me when
I am happy, and sits with me when words aren't necessary.
I want to give that back in return."—*Annie*

We hunger for someone who doesn't ask how she can help, but immediately begins to pitch in when our load grows too heavy, with whom we can be completely honest without the fear of rejection or condemnation, with whom we can share our victories and successes without the fear of jealousy or competition, and with whom we can confide our personal and spiritual struggles without fear of judgment or lecture.

We yearn for a friend who is on our team, cheering us on as we run the great race of life and encouraging us to get up when we fall. We desire someone who will listen to our problems and offer advice sparingly when asked, who will dream dreams with and for us and then help us accomplish those dreams, who looks for gifts God has given us and helps us develop those gifts.

In my years of working with women, I have observed clusters of friends. Just today I had lunch with three dear women, almost 20 years my senior, who share such a love and a bond I did not need food to receive nourishment. Their conversation and laughter fed my soul. I was with them because they invited me to join them, but I was not one of them. Oh, they love me dearly, but the three of them share a special connection that is woven after many years of struggle, sadness, sorrow, loss, laughter, lunches, shopping, phone conversations, and prayer. It was a privilege and an honor to sip from the deep well they shared.

In 2002, clusters of women gathered in darkened cinemas with popcorn, soft drinks, and wounded hearts to watch the movie *Divine Secrets of the Ya Ya Sisterhood*. I was among such a group. It is the story of four little girls who made a pact to be lifelong friends. We were allowed to follow their passing years and observe how that bond carried them through the storms, how they were stretcher bearers during the difficult years, and how they loved and laughed through it all. But the reality is, lifelong friends like the four women in the Ya Ya Sisterhood are very rare. To find one such friend is a treasure indeed.

Friendship Is God's Design

I believe that God, our Father, understands a woman's desire to have a bosom friend. He created us to be in relationship. In Luke 1, the angel Gabriel delivered some pretty incredible news to young Mary. While still a virgin, she was going to conceive a child by the Holy Spirit and give birth to the Savior of the world. Before Mary could catch her breath, the angel continued by telling her, "Oh, by the way, your supposedly barren cousin, Elizabeth, is also with child in her old age" (Jaynes version). Gabriel knew the young girl was going to need the encouragement of a friend who would understand, so before she could even ask, he sent her to Elizabeth.

"Someone who will call me or I can call at the drop of a hat. Someone who I can be myself with, who will love me and never stop being my best friend. That's what I dream about."—*Helen*

So Mary, probably around 16 years old, traveled 100 miles from Galilee to Judea to spend three months with her cousin. When Mary walked into Elizabeth's home, the older woman gave her a blessing: "Blessed are you among women, and blessed is the child you will bear! But why am I so favored, that the mother of my Lord should come to me? As soon as the sound of your greeting reached my ears, the baby in my womb leaped for joy. Blessed is she who has believed that what the Lord has said to her will be accomplished!" (Luke 1:42-45).

Can you imagine the turmoil Mary felt as she traveled to Judea? *No one is ever going to believe me. Joseph is going to put me away. And what will my parents think?* And can you imagine how Elizabeth's words of encouragement were a balm to the young girl? God divinely revealed His plan to Elizabeth, and she in turn affirmed Mary before she revealed her news. What a precious Lord we serve!

Mary was so encouraged, she broke out into song. She stayed with Elizabeth for about three months, no doubt helped with the labor and delivery of John, and then returned home.

Jesus and His Friends

Jesus Himself had best friends. Think of concentric circles with graduated smaller ones inside the larger ones, like an archery target. His first and largest realm of influence was to the multitudes. Next, He gave special attention to 72 men He sent out to heal and cast out demons. Smaller still, Jesus gathered 12 men to be His good friends whom He closely discipled. But then He chose an even smaller group of three to be His best friends—Peter, James, and John. These three men were privy to Jesus' transfiguration (Mark 9:2), His deep sorrow in the Garden of Gethsemane (Mark 14:32), and the first in the empty tomb (John 20:3).

But there was also the bull's-eye of friendship, if you will, that Jesus shared with no man. It was a place reserved for God alone. Before His arrest, Jesus took Peter, James, and John with Him to Gethsemane to pray. However, He left the three and went "a little farther" to be alone with His Father. It was a place where no man could join Him, no man could calm Him, no man could reassure Him. He had to go alone. I honestly believe that is a place we rarely go, but a place where Jesus longs for us to join Him.

"When I was young, I dreamed of having wonderful friends that would do special things for me, like the popular kids at school."—*Donna*

Dee Brestin, in her book *The Friendships of Women,* describes our relationships this way: "Like gently moving streams joining into one river, we round the difficult bends of life together, strengthening each other with a fresh water supply. We are free and flowing and unconcerned with boundaries. . . .We are afraid to run toward the ocean alone."[8]

What a beautiful picture of the refreshing, refueling, and renewing power of friendship. However, our friends were never intended to meet our greatest need to be in relationship. No woman—or man—can fill all our emotional needs. If we look to one friend or a few for everything, we'll be doomed to disappointment. That is an empty place only Jesus can fill.

I have found that when I feel empty inside and try to grasp desperately at friends to fill the void, I come up emptier than before. At those low points, friendships seem to elude me. The more frantically I grasp, the more elusive true friendships appear. However, if I go to Jesus Christ and allow Him to fill me with His love, I move from needy to full, and from being a taker to a giver. Then I find friendships are plentiful. When God calls us to come "a little farther" away to be completely alone with Him in the garden of our souls, but we go to our friends instead, we will be sorely disappointed. People are a poor substitute for God. So let's take a moment and look at the best friend a girl could ever have—Jesus Christ.

Jesus—Our Bosom Friend

One of the most intimate times Jesus spent with His 12 best friends occurred in the Upper Room the night before His arrest. He assured them, "Greater love has no one than this, that he lay down his life for his friends. You are my friends if you do what I command. I no longer call you servants, because a servant does not know his master's business. Instead, I have called you friends, for everything that I learned from my Father I have made known to you" (John 15:13-15).

No matter how close we may feel to our earthly friends, they will inevitably disappoint us. Human beings were never intended to fill the God-shaped void in our lives. Yes, we may have a bosom friend, as Anne of Green Gables described, but there is a place in our bosom that's meant for Jesus Christ alone. He is the Friend of our dreams.

Let's look at some ways that Jesus truly is our best Friend, using A through Z.

A Jesus *accepts* us just as we are. I'm always encouraged that He didn't tell the ones He called to change first and then follow Him. No, He told them to follow Him because He knew they would change along the way as they stayed close to Him.

B Jesus *believes* in us and encourages us to do even greater things than He did while He was on earth (John 14:12). He even appoints us to be His ambassadors or representatives here on earth.

C He *counsels* us with His Word when we have difficult decisions to make (Isaiah 9:6).

D He *defends* us in spiritual warfare to make us more than conquerors (Romans 8:37).

E Jesus *encourages* us: "You give them something to eat," He encouraged the disciples as they looked on the hungry crowd of 5,000 men plus women and children. "Come," He called to Peter as He held out His hand urging him to walk on the water with Him (Matthew 14:29). "Go," He commanded His 12 disciples as He sent them out with authority to drive out evil spirits and heal every disease and sickness (Matthew 10:1). Jesus doesn't need our help, but He encourages us to join Him and thus fulfill our dreams.

F A true friend forgives, and Jesus *forgives* us when we fail, just as He forgave Peter who denied he even knew Jesus the night of His arrest (Matthew 26:69-75).

G The ultimate test of friendship is found in the fact that Jesus *gave* His life for us: "Greater love has no one than this, that he lay down his life for his friends" (John 15:13).

H What a friend we have in Jesus! He *helps* us when we call on Him: "The Lord is my helper; I will not be afraid. What can man do to me?" (Hebrews 13:6).

I He lives to make *intercession* for us, praying for us constantly (Romans 8:34).

J Jesus is *joyful* when we have victory in our lives. When the 72 disciples came back home telling how they cast out demons and healed the sick in His name, Jesus was full of joy (Luke 10:21). That Greek word for joy, *agalliao,* means to leap for joy or to show one's joy by leaping and skipping; excessive or ecstatic joy and delight.[9] It's not a picture depicted often of Jesus, but I dare say He jumps for joy over our triumphs!

K Not only is Jesus a true *kindred* spirit, as Anne of Green Gable desired, but Jesus and believers share the same spirit—the Holy Spirit (John 14:17). You can't get much closer than that.

L A true friend is one who *listens*, and Jesus is a great listener. Even while dying on the cross, He took the time to listen to the thief being crucified with Him and offer him the promise of eternal life (Luke 23:43).

M He is our *mediator* who bridges the gap between God and man: "For there is one God and one mediator between God and men, the man Christ Jesus, who gave himself as a ransom for all men— the testimony given in its proper time" (1 Timothy 2:5-6).

N One of the best facets of having Jesus as our best Friend is that He *never changes.* He's the same yesterday, today, and tomorrow (Hebrews 13:8).

O He's *omnipotent* (all-powerful), *omnipresent* (everywhere at once), and *omniscient* (all-knowing). We'll do well to remember that He is the *only* Friend who possesses those qualities.

P Betrayal, according to a test administered by *Psychology Today* to 40,000 people, is the main reason close friendships end.[10] But with Jesus as our best Friend, betrayal is not a possibility. He is a *Promise Keeper* who cannot lie because He is Truth (John 14:6).

Q Jesus *quiets* our fears with peace (John 14:27).

R He *restores* our souls with Living Water (John 4:10).

S He is our *Shepherd* who prods us with His staff when we are moving too slowly and pulls us back with the Shepherd's crook when we start to stray (John 10:11).

T But like a good Shepherd, He *tenderly* cares for us and has compassion for our weakness (Matthew 15:32). He wept when He saw how the friends of Lazarus mourned at his death. Jesus had compassion on the crowds who were sick and diseased, a woman caught in adultery, lepers with rotting bodies, a woman who had been bleeding for many years, a man blind from birth, a soldier with a sick child, and a little girl from eastern North Carolina born into a home with unsaved parents—me. What a friend!

U Webster's dictionary defines a friend as a person "on the same side of a struggle." Jesus *understands* our weaknesses because He has lived on this side of heaven in the confines of a human body (Hebrews 4:15).

V Jesus loved to *visit* people's homes while He was walking the earth as a man, and He still loves to visit our homes today. In *The Message*, Eugene Peterson paraphrased John 1:14 this way: "The Word became flesh and blood, and moved into the neighborhood." He loves to make house calls!

W From the very beginning, people were amazed at Jesus' *wisdom*. When He taught in the synagogue, the people asked, "Where did this man get this wisdom and these miraculous powers?" (Matthew 13:54). When we know Him, He doesn't keep that wisdom to Himself, but shares that same wisdom with us: "Christ, in whom are hidden all the treasures of wisdom and knowledge" (Colossians 2:3).

X Jesus promises to never *X* us off His list or let anything or anyone separate us (Romans 8:35).

Y We are *yoked* together for all eternity (Matthew 11:29).

Z He is *zealous* about His friendship with us.

I don't know about you, but I'm absolutely crazy in love with this best Friend of mine. I do know this about Him: He's crazy in love with you!

> Christ Jesus:
> Who, being in very nature God,
> did not consider equality with God something to be grasped,
> but made himself nothing,
> taking the very nature of a servant,
> being made in human likeness.
> And being found in appearance as a man,
> he humbled himself
> and became obedient to death—
> even death on a cross!
> Therefore God exalted him to the highest place
> and gave him the name that is above every name,
> that at the name of Jesus every knee should bow,
> in heaven and on earth and under the earth,
> and every tongue confess that Jesus Christ is Lord,
> to the glory of God the Father.
> Philippians 2:5-11

He did that for you. What a friend!

Anne Finds Her Bosom Friend

"Oh, Diana," said Anne at last, clasping her hands and speaking almost in a whisper, "do you think—oh, do you think you can like me a little—enough to be my bosom friend?"

Diana laughed. Diana always laughed before she spoke.

"Why, I guess so," she said frankly. "I'm awfully glad you've come to live at Green Gables. It will be jolly to have somebody to play with. There isn't any other girl who lives near enough to play with, and I've no sisters big enough."

"Will you swear to be my friend forever and ever?" demanded Anne eagerly.

Diana looked shocked.

"Why, it's dreadfully wicked to swear," she said rebukingly.

"Oh no, not my kind of swearing. There are two kinds, you know."

"I never heard of but one kind," said Diana doubtfully.

"There really is another. Oh, it isn't wicked all. It just means vowing and promising solemnly."

"Well, I don't mind doing that," agreed Diana, relieved. "How do you do it?"

"We must join hands—so," said Anne gravely. "It ought to be over running water. We'll just imagine this path is running water. I'll repeat the oath first. I solemnly swear to be faithful to my bosom friend, Diana Barry, as long as the sun and moon shall endure. Now you say it and put my name in."

Diana repeated the "oath" with a laugh fore and aft. Then she said, "You're a queer girl, Anne. I heard before that you were queer. But I believe I'm going to like you real well."[11]

PART TWO

Women in the Bible and Their Dreams

6

Sarah—A Woman Who Interfered with God's Dreams

Sarai reclined on her scarlet-and-purple-tapestry-covered sofa and looked around at the blessings that surrounded her on every side.

Yes, she thought to herself, *I have everything a woman ever dreamed of. I have a husband who adores and respects me, which is more than most Hebrew women, who are treated like chattel, can boast. We have great wealth—even if some of our inheritance did come from my father-in-law's idol-making business. We have a beautiful cedar and stone home with servants to care for our every need. And, if I am to believe the accolades of the men and women in our town, I have beauty that seems to defy my years. Yes, I have everything a woman could want.*

Just then, Sarai heard a baby's cry carried on the wind and right to her heart. Suddenly, as quickly as an approaching storm cloud looms on a clear summer day, a longing deep within her soul overshadowed Sarai's countenance. There was one thing she did not have, one thing she would gladly give all her worldly possessions to obtain. She wanted to be a mother, to suckle a babe at her breast, and give her husband an heir.

Sarai was startled from her dark musing by her husband, Abram, bursting through the front door.

"Sarai, I have some news."

"What is it, Abram, that you startle me so!" she said.

"God spoke to me today. He told me that we are to leave this place and go to a place He will show us."

"That's it?" she asked quizzically. "Just pick up and go? He'll tell us where later?"

"That's it. Just go," Abram answered. "Well, there was one more little detail. God said He would make of me a great nation."

The cloud returned. The word *barren* echoed in her head. "How long will we be gone? Who will take care of your father? What will we do with all of our furniture? I am 65 and you are 75. It's time to start thinking about slowing down—not moving on to a new place and starting over! What are you thinking?!"

"I don't know the answer to any of those questions. I only know what God said," Abram responded.

"What did God say—exactly?" Sarai asked.

"He said, 'Leave your country, your people, and your father's household and go to the land I will show you. I will make you into a great nation and I will bless you; I will make your name great, and you will be a blessing. I will bless those who bless you, and whoever curses you I will curse; and all peoples on earth will be blessed through you.' That is what He said."

Sarai got up from her seat, called her servant girls, and began to pack. She could argue with Abram, but she knew better than to argue with God. The couple bade farewell to their family and friends and began a journey to only God knew where.

After Abram and Sarai settled down in their goatskin tent in the land of Canaan, God spoke to Abram again. "Look up at the heavens and count the stars—if indeed you can count them. . . . So shall your offspring be" (Genesis 15:5). This was the second of seven times God would speak to Abram. Each time, he "believed the LORD, and [God] credited it to him as righteousness" (Genesis 15:6). Sarai, on the other hand, got tired of waiting on God and decided to interfere.

On their wedding day, Sarai had promised Abram a son to carry on the family name. It was customary in those days for a barren woman to offer her maidservant to her husband to serve as a surrogate mother. So Sarai made Abram the offer: "The LORD has kept me from having children. Go, sleep with my maidservant; perhaps I can build a family through her" (Genesis 16:2).

"But God specifically said . . ." Abram argued.

"I know what God said," she interrupted, "but I'm 75 years old."

Abram believed God, but he was swayed by his beautiful wife. He gave the same answer Adam gave to Eve in the garden when she offered him the forbidden fruit—"Yes, dear."

Sarai's maid, Hagar, quickly conceived and began to act arrogantly toward her barren mistress. Sarai's interference had created a monster in Hagar (as our interference often does). Abram was taken aback when Sarai stormed into the tent in a huff.

"This is all your fault. I put my servant in your arms, and now that she knows she is pregnant, she despises me." (Have you ever interfered and then blamed the consequences on someone else?)

At a loss, Abram said, "Do whatever you think best." He murmured as she stomped out of the room, "You always do anyway."

Sarai began mistreating Hagar so severely, the servant girl ran away into the desert. But the Lord appeared to Hagar and encouraged her to go back to her mistress and submit to her. He also gave Hagar a promise regarding her son: "You shall name him Ishmael, for the LORD has heard of your misery. He will be a wild donkey of a man; his hand will be against everyone and everyone's hand against him, and he will live in hostility toward all his brothers" (Genesis 16:11-12).

Hagar did return and a few months later gave the 86-year-old Abram a son. They named him Ishmael, just as God commanded.

Thirteen years later, God came to Abram again and reminded him of His promise to make of him a great nation through his wife, Sarai. This time, Abram fell facedown and laughed (Genesis 17:17). He was 99 and Sarai was 89. God reinforced the promise by establishing a covenant and changing Abram's name to Abraham, which means, "father of many nations" or "father of a multitude." God changed Sarai's name to Sarah, which means, "princess and mother of many" or "one whose seed would produce kings."[1]

When three angels came back a few months later, Sarah overhead them telling Abraham that Sarah would birth a child before year's end. This time, Sarah burst out laughing. Apparently, the angels heard her laugh and said, "Is anything too hard for the LORD?"

Sarah laughed at the angels' prediction, but the joke was on her. One year later, she gave birth to a baby boy and named him Isaac, which means "laughter." Through this baby, God made Abraham a great nation, with more descendants than the stars in the sky.

And what of Ishmael? He was about 14 when Isaac was born, and he wasn't too pleased. He mocked Sarah's son and eventually she sent Abraham's firstborn and his mother away to the desert. Hagar and her son were on the verge of dehydration and starvation, but God led her to a spring of water and renewed His promise to take care of them.

In time, Ishmael became the father of the Arab people, and Isaac became the father of the Jewish people. I have to wonder about the constant conflict we see between the two nationalities even today. What would have happened if Sarah had not interfered with God's dream for her life? She made a decision that has affected the entire world and will for many years to come.

What Can We Learn from Sarah?

Our interference can have devastating results. God had an incredible plan for Abraham and Sarah. While His plan was still accomplished despite Sarah's scheming, her interference caused much heartache and strife. Many times we have a tendency to run ahead of God when we feel He is not acting quickly enough. We connive, cajole, coax, and conspire. We hamper, hinder, hassle, and hurry.

Jeremiah 29:11 promises that God has a plan for each and every one of us: " 'For I know the plans I have for you,' declares the LORD, 'plans to prosper you and not to harm you, plans to give you hope and a future.' " He does not need our interference to accomplish that plan. He desires our obedience and cooperation to walk in tandem with Him.

God has given us a free will and allows us to storm ahead, but He also allows the consequences of our interference to affect our lives. Because of Sarah's interference, Hagar's son, Ishmael, was born. Muhammad, the founder of the Muslim people and Islam faith, came from Ishmael's family tree. God predicted tension between the offspring of Ishmael and Isaac, and we see that conflict raging even today.

Have you ever interfered with God's plans? I admit I have on many occasions. For example, I have a wonderful marriage and want everyone else to be as happily married as we are. (I bet you know what's coming.) I confess the sin of matchmaking. Now I know it's not really a sin, but trying to fix other people's lives and interfere with God's plan for them is.

I had this tendency to make matches before I was married. When I was in high school, a friend of mine came home after two years of college very discouraged and defeated. He had made many bad choices and was going to have to drop out of school. The same day he told me about his plight, I met a girl at the local mall who was visiting her cousin, a friend of mine.

"Robby," I said, "I just met a girl I think you'd really like. Her name is Beth and she's here visiting her cousin, Claire. Why don't you give her a call? I bet she'd perk you up."

Well, he gave her a call and six months later asked her to marry him. But there was a problem: Beth was a Christian and Robby was not. I was exasperated because I had made the match. I begged Beth not to marry him.

"Please," I begged, "God says for Christians not to be unequally yoked to nonbelievers. Please don't marry him. Give it some time."

"I know he's not a Christian," she rationalized, "but God can change his heart. I believe that my love will draw him to Christ."

All my arguments fell on deaf ears. Beth married Robby, and they had 25 years of hardship and heartbreak until he finally left her for another woman. I often wonder what would have happened if I had not interfered and encouraged Robby to call Beth. I'll never know.

Our interference can have devastating results.

No one wins the blame game. After Sarai convinced Abram to sleep with Hagar and conceive a child, she turned and blamed Abram for the tension that was birthed between her and her maid. I read those words and shook my head—how silly. Then I read them again and thought—how familiar.

Isn't that what Eve did? "The devil made me do it. It's all his fault," she said.

How many times do we interfere with God's plans and then blame someone else for the consequences? We blame our misguided parents, our difficult spouses, our unreasonable bosses, our unruly children, and the list goes on. Admitting one's mistakes and failures is the first step to becoming a Christian and the stepping-stones to maturity along the way. The book of 1 John reminds us that "If we confess our sins, he is faithful and just and will forgive us our sins and purify us from all unrighteousness" (1 John 1:9). The book of James echoes, "Therefore confess your sins to each other [admit your mistakes] and pray for each other so that you may be healed" (James 5:16).

When my son was young, I tried to teach him how to ask for forgiveness and say, "I'm sorry." His tendency was to follow "I'm sorry" with the rationalization behind why he committed the offense. However, in true repentance, one takes full responsibility for his or her actions and commits to turn and go in the opposite direction.

The devil never "makes us do it," but he sure does offer some powerful suggestions. The good news is that God promises we will never be tempted beyond what we are able to resist, but will always provide a way out (1 Corinthians 10:13). That includes the temptation to interfere with His plans.

God can use what God does not choose. The sexual relationship between a man and a woman is a beautifully exciting act of love ordained by God. However, the Bible is very clear that sex outside of marriage is out of His will. Adultery and premarital sex have caused insurmountable ills in our world today: broken homes, illegitimate children, sexually transmitted diseases, depression, sterility, and infertility. One such consequence is children born without the security of a mother and father living in a monogamous, heterosexual relationship bound together by the covenant of marriage. Regardless of how a child comes into the world, God still loves that child.

No, God did not will for Abraham to father a child with Hagar, and yet He had compassion on her and her son. He did not leave Hagar and Ishmael in the desert to die but rather heard their cry for help and came to their aid. In the first incident, when Hagar ran away from home, God sent a spring of water in the desert and encouraged the maid to return and submit to her mistress. In the second incident, when Hagar was sent away from home, God again provided a spring of water. "God was with the boy as he grew up. He lived in the desert and became an archer. While he was living in the Desert of Paran, his mother got a wife for him from Egypt" (Genesis 21:20-21).

There is a well-known story of some men in Scotland who had spent the day fishing. That evening they were having tea in a little inn. One of the fishermen, in a characteristic gesture to describe the size of the fish that got away, slung out his hands just as the little waitress was getting ready to set the cup of tea at his place. The hand and the teacup collided, dashing the tea against the white-washed wall. Immediately an ugly brown stain began to spread over the wall.

The man who did it was very embarrassed and apologized profusely, but one of the other guests jumped up and said, "Never mind." Pulling a pen from his pocket, he began to sketch around the ugly brown stain. Soon there emerged a picture of a magnificent royal stag with his antler spread. The artist was Sir Edwin Lanseer, England's foremost painter of animals.[2]

What a wonderful picture that is of God taking our mistakes and somehow creating a beautiful work of art.

God's timetable is not our timetable. God is omnipotent (all powerful), omnipresent (everywhere at once), and omniscient (all knowing). And often, He shows His power in the last moments of desperation when all we have left is to trust in Him. God could have provided Sarah with a child when she was 40 or 50, but by waiting until she was 90, everyone knew this was nothing short of a miracle.

Being involved in ministry has been a tremendous tool to teach me to depend on God for financial needs. At Proverbs 31 Ministries we have seen many days when we didn't know how we were going to pay tomorrow's bills, and then an unexpected check would come in the mail.

On one particular occasion, we needed $3,000 to meet the end of the month's bills. We prayed and I worried. I called the office and spoke to our executive director: "Joel, I'm just going to write a personal check to cover the bills."

"No," he said. "God called you to this ministry, but He did not call you to fix every problem. I believe that we need to let God handle this."

I was amazed at his faith, especially since he was in charge of the finances, and my offer would have solved his dilemma.

The next day Joel called. "Sharon," he said, a little choked up, "we got a check today from a church. It was for $3,000."

What would have happened if I had interfered the day before? I'm not sure. But I do know that God did not need me to fix the problem. He had everything under control. God's timetable is not our timetable. It may seem as though He is moving too slowly, moving too quickly, or has forgotten our dream altogether. However, He has everything under control. Our job is to trust Him.

7

Naomi—A Woman Who Forgot Her Dreams

Naomi was a young girl when she met and married Elimelech. His name meant "God is King," and she knew that he would always serve the living God of Israel. She had a dream to live all her days in the fertile land of Bethlehem, which meant "house of bread." She also dreamed of having many strapping, robust young sons, beautiful, wise daughters, and a passel of grandchildren crowding around her feet in her later years.

Naomi did have two sons, but they weren't quite what she had expected. From the time they entered the world and gave their first cries,

Naomi could tell they were not exactly warrior material. One boy she named Mahlon, which means "puny or weakling," and the other she named Kilion, which means "pining."

When the boys were still young lads, a terrible famine hit the land of Bethlehem. In an effort to provide for his family, Elimelech decided they should move to Moab, a grain-filled plateau east of the Dead Sea. It was not a land suitable for farming, but he could raise goats and sheep on the plentiful grain. The boys grew older, if not stronger, and married Moabite women. This was not Naomi's dream for her boys; after all, God's law forbade Israelites from marrying Moabites (Deuteronomy 7:1-4). But what was she to do when Elimelech agreed to the unions?

Naomi made new friends and tried not to think of the homeland she had left behind. But suddenly, her life took a drastic turn for the worse. Her husband died. Then over the next ten years, both her sons died. With the death of these three men, Naomi's hopes and dreams died as well. She felt discouraged, dejected, and depressed with no one to take care of her. She did have two wonderful daughters-in-law, but without husbands to bring children into the world and carry on the family name, her future and theirs were barren.

"Girls," Naomi announced one day after much contemplation, "I have heard news from my homeland. God has remembered Bethlehem and the famine has passed. There is no reason for me to stay in Moab, and I have decided to return to the land of my people. I want you both to go back to your mothers' houses and find other nice young men to marry. I pray God will be as kind to you as you have been to me."

Naomi kissed each of the girls as they wept loudly. "We will go back with you to your people," they cried. "No, my daughters," Naomi said. "Go back home. There's no reason for you to come with me. I know it is the custom for you to marry another son in a family if your husband dies, but I'm not going to have any more sons. Even if I did, I wouldn't want you to wait around until they were old enough to marry. Now, go back to your mothers' houses. That is the best solution. The Lord's hand has gone out against me. My dreams are buried with Elimelech, Mahlon, and Kilion."

The two women loved their mother-in-law dearly and clung to her robe with tears streaming down their cheeks. After what seemed like hours, one of the girls, Orpah, kissed her mother-in-law goodbye and turned to walk away.

The other girl, Ruth, embraced Naomi and begged to go with her: "Don't urge me to leave you or to turn back from you. Where you go I will go, and where you stay I will stay. Your people will be my people and your God my God. Where you die I will die, and there I will be buried. May the LORD deal with me, be it ever so severely, if anything but death separates you and me" (Ruth 1:16-17).

Naomi and Ruth both knew that most Israelites despised Moabites. They had never forgiven the Moabites for hiring Balaam to place a curse on them after they left Egypt for the Promised Land many years before (Numbers 22–24). Regardless of the opposition Ruth knew she would face, she still desired to go and take care of her friend.

So Naomi gave in and allowed Ruth to return to Bethlehem with her. After an arduous journey, the two dusty and exhausted women reached their destination. The twosome caused quite a stir, and the townspeople began to whisper among themselves, "Could this be Naomi? It looks like her and yet it doesn't."

She was so depressed, downcast, and discouraged that her very countenance disguised the woman she had been before. Naomi heard the whispers as she walked by and stopped in her tracks. "'Don't call me Naomi,' [which means "pleasant"] she told them. 'Call me Mara, [which means "bitter"] because the Almighty has made my life very bitter. I went away full, but the LORD has brought me back empty. Why call me Naomi? The LORD has afflicted me; the Almighty has brought misfortune upon me'" (Ruth 1:20-21).

Ruth felt a pang in her heart at the words *brought me back empty.* Part of her thought, *What about me?* But the other part knew Naomi was speaking out of her loss and hurt.

Naomi was a woman who had forgotten her dreams and saw no hope of finding happiness or fulfillment ever again. She was blinded by bitterness and didn't even recognize the answer to her prayers walking right beside her in the form of a Moabite girl whose name meant "woman friend." Even though Naomi had lost her dreams, God had a plan to restore them.

The next day, Ruth went out to glean in the barley fields. It was customary for the farmers to allow the poor to come behind the workers and pick up the barley that was left scattered on the ground after the harvesters had completed their work. Most likely, Ruth and Naomi knew that it would be dangerous for a Moabite woman to venture into the field because of the generational hostility toward them. However, Ruth took a chance in order to provide food for her friend.

It just so happened that Ruth went to the field owned by a man named Boaz. I hope you don't believe that for a second. There are no "it just so happened" occurrences in the kingdom of God. He led Ruth to this field. He was in the process of restoring Naomi's dreams and placed Ruth in the middle of a field owned by the one who would make those dreams come true.

"Who is that young woman?" Boaz, the owner of the field, asked his foreman.

"She is the Moabitess who came back from Moab with Naomi. She said, 'Please let me glean and gather among the sheaves behind the harvesters.' She went into the field and has worked steadily from morning till now, except for a short rest in the shelter" (Ruth 2: 6-7).

Something began to stir in Boaz at the sight of this one so faithful to the older woman who had lost so much. He had heard how she left her homeland and her people to care for her discouraged mother-in-law. Boaz called Ruth over to himself.

"My daughter, listen to me. Don't go and glean in another field and don't go away from here. Stay here with my servant girls. Watch the field where the men are harvesting, and follow along after the girls. I have told the men not to touch you. And whenever you are thirsty, go and get a drink from the water jars the men have filled" (Ruth 2:8-9).

"At this, she bowed down with her face to the ground. She exclaimed, 'Why have I found such favor in your eyes that you notice me—a foreigner?'" (Ruth 2:10).

"Boaz replied, 'I've been told all about what you have done for your mother-in-law since the death of your husband—how you left your father and mother and your homeland and came to live with a people you did not know before. May the LORD repay you for what you have done. May you be richly rewarded by the LORD, the God of Israel, under whose wings you have come to take refuge,'" (Ruth 2:11-12).

Ruth had a very fruitful day of gleaning. She noticed that some of the workers she followed pulled out the choice barley from their bundles and left it on the ground for her to pick up. Boaz invited her to have lunch with him and his men, eating all the roasted barley she could hold and drinking from the wine and vinegar.

When Ruth went back home that evening, arms overflowing with choice barley, Naomi asked, "Where did you glean today to gather such a bountiful load?"

"His name was Boaz," Ruth replied, "and he was quite handsome, I might add."

"Boaz! I had forgotten all about him. He is one of our relatives—one of our kinsmen-redeemers."

"What is a kinsman-redeemer?" Ruth asked.

"In our customs, a kinsman-redeemer is a man who is responsible for protecting the interests of needy members of his extended family. He might provide an heir for a brother who has died, buy back land that a poor relative sold outside the family, or buy back a relative who had been sold into slavery."

Ruth noticed a flicker in Naomi's eyes that she had not seen since the loss of her husband and two sons. Yes, they had a wonderful dinner, and Ruth feasted on Naomi's much-missed chatter.

After the barley harvest passed, Naomi devised a plan: "Ruth, tonight, I want you to take a long bath, put on your best dress, and wear ample perfume. After dark, go down to Boaz's threshing floor. Don't let anyone see you. After Boaz has had plenty to drink and eat and lies down for the evening, note where he is sleeping. When you hear the heavy breathing that lets you know he is sound asleep, tiptoe over to him, uncover his feet, and lie down. He will tell you what to do when he wakes up."

"Is this another one of your Hebrew customs?" Ruth asked.

"Yes. Now listen carefully. When you uncover his feet and lie at the foot of his pallet, you are making known your desire for him to become your kinsman-redeemer and marry you. We call such a man as this a *go'el*. When he awakes, ask him to take the corner of his blanket and cover you. If he does, then he is agreeing to marry you."

"But suppose he doesn't want me?"

"Don't worry about that, child. From the rumors I've heard about the way he watches you in the fields, I don't think rejection is likely."

Ruth blushed at Naomi's comment and responded, "I'll do exactly what you say."

That night, Ruth snuck onto the threshing floor where Boaz and his men slept to protect the harvested barley. Just as Naomi instructed, she waited until Boaz was asleep, uncovered his feet, and lay down to wait until morning.

During the night, something startled Boaz and he woke up, noticing a woman at his feet!

"Who are you?" he asked, not able to recognize her in the darkness.

" 'I am your servant Ruth,' she said. 'Spread the corner of your garment over me, since you are a kinsman-redeemer' " (Ruth 3:9).

" 'The LORD bless you, my daughter,' he replied. 'This kindness is greater than that which you showed earlier: You have not run after the younger men, whether rich or poor. And now, my daughter, don't be afraid. I will do for you all you ask. All my fellow townsmen know that you are a woman of noble character. Although it is true that I am near of kin, there is a kinsman-redeemer nearer than I. Stay here for the night, and in the morning if he wants to redeem, good; let him redeem. But if he is not willing, as surely as the LORD lives I will do it. Lie here until morning,' " (Ruth 3:10-13).

The next morning, Boaz filled Ruth's shawl with barley and sent her back to Naomi. "What did he say? What did he say?" Naomi asked as Ruth came bursting through the door.

"He thanked me! Can you image that? He thanked me for asking!" Ruth replied. Then she filled her in on all the details.

In God's providence, the other relative was not interested in becoming Ruth's *go'el,* which opened the door for Boaz to marry her. What a joyous day when Boaz and Ruth became man and wife. Shortly thereafter, Ruth conceived and bore a son and named him Obed, who became the father of Jesse, who became the father of David, the most famous and powerful king in Israel's history.

I suspect Naomi told her friends to stop calling her Mara, for she was no longer bitter but ecstatically joyous. Her friends proclaimed, "Praise be to the LORD, who this day has not left you without a kinsman-redeemer. May he become famous throughout Israel! He will renew your life and sustain you in your old age. For your daughter-in-law, who loves you and who is better to you than seven sons, has given him birth" (Ruth 4:14-15).

What a glorious story. Naomi was a woman who forgot her dreams, yet God restored them and took her from a place of emptiness to fullness. He even placed her in the family tree of Jesus! Why do we ever doubt God's plans for our lives? He wants to give us exceedingly abundantly more than we could ever ask or think, and yet we tend to give up when times get hard. Admittedly, losing a husband and two sons is enough to devastate any woman, but what a wonderful picture that God will never leave or forsake us. He will provide someone to take care of us, even in the hardest, most difficult situations imaginable.

God provides a kinsman-redeemer. His name is Jesus Christ.

What Can We Learn from Naomi?

God sometimes uses other people to help restore our dreams. Naomi had become very bitter, and that bitterness blinded her from seeing God's provision of love, strength, and resources through Ruth.

After I lost a child through miscarriage, I didn't want to be around anyone for several months. The only people I did want to talk to were those who had experienced the same pain of losing a child. One friend in particular, Leigh Ann, sent me a poem that I still refer to today.

My Father's way may twist and turn.
My heart may throb and ache.
But in my soul I'm glad I know
He makes no mistake.

My cherished plans may go astray.
My hopes may fade away.

But still I'll trust my Lord to lead
For He does know the way.

Tho night be dark and it may seem
That day will never break;
I'll pin my faith, my all in Him,
He makes no mistake.

There's so much I cannot see,
My eyesight far too dim;
But come what may, I'll simply trust
And leave it all to Him.

For by and by the mist will lift
And plain it all He'll make
Through all the way, tho dark to me,
He made not one mistake.

A. M. Overton (1932)

God used Leigh Ann to help me remember that He does have a plan, and though I might not understand it, He makes no mistakes. While I did not have another child, God gave me a dream to be a spiritual mother to many.

God may use us to restore someone's broken dreams. When Naomi returned to town, her old acquaintances recognized that she was depressed and had suffered a great loss. She had gone away married and wealthy and had returned home widowed and poor. However, we see no signs that they offered to alleviate her pain or minister to her in any way.

Ruth gives us such a wonderful example of how to fan the dying embers of a friend's smoldering dreams. She didn't reprimand, lecture, or remind Naomi why she needed to be thankful or tell her to stop feeling sorry for herself. She simply loved her unconditionally, cared for her unceasingly, and supported her unselfishly. She certainly lived up to her name, *woman friend*.

In the South, we have a tradition similar to Ruth's action. When someone is hurting, we fix them a good meal. Whether someone has a baby, loses a loved one, or is sick for an extended period of time, it is common for her "sisters" to bring by casseroles of every kind. Ruth made sure Naomi had food to eat and plenty of it. But that was just the beginning. She carried Naomi's burdens too.

Paul encourages the Galatians, "Carry each other's burdens, and in this way you will fulfill the law of Christ" (Galatians 6:2). The word *burden* here means overburden, such as the loss of a child, a divorce, or a serious illness. These are all situations that tend to destroy our dreams for the future. As a "woman friend," God may be using us to restore someone's dreams by walking alongside them, taking care of their physical needs, or being their spiritual and emotional support until the cloud has passed. When we allow God to use us this way, we in turn will be richly blessed.

In her book *Running on Empty,* Jill Briscoe writes, "Ruth was a wise woman. It is in companionship that gives itself unselfishly, without looking for returns, that we receive the very things we are looking for ourselves."[1]

God desires for us to become better, not bitter. Naomi blamed God for her afflictions. In one sense, she was correct. God is sovereign and in control of every aspect of our lives. However, He was not "out to get her." His hand was not "against her" as she claimed. Naomi became very bitter about what had happened to her, so much so that she changed her name to Mara, which means "bitter." God never desires for us to become bitter, but longs to make us better. The way we become better is by learning to lean on Him and trust His ways.

In Jesus' last words to His disciples, He compared their relationship to Him to that of a vine and the branches: "I am the true vine, and my Father is the gardener. He cuts off [lifts up out of the dust][2] every branch in me that bears no fruit, while every branch that does bear fruit he prunes so that it will be even more fruitful" (John 15:1-2).

When our dreams seem to be lost, it can feel like God's giant gardening shears have lopped off part of our life that seems vital to our existence. However, His desire is for us to bear as much fruit as possible, not become stunted by bitterness. Bruce Wilkinson, in his book *Secrets of the Vine,* notes, "God isn't trying to just take away; He's faithfully at work to make room to add strength, productivity, and spiritual power in your life. His goal is to bring you closer to the 'perfect and complete' image of Christ."[3]

He goes on to say, "Not every painful experience is the result of pruning. Is your heart breaking because your teenager is experimenting with drugs and sex? God did not cause your son to do these things in order to prune you. Are you suddenly facing a future with diabetes or cancer? God isn't purposefully constraining your life just to see how you'll react. Yet every trial you face is an opportunity to let Him work in your life for abundance. If you invite Him into your circumstances, He will keep His promise to work everything together for your good (Romans 8:28)."[4]

Have you noticed the only difference between the words *bitter* and *better* is the letter i? When we get I out of the way and stop focusing on ourselves, God can have His way. If He prunes away a dream, it is only because He has a greater dream in store that will produce more fruit.

"It just so happened" never happens in God's economy. Divine providence is behind every event in the story of Ruth and Naomi: the famine that led the family to Moab, the marriages to Moabite women, the deaths of Elimelech and Naomi's sons, the lifting of the famine in Bethlehem and Naomi's return to her homeland, the choice of Boaz's field as a place for Ruth to glean, his notice of her, the refusal of the next in line to be Ruth's kinsman-redeemer, and Boaz and Ruth's subsequent marriage.

Have you ever noticed such a chain of events in your own life? My friend Gayle shared a wonderful story of divine intervention in her life. She started having trouble with her knees in her early 30s. Chronic pain in her right knee sent her to the doctor's office on a regular basis for cortisone injections. Because Gayle's mother had joint pain in her knees for most of her adult life, Gayle resigned herself to the same fate—arthritis. The doctor never x-rayed or performed an MRI to diagnose the problem, but prescribed treatment according to symptoms and a family history of joint pain.

One night, after five years of cortisone injections, Gayle, her husband, Joe, and another couple attended a basketball game at their alma mater. On the way home, Gayle had twisted around in her front seat to face the couple in the back. As they chatted, she noticed an 18-wheel semi-trailer's headlights rapidly approaching their car. *Surely he's going to slow down,* she thought. But before she could even warn the other passengers, the truck plowed into the back of their car at 55 miles per hour. Because of Gayle's position, her knees were smashed into the dashboard.

The driver of the truck had fallen asleep at the wheel and never even applied the brakes before impact. Gayle and Joe's car, a heavy Lincoln Continental, was totaled, but no one in the car was hurt except Gayle. Her knees became black, blue, and swollen within a couple of hours.

When Gayle went to the doctor the next day, he decided to take an x-ray to make sure there were no broken bones. "Gayle," he said, "I don't know how to tell you this, but you have a slow-growing tumor in your right knee."

"A tumor? How long has it been there?" she asked.

"Well, this is a very slow-growing type of tumor that has probably been there for several years. The pain you've been experiencing in the past has most likely been due to the tumor causing the bone to expand as the tumor grows. We're going to have to remove it right away."

"I can't do it right away," she answered. "I have a two-week counseling course I'm going to next week. I've been on the waiting list for two years, so this tumor is going to have to wait. You did say it was slow growing, correct?"

"Yes," he answered, "but I wouldn't wait a day longer than necessary. You are a very lucky young lady. If you had not been in that car accident, we may not have found the tumor until it was too late."

Gayle smiled. Luck had nothing to do with it. God was in control. She did go to the counseling seminar, where 750 committed Christians gathered around her on the last night and prayed for her knee. The next day, when the doctor went in to remove the tumor, he was amazed to find that this slow-growing tumor had rapidly begun to shrink.

"Once again," the doctor said as he showed Gayle the new pre-op x-ray of a much smaller tumor, "you are a lucky girl. The tumor was smaller today than it was two weeks ago."

Gayle knew luck had nothing to do with it. She then shared with the doctor about the 750 people who had prayed for her the night before.

Many times when something seemingly bad happens in our life, we need to remember that God is the director of the drama. We may not understand the "whys" or the "what fors," but we can trust in the God who controls it all. Kathy Collard Miller said it so well: "Nothing that happens to the child of God is a coincidence, and when we look at every situation and encounter as God-directed, we will more easily fulfill His plan. This knowledge should also make each of us feel needed, valuable, and important: we are fulfilling God's purposes for His Kingdom."[5]

Just when it looks like our dreams have been shattered, God picks up the pieces and creates a beautiful mosaic—a work of art that He planned all along.

8

Esther—A Woman Who Fulfilled God's Dream

Tucked in between the Old Testament books of Nehemiah and Job is the little book of Esther. We don't know much about Esther's childhood, but I imagine her dreams were not that different from those of other little Hebrew girls growing up around 460 B.C. She probably had dreams of marrying a handsome Jewish husband and having a quiver full of children with names like Isaac, Mariah, Daniel, and Rebekah. I imagine she dreamed of the day when her prospective groom would come to her father, ask for his daughter in marriage, and pay the *mohar*.

131

"And what will you pay for my daughter?" her father would ask.

"For one so lovely, I will pay 1,000 sheep, 20 heifers, and 40 pieces of gold," her handsome suitor would reply.

Perhaps Esther dreamed she would live in a house next to her in-laws so they could watch the children on the weekends while she and her husband attended the camel races. Or perhaps she dreamed of having her own well in the backyard—that would really be a dream house.

But life didn't turn out the way Esther had imagined. We don't know exactly what happened to her parents, but at some point in her young life, both mother and father died. When we meet Esther, she is living with her Uncle Mordecai, who has agreed to take care of her.

During this time in history, Esther's hometown of Susa was ruled by King Xerxes (Ahasuerus in the Hebrew). He was a very powerful king who ruled over 127 provinces stretching from India to Ethiopia. While he was famous for his great wealth and territorial rule, he was most widely known for his grand parties that lasted for months on end.

As the book of Esther opens, we find him throwing a party that lasted for 180 days. King Xerxes was planning to wage war against Greece, the only part of the known world not under his reign, and he hoped the lavish party would build confidence in his war plans among his peers. During the last seven days of the festivities, all the people from the least to the greatest who were in the citadel of Susa were invited to eat their fill and drink from handcrafted golden goblets; there were no two alike. While the men were carousing in the gardens, Queen Vashti entertained the ladies at a party of her own in the palace.

On the final day of the festivities, King Xerxes sent word for Queen Vashti to come before the men wearing her royal crown in order to display her beauty to the people and nobles. However, the queen refused to be put on display before the drunken crowd.

"What does she mean, she won't come!" the king exclaimed.

"She just said, 'No, Sire,' " the messenger reluctantly relayed.

The king was infuriated at her refusal, but perhaps more than anger, he felt embarrassment at his lack of control over his own wife.

"What am I going to do about her insolence?" the king asked his counselors.

"Queen Vashti has done wrong, not only against the king but also against all the nobles and the peoples of all the provinces of King Xerxes. For the queen's conduct will become known to all the women, and so they will despise their husbands and say, 'King Xerxes commanded Queen Vashti to be brought before him, but she would not come.' This very day the Persian and Median women of the nobility who have heard about the queen's conduct will respond to all the king's nobles in the same way. There will be no end of disrespect and discord" (1:16-18).

So the King's counselors suggested that Queen Vashti be removed as queen and the crown be placed on someone more deserving. The king agreed to their suggestion and issued a royal decree for a search for a new queen.

Among the young virgins brought to the palace was Esther. She was entrusted to Hegai, a eunuch who was in charge of the King's entire harem. Immediately, Esther won Hegai's favor. But there was one little detail Esther and her uncle failed to mention: She was Jewish.

Esther had one year at the king's spa before she went before him: six months with oils and six months with perfumes and cosmetics. She was also assigned seven maids to take care of her every need. At the end of her beauty treatment, the king chose Esther to be the next queen. She was not only beautiful in form and feature, but gentle and kind. If there had been a Miss Susa contest, Esther would have won the crown and Miss Congeniality at the same time. After he selected Esther as the queen, the king gave a great banquet in her honor and proclaimed a holiday throughout the provinces.

Now lest we think being Xerxes's queen sounds like a dream come true, there are a few facts we need to understand. Esther was not a cherished wife as she had hoped to become. She was one of many wives and concubines who served as the king's possessions and objects of sexual satisfaction. As part of his harem, she rarely saw the king and had very few rights.

She did not live with her husband as you and I think of a marriage relationship today, but could approach the king safely only when he summoned her. If she went before the king and he was not pleased, he could have her put to death. Also, Esther would never carry on her Jewish heritage by having a quiver full of Hebrew children. The king was a gentile—not what she had dreamed of.

But God had another dream for Queen Esther: to save the entire Hebrew nation. A few months after Esther was named queen, her Uncle Mordecai overheard a plot to kill the king. He reported this to Esther, who reported it to the king. The would-be assassins were hanged, and Mordecai's name was written in the record books for saving the king's life.

Sometime later, Haman, one of the king's officials, was elevated to a place of honor above all the other nobles of the empire: "I command all the royal officials at the king's gate to kneel down and pay honor to Haman when he passes by," the king proclaimed.

But because Mordecai bowed only to the one true God of Israel, he refused to bow to Haman. If Haman had been king, Mordecai possibly would have bowed, but Haman was an Amalekite, an enemy to the Jews.

This infuriated Haman, and he began to plot Mordecai's demise. "Who is this man who refuses to bow before me?" Haman raged. "I'll have him killed. Better yet, I will have his entire nationality exterminated. Every Jew in the nation will be killed because of this man's insolence!"

Haman went before the king and explained, "There is a certain people dispersed and scattered among the peoples in all the provinces of your kingdom whose customs are different from those of all other people and who do not obey the king's laws; it is not in the king's best interest to tolerate them. If it pleases the king, let a decree be issued to destroy them, and I will put ten thousand talents of silver into the royal treasury for the men who carry out this business" (3:8-9).

The king, feeling very indifferent toward Haman's request, took his signet ring from his finger and gave it to Haman. " 'Keep the money,' the king said to Haman, 'and do with the people as you please' " (3:11).

As the news of the Jews' planned demise spread across the land, the king and Haman sat down to drink, but the city of Susa was bewildered. When Mordecai heard of the news, he tore his robe, put on sackcloth, sprinkled ashes on his head, and went about the city wailing loudly.

Esther heard of her uncle's strange behavior at the city gate and sent one of her attendants to find out what was wrong. "Mordecai, what is wrong?" the eunuch inquired. "The queen has heard about your deep sorrow. She has even sent me to bring you clothes instead of the sackcloth."

"I cannot accept them," Mordecai answered through his tears. "The king has issued a royal decree to have all the Jewish people annihilated. He is doing this at the request of Haman because I refused to bow before this elevated Amalekite. Here, this is a copy of the actual decree. Take this back to Esther. Tell her that she must go before the king and plead for mercy for her people."

The eunuch went back and reported to Esther all that Mordecai had said. She sent him back to Mordecai with this message: "All the king's officials and the people of the royal provinces know that for any man or woman who approaches the king in the inner court without being summoned the king has but one law: that he be put to death. The only exception to this is for the king to extend the gold scepter to him and spare his life. But thirty days have passed since I was called to go to the king" (4:11).

The eunuch returned to Mordecai with Esther's message. He responded, ["You tell Esther,] 'Do not think that because you are in the king's house you alone of all the Jews will escape. For if you remain silent at this time, relief and deliverance for the Jews will arise from another place, but you and your father's family will perish. And who knows but that you have come to royal position for such a time as this?' " (4:13-14).

"Then Esther sent this reply to Mordecai: 'Go, gather together all the Jews who are in Susa, and fast for me. Do not eat or drink for three days, night or day. I and my maids will fast as you do. When this is done, I will go to the king, even though it is against the law. And if I perish, I perish'" (4:15-16).

So Esther fasted and prayed. After three days, she bathed, perfumed, put on her royal robe, and went before the king. He was sitting on his throne, facing the entrance and saw her as she approached the forbidden inner court. At her appearing, he was pleased and extended the gold scepter. Esther approached the king and touched the tip of the scepter.

"What is it, Queen Esther?" he asked. "What is your request? Even up to half the kingdom, it will be given you" (5:3).

" 'If it pleases the king,' replied Esther, 'let the king, together with Haman, come today to a banquet I have prepared for him' " (5:4).

Esther knew the way to the king was through his stomach. She invited him to dinner and then, afterward, invited him to join her again the following evening. The king knew that Esther had a request, and she promised to reveal it on the second evening. Of course, Haman felt quite smug about being invited to dine with the queen.

When the king and Haman joined her the following evening for dinner, Queen Esther announced her petition and reason for disturbing the king. "If I have found favor with you, O king, and if it pleases your majesty, grant me my life—this is my petition. And spare my people—this is my request. For I and my people have been sold for destruction and slaughter and annihilation. If we had merely been sold as male and female slaves, I would have kept quiet, because no such distress would justify disturbing the king" (7:3-4).

"Where is the man who has dared to do such a thing?" Xerxes asked (7:5). (He had never even asked Haman who the people were he wished to exterminate.)

Esther turned and pointed across the table. "It is Haman!"

Furious, the king stood and marched into the garden to let his anger cool down. Then Haman threw himself at the queen as she was still reclining on the couch. "Please spare me, my queen!" he begged.

Haman's timing couldn't have been worse. The king entered and saw Haman throwing himself on the queen. "What! Will you even dare to molest the queen while she is in the palace?"

"I wasn't . . ."

"Silence!" the king shouted.

The next day, Haman and his sons were hanged on the gallows that Haman had built to hang Mordecai. While the king could not revoke a royal decree, he issued another decree that allowed the Jews the right to assemble and protect themselves; to destroy, kill, and annihilate any armed force of any nationality or province that might attack them and their women and children; and to plunder the property of their enemies. Thus, on March 7, 473 B.C., the entire Hebrew nation was spared. Even to this day, the Jews celebrate the Feast of Purim to commemorate Queen Esther's brave act that saved the Hebrew nation.

Queen Esther had dreams for her life. They were perhaps very simple—a husband, children, a home, a quiet and peaceful existence. However, God had a much larger dream for this little orphaned girl. He had a dream to make her a queen and an instrument to save an entire nation, the nation from which the Savior of the World would be born.

It is interesting that God's name is not mentioned in this small book of the Bible, but His fingerprints are on every page. William M. Taylor noted, "It was not needful that the name of God should be introduced into it, because His hand is everywhere so manifest throughout it."[1]

Esther experienced fear in her high calling, but she overcame her fear by depending on God for wisdom, strength, and courage. She was a woman who fulfilled God's dream.

What Can We Learn from Esther?

God has bigger dreams for our lives than we can ever imagine. Can you guess what young Esther would have thought if someone had come up to her at the market while gathering produce for her uncle and told her that she was going to be the next queen of Persia and save her people from annihilation? I think she would have laughed or run for cover from the lunatic making such a prediction. But God had a plan. He took a lonely orphan girl and used her to rescue the Jewish nation.

If someone had come to me 20 years ago and told me that I would be spreading the gospel through an international radio program, speaking at women's conferences, and authoring several books, I would have quickly informed that person that she had a serious case of mistaken identity. As a matter of fact, when God called me into ministry, that's precisely what I told Him. But praise the Lord, I began to take those first steps of obedience and to see that God had bigger dreams for my life than I had ever imagined.

While God has probably not called you to save an entire nation from destruction, He has called you to be a woman He can use. Missionary Amy Carmichael wrote, "Often his call is to follow in paths we would not have chosen."[2] "'For my thoughts are not your thoughts, neither are your ways my ways,' declares the LORD. 'As the heavens are higher than the earth, so are my ways higher than your ways and my thoughts than your thoughts'" (Isaiah 55:8-9).

Whether God is calling us to be a catalyst for saving someone from physical death or to be a catalyst for saving someone from eternal separation from God by offering him or her eternal life, He can use us as instruments of salvation. He has called each of us to share His plan of salvation to a lost and hurting world. That is a big dream, my friend.

"For we are God's workmanship, created in Christ Jesus to do good works, which God prepared in advance for us to do" (Ephesians 2:10). He created Esther for a purpose, just as He has created you and me for a purpose.

God's dreams require courage to fulfill. Hearing God's call on our life is the first step. Obeying that call is the second. Making the leap between hearing and obeying may be one of the most difficult moves of our lives. Because of Esther's willingness to transcend her fears, the nation was saved and she was the vehicle to bring about an amazing miracle.

Anne Graham Lotz, one of Billy Graham's three daughters, was comfortable being the wife of a dentist and mother of three. But God had a bigger dream for Anne—not to replace her role as wife and mother, but to add to it. A few years ago, on a visit to southern India, a group of people took her to a soccer stadium full of thousands of expectant people. They asked her to deliver an evangelical message like her daddy does. Anne explained to her hosts that was not what she did. Yes, she spoke to Bible studies and to smaller crowds, but not to large arenas. Nevertheless, God had a call on Anne, a dream for her life. She laid her fears aside, stepped into the pulpit, and preached.

"I was sitting there thinking, *I'm an American housewife. I don't belong here,*" she recalled. "But I just stepped aside and let God take over. And it's amazing what he can do."[3]

Mary Slessor had a remarkable missionary career in Calabar, which is now part of modern Nigeria. At the beginning, she prayed, "Lord the task is impossible for me but not for Thee. Lead the way and I will follow. Why should I fear? I am on a royal mission. I am in the service of the King of Kings."[4]

God can take a painful childhood and turn it into a fruitful adulthood. Reading the story of Esther gives me so much hope as I listen to story after story of painful childhood memories of men and women today. While we don't know much about Esther's parents, we do know that she was an orphan who was raised by her uncle, Mordecai. As far as we can tell, she had no feminine influence in her life. And yet she grew to be a gracious, lovely woman who won the favor of everyone she encountered.

Perhaps your childhood was less than ideal. Perhaps you had an alcoholic father, an abusive mother, poverty level income, or grew up in an orphanage, a foster home, or with parents who felt you were a bother instead of a blessing. It doesn't matter how you start; what matters is how you finish.

The apostle Paul said, "But one thing I do: forgetting what lies behind and reaching forward to what lies ahead, I press on toward the goal for the prize of the upward call of God in Christ Jesus" (Philippians 3:13-14, NASB). Paul had to put his past behind him to accomplish what God called him to do. Likewise, when we put our painful pasts behind us and obey what God is calling us to do in the present, we will lead a fruitful, fulfilling, fascinating adulthood. He can take those miseries of the past and turn them into ministries in the present. God took a frightened orphan girl and used her to accomplish a great mission. He did it for Queen Esther. He wants to do it for you.

When we move forward in obedience, God provides what we need. When the angel of the Lord came to call Gideon to be the leader of the Israelite army, Gideon was in a wine press threshing wheat (Judges 6). Now you don't thresh wheat in a wine press. You thresh wheat by throwing it up into the open air and letting the chaff blow away and the heavier grain fall to the ground.

So why was Gideon in the wine press? He was hiding. That's right. He was so terrified of his encroaching enemies, he was hiding. And yet, when the angel of the Lord addressed Gideon, He said, "O valiant warrior." I imagine Gideon looked to the left and the right and then asked, "Are you talking to me?"

God doesn't see as we see. We tend to look on our present resources, gifts, and abilities. But God looks much deeper. He sees what we can be if we trust in Him. He saw what Gideon could be if he trusted in Him. He sees what we can be if we trust in Him to provide. He provided sight for the blind, strength for the weary, food for the hungry, wisdom for the confused, peace for the worried, and courage for the fearful. Whatever dreams God has for our lives, He will provide what we need to accomplish them each step of the way. The catch is, He often doesn't provide until we take that first step in faith.

PART THREE

Big Girls' Dreams

9

Shattered Dreams

Steve and I were reveling in our time with good friends from college days, Larry and Cynthia Price. It had been almost a year since our last visit, and I was hungry to hear the latest family news about their children: Daniel, Julianna, and Laura Beth. While the four adults feasted on grilled teriyaki chicken, steamy baked potatoes, and tossed salad with home-grown tomatoes, the kids ran out the door to attend the Friday night high school football game. For over an hour, conversation and sweet tea flowed like a mountain stream. We were just finishing the last bites of chocolate silk pie when our laughter was interrupted by the ringing phone.

"Hello," Cynthia answered.

I could hear only one side of the conversation, but I could tell something was terribly amiss.

"Daniel, calm down! What's wrong? Talk slower," she urged. "Oh God, no," Cynthia gasped. "OK, Daniel. I'll meet you at the hospital."

An ashen Cynthia turned to her husband and could barely force the words out of her mouth. "Larry, Daniel said that Will took a bad hit at the football game. He went in for a tackle. They hit. Will stood up. Fell on the ground. And he never got back up. They are taking him to the hospital in Clinton."

"Cynthia, you two go on to meet them. Don't even think twice about us," I assured her. "I'll clean up and take any calls that come in."

"Are you sure?" she asked. "I hate to leave you here."

"Absolutely; now scoot!"

Before they left, we held hands and prayed for Will; his mother, Luanne; his dad, Bob; his two brothers; and little sister who were all at the game.

"I am disappointed with my life. I had hoped to be a better mother and wife. I've spent my life doing everything in my own strength instead of relying on God."—*Collette*

Larry and Cynthia drove down their mile-long driveway, and my mind rushed back to another time 14 years earlier when I first met Luanne Johnson. She was Cynthia's best friend in the sleepy rural town of Rose Hill, North Carolina, four hours from our home. She had just given birth to her third child, Bailey, who was born with a hole in his heart. When he was seven months old, Luanne kissed his cheek as the doctors and nurses rolled him into the operating room to attempt to correct the defect. The physicians assured the Johnsons that the procedure had a 98 percent success rate and there was no cause for alarm. While Bailey came through the surgery just fine, he developed complications a few days later and had to go back in for a second procedure. This operation was not successful.

Bailey died on the operating table on his brother Will's third birthday. Now this.

I pictured Luanne riding in the ambulance or perhaps following in a car close behind the blaring sirens. I recalled the words I had penned in another book: "There is an inexplicable bond that exists between a mother and her child. Even though the umbilical cord is severed in the delivery room, a cord of love connects them for the rest of their lives." Luanne already had one deposit in heaven. The thought of a second was almost too painful to imagine.

Oh, he'll be okay, I thought. I'd grown up in a small North Carolina town where high school football was a part of life for the entire community. When I was elementary school age, I went to Friday night games and ran around under the bleachers, paying very little attention to the pigskin on the field. When I was a teenager, I was a cheerleader and paid attention to the game just enough to know which cheers to yell when. My father-in-law had been a coach. Boys were constantly "down on the play." But they always got up. Didn't they?

I'm not sure how much time passed, but Cynthia's phone call startled me back to reality.

"Sharon, this is Cynthia. Will didn't make it."

"What do you mean 'didn't make it'?" I asked.

"Will died on the field," she said.

Somehow the news spread through the quiet little town that Will Johnson had been hurt at the football game. All through the night I fielded calls that came to the Prices' home. Cynthia was Luanne's best friend, and Daniel had been Will's.

The next day, the news reported the story. Will had gone in to make a tackle and instead of grabbing his opponent at the waist, he hit the boy carrying the ball much too high. His opponent's helmet crashed into Will's chest, causing a concussion to his heart. He stood up and said,

"Coach, I think I need to come out." Then he collapsed, and his heart never beat again.

I was just a visitor from 200 miles away. I didn't know most of these people, but one thing was clear: What affected one, affected them all. A mother's dreams had been shattered, and the entire town felt her pain.

Shattered dreams are a part of life. Children die, husbands leave, jobs are lost, cancer tests come back positive, proposals are rejected, teenagers rebel, houses burn, terrorists attack, and the list goes on. Part of the pain is the feeling that God has forgotten us, grown deaf to our cries, or lost our address. Zion cried, "The LORD has forsaken me, the Lord has forgotten me" (Isaiah 49:14). David lamented, "My God, my God, why have you forsaken me? Why are you so far from saving me, so far from the words of my groaning? O my God, I cry out by day, but you do not answer, by night, and am not silent" (Psalm 22:1-2). Even Jesus called out from the cross, "My God, my God, why have you forsaken me?" (Matthew 27:46).

I have cried, "Where are you, God? How could you do this to me? Have you forgotten all about me?" Then He answered, "Can a mother forget the baby at her breast and have no compassion on the child she has borne? Though she may forget, I will not forget you! See, I have engraved you on the palms of my hands" (Isaiah 49:15-16).

Ah, the string around His finger, the brand on His palm, the scar on His heart. No, He doesn't forget.

Mary and Martha's Shattered Dream

In the New Testament, we find a story about two sisters whose dreams were shattered by a death in the family. Jesus received word that one of His best friends, Lazarus, was sick. In reality, by the time the messenger made the one-day journey to inform Jesus about Lazarus's illness, he had already died. Jesus didn't leave right away, but tarried two days before making the journey to Bethany. When He arrived, Lazarus had been in the tomb for four days. His death shook the entire village, and many Jews from surrounding cities went to mourn their loss. For these two women, their dreams for the future were bleak: no husbands, no children, no father, and now, no brother to take care of them.

When Martha heard Jesus was coming, she ran to meet Him. "'Lord,' Martha said to Jesus, 'if you had been here, my brother would not have died'" (John 11:21). Can you relate to Martha? Have you ever thought, *Lord, if You had been here, this would not have happened to me. Where were You? Where are You now?*

Then it is as if she thought better of the words that had escaped her lips. Martha added, "But I know that even now God will give you whatever you ask."

"People in my life destroyed the dreams of a little girl. My dreams turned into nightmares."—*Tansy (a homeless woman)*

Jesus said to her, "Your brother will rise again."

Martha answered, "I know he will rise again in the resurrection at the last day."

Jesus said to her, "I am the resurrection and the life. He who believes in me will live, even though he dies; and whoever lives and believes in me will never die. Do you believe this?"

"Yes, Lord," she told Him, "I believe that you are the Christ, the Son of God, who was to come into the world" (John 11:22-27).

Martha went back to her home and told Mary that Jesus was on the way. Like Martha, Mary ran to meet Him and said, "Lord, if you had been here, my brother would not have died." Do you see a pattern? *If You had been here, this would not have happened to me. Where were You?*

Do you think God hurts when we hurt? Oh yes, dear sisters, God hurts. Jesus wept when He saw the pain of those around Him. He wept for the two sisters, and I suspect He wept for a people who did not understand the power of God.

After four days, Lazarus's body had already begun to decay. Make no mistake about it: God was about to do something so incredible, no one would refute His power. Jesus ordered the stone rolled away from the mouth of the cave that served as Lazarus's tomb. "Then Jesus said, 'Did I not tell you that if you believed, you would see the glory of God?'

"I tried not to have dreams when I was young because I did not want to be disappointed."—Kelly

"So they took away the stone. Then Jesus looked up and said, 'Father, I thank you that you have heard me. I knew that you always hear me, but I said this for the benefit of the people standing here, that they may believe that you sent me.' When he had said this, Jesus called in a loud voice, 'Lazarus, come out!'" (John 11:40-43).

And he did.

Jesus resurrected Mary and Martha's dream.

Those of us who have lost a loved one may be thinking, *God didn't bring my brother back. God didn't save my child. God didn't resurrect my dead marriage. God didn't bring Will back to life.*

Let's go back to Will for a moment. Did resurrection power take place after Will's death? His mother would say a resounding "yes." Luanne shared with me that just days before Will's final football game, he said,

"Mom, I'll be glad when this is all over. Now that I'm older, I see just how unimportant all this sports stuff is."

As Luanne knelt beside her boy on that football field, she begged him to keep breathing. But then, as she felt him take his last breath, his words echoed in her heart: "I'll be glad when this is all over."

"It's all over, son," Luanne whispered. "Go on home."

At Will's funeral a few days after his death, Luanne stood and shared the gospel message about the Jesus Will loved so. What was the result? Thirty people attending the service committed their lives to Christ or renewed their passion for serving Him.

"Mrs. Johnson, I gave my life to Christ today."

"Luanne, I haven't been following Jesus like I should. I recommitted my life to Him today, and I'm going to get serious about my relationship with Him."

"Luanne, our family was in a shambles, and I was thinking about leaving my husband. After today, I have decided to make our marriage work. I see how important family is."

"I have been putting my family on the back burner and letting everything and anything come before them. After today, I'm putting my family second only to God."

The Johnson family continues to minister all across the state about the power of Jesus Christ that sustains us when our dreams are shattered. Because of Will's death, hundreds have come to Christ and many family relationships have been restored. Churches have torn down denominational walls as the Presbyterians, Methodists, Baptists, and Pentecostals in the tiny little town have made a historic move to worship together. Being from a small North Carolina town myself, believe me, I know that is a miracle.

The Bible says that before we know Jesus Christ, we are dead in our transgressions. We inherited a dead spirit from our father, Adam. However, when we accept Jesus Christ as our Savior, God gives us a new heart and a new spirit that are fully alive. This is resurrection power at its best.

Why did God allow Lazarus to die? He allowed it so His Son could be glorified through it. Why did God allow His own Son to die on the cross? To bring salvation to all who believe. I suspect that is the same for Luanne and Bob's son as well.

The Death of the Disciples' Dream

If ever there was a group of people who lost their dream, it was Jesus' disciples and the women who ministered to and with them. They had such high expectations that Jesus would be the next political leader of Israel (Luke 24:21). They had witnessed His power in feeding 5,000 men plus women and children with two loaves and five fishes. They felt the waves beneath their tiny boat subside at His command.

They had watched Him breathe life into a lifeless child, open the eyes of a man blind from birth, create new skin from rotting flesh on the limbs of lepers, and command a lame man to take up his pallet and walk. They had seen him walk on water, outwit the Pharisees, and win the lost.

In their narrow scope of hopes for a political leader to save the Jews, they missed the bigger picture of God's plan for a Savior to free mankind from the bondage of sin. While Peter realized Jesus' identity ("You are the Christ"), he did not understand His destiny. Peter was shocked when Jesus explained that He had to go to Jerusalem, suffer, be killed, and on the third day rise from the dead. Peter even took Jesus aside: " 'Never, Lord!' he said. 'This shall never happen to you!' " (Matthew 16:22). Christ's death was not part of Peter's dream. Suffering did not fit into his plan.

"Jesus turned and . . . rebuked Peter. 'Get behind me, Satan!' he said. 'You do not have in mind the things of God, but the things of men' " (Mark 8:33).

Call me stupid, but don't call me Satan. Yet, that is how Jesus sees it when we try to block God's plans. He sees us as an instrument of darkness, an offense, a hindrance, and a snare. It is amazing that one minute Peter could be a building block and the next a stumbling block. But that's the trap we all fall into when we have our minds set on the world instead of on the things of God.

Jesus told His disciples, "If anyone would come after me, he must deny himself and take up his cross and follow me. For whoever wants to save his life will lose it, but whoever loses his life for me will find it" (Matthew 16:24-25).

Does that mean we give up our dreams? I can promise you this: Whatever dreams you have for your life, God's dreams are greater. The power of the Holy Spirit the disciples received after Jesus' resurrection and the impact they made on the world thereafter was beyond their wildest dreams. That's what God does with a heart that is wholly yielded to Him. That's what He does when we give our shattered dreams to Him.

Our Reaction to Shattered Dreams

Even though Jesus forewarned the disciples of His death and resurrection, they fled when the soldiers came to arrest Him and hid when they hung Him on a cross to die. When Jesus was sealed in the tomb, their hopes and dreams were sealed in the darkness with Him.

Every day, I receive e-mails from women who have had their dreams shattered. A husband has an affair, becomes addicted to pornography, abuses the children, or deserts the family. A child gets caught with drugs, becomes pregnant, or dies in a car accident. Parents divorce, friends betray, careers come to an abrupt halt.

The list is endless. So what do we do when our dreams are seemingly destroyed? The answer to that will shape the rest of our life.

The entire book of Job is about a man who lost his dreams. He was a man who was blameless and upright; he feared God and shunned evil.

Then one day, Satan came before God "from roaming through the earth and going back and forth in it" (Job 1:7). God pointed out His servant Job, and Satan said, "Does Job fear God for nothing? . . . Have you not put a hedge around him and his household and everything he has?" (Job 1:9-10). (In other words, "Of course he loves You. You give him everything he wants!") "But stretch out your hand and strike everything he has, and he will surely curse you to your face," Satan continued (Job 1:11).

God allowed Satan to strike Job. He lost his children, his wealth, and his health. Just about the only thing he didn't lose was his nagging wife, who told him to curse God and die. But in the end, Job confessed, "I know that you can do all things; no plan of yours can be thwarted" (Job 42:1). He also said, "My ears had heard of you but now my eyes have seen you" (Job 42:5).

When our dreams are shattered, we have a greater opportunity to see with our eyes what we have heard with our ears. In the end, God, the Restorer of Dreams, blessed Job, "made him prosperous again and gave him twice as much as he had before" (Job 42:10).

Satan, the Destroyer of Dreams

Did you notice a common theme with Sarah, Naomi, and Esther? With each woman, the heritage of the Jewish nation and the family tree of Jesus Christ was at stake. Sarah gave birth to Isaac, and her husband, Abraham, is called the father of the nation of Israel. Naomi's daughter-in-law gave birth to Obed, who was the father of Jesse, who was the father of David, who was the father of Solomon. And after many more fathers, we get to Jesus. Esther saved the Jewish nation from annihilation by the Persians.

As I looked at each one of these women and their dreams that teetered on the brink of extinction or fulfillment, I asked myself these questions: Who was the real enemy? Who was trying to destroy their dreams? Who was trying to destroy God's plan to bring the Savior of the world through the Jews?

I believe there was only one antagonist in each of these stories. It wasn't Ishmael, Hagar, or Haman. It was Satan himself. Just as God's fingerprints ran throughout the book of Esther, so did Satan's claw marks jump out from the words and schemes of Haman. Likewise, as we begin to think about the dreams God has for our life, we need to be cognizant of the enemy who tries to prevent those dreams from coming to fruition—the roaring lion that prowls around looking for someone to devour, someone's dreams to destroy.

There are circumstances in each of our lives that cannot be reconciled other than by trusting that God's ways are not our ways. Satan's desire is to take those circumstances, destroy our dreams, and prevent us from accomplishing the greater dreams that God has for our lives. He whispers, *If God loved you, He would have not let that happen to you. If He cared for you, He would provide what you want: He'd give you a husband who would meet your needs, children who would obey, a career that would help you meet your goals,* and on and on.

"I always wanted to be a mother. As much as I loved having four babies, they were much harder to deal with and more time-consuming than I thought they would be."—*Cathy*

Satan has one basic weapon he uses to destroy or block our dreams: lies. "He [Satan] was a murderer from the beginning, not holding to the truth, for there is no truth in him. When he lies, he speaks his native language, for he is a liar and the father of lies" (John 8:44).

While lies are Satan's primary weapon of choice, causing us to doubt God is his primary hoped-for result. During my years of struggle with infertility and miscarriage, Satan taunted me with such lies: *If God loved you, He would answer your prayer. You must not be a very good mother for God not to give you other children. You are a failure as a woman. Believing the promises of God works for other people, but apparently they aren't meant for you.* On and on he lied. Unfortunately I believed many of those lies.

Eve was a woman who had everything a girl could ever hope for. She was beautiful, had a perfect husband, and walked with God in the cool of the evening; all her needs were provided for. But then Satan came along and tempted her with his lies. The basis of his lies was that God was holding out on her. There was more to be had, and it was at her fingertips. She bought his lies and disobeyed the one restriction put on her by her heavenly Father. Satan caused Eve to doubt God and His justice.

Satan tempted Jesus the same way, not in a garden, but in a desert. However, Jesus did not give in to Satan's temptations, but fought him with the truth. Each time Satan hurled a temptation that would have destroyed God's dreams, Jesus fought back with Scripture. His response to each of Satan's temptations was, "It is written . . ." Author Neil Anderson said, "You don't have to out shout him or out muscle him to be free of his influence. You just have to out truth him."[1]

Satan still roams the earth spreading venomous lies today. Even when he left Jesus in the desert, the Bible says, ". . . he left him until an opportune time" (Luke 4:13). He would be back. He's always looking for the opened door, the chink in the armor, the opportune time. The apostle Peter describes Satan as a roaring lion roaming the earth seeking someone to devour (1 Peter 5:8). He wants to rip our dreams apart and leave us bleeding to death on the side of the road. The only way to fight a lion such as this is with the truth.

De is a prefix that means "to reduce." Satan deceives, defeats, demeans, devalues, and destroys. *Dis* is a prefix that means "to deprive of, remove, exclude." Satan also discourages, disappoints, and disillusions. We are in an all-out battle for our dreams.

In any battle, if you could send in a spy to retrieve the enemy's battle plan, victory would be sure. It's the surprise attacks that catch us off guard and defeat us. This was never more evident than during the Japanese attack on Pearl Harbor, December 7, 1941. While the U.S. secretary of state was having peace meetings with two Japanese diplomats in Washington, D.C., the Japanese military had already launched the attack on the U.S. military base at Pearl Harbor.

Vice Admiral Chuichi Nagumo led a 33-ship Japanese striking force under the cover of night and launched 350 airplanes against the U.S. fleet anchored in the peaceful waters of Oahu, Hawaii. The attack killed 2,388 people and wounded approximately 2,000 more. One ship, the U.S.S. *Arizona,* sits upright on the bottom of the harbor with more than 1,000 men entombed aboard. A memorial above the ship's resting place allows about 1.5 million visitors each year to view the names of those who died and remember the surprise attack. Even today, bubbles of oil rise to the surface where the *Arizona* lies in its watery grave. They remind us what can happen when we are caught off guard by the enemy.

Paul reminded us that we must not be unaware of the enemy's schemes (2 Corinthians 2:11).

Vulnerability to Attacks

During hurtful times in our lives when we don't understand what God is doing, when we feel that our dreams have been unfulfilled or shattered, we are the most vulnerable to the lies of the enemy. He taunts us with lies: God doesn't love you. If God loved you, He wouldn't have let this happen. He could have saved your brother, but He didn't. He must not think you are worthy of having a child. God may work for some people, but he doesn't work for you. If God cared about you, He would give you a husband . . . give you children . . . make your husband love you the way you deserve to be loved . . . make your teenager obey . . . give you a bigger house . . . find you a better job . . .

He whispers lies even though he knows the truth. Satan doesn't doubt God's control or God's power; he just wants to cause *you* to doubt. He says to the woman sitting alone in church, *Look at that family in the pew in front of you—Dad, Mom, and two beautiful children. Why hasn't God blessed you with a family like that? You could be happy with a home like theirs.*

"It was in my mid to late 20s that I started worrying God might not give me my ideal 'picture of life.' That ideal was a middle-class Ameri-can picture: a husband who loved me, healthy children, and at least one dog and cat. And we would live in a cozy home with a fireplace. I had been a little fearful before, but my fear was increasing with my age. The older I got, the more I feared I might not marry."—*Mariana*

Maybe what you don't know is that the father just lost his job, with no employment opportunity in sight. Just this morning the mother discovered a lump in her breast. One child got caught lying at school, and the other was going on the Internet where he shouldn't have been. And yet, the enemy whispers, even though he knows the truth. If Satan can get us to doubt God's justice and divine plan, then he knows we will be more easily swayed to try to make our dreams come true in our way, apart from Christ.

Another one of Satan's weapons is to continue bringing up your past mistakes and failures. When we confess our sins and ask God to forgive us, He throws them into the deepest of seas and wipes the slate clean. Satan, on the other hand, keeps bringing them to the surface. He has no future, so he keeps bringing up your past. He throws it in your face every chance he gets. What we need to do is throw it right back at him.

God never asks you to ignore your difficult or sinful past. But He will never define you by it. As we drive down the road of life, if we keep looking in our rearview mirror instead of straight ahead, we're bound to have a lot of wrecks.

Pain with a Purpose

Our broken or unfulfilled dreams undoubtedly will cause us great pain. However, that pain can be used to serve a purpose. Like Naomi, it will do a work in our lives to make us bitter or better. The choice is ours. Hopefully, a shattered dream will stir our appetites for a higher purpose or a higher calling or a higher love or a higher trust. Can we love God no matter what? Will we trust Him regardless of our earthly circumstances? Do we believe He has greater dreams for our lives than we ever imagined?

Author and counselor Larry Crabb writes, "Shattered dreams open doors to better dreams, dreams that we do not properly value until the dreams that we improperly value are destroyed. Shattered dreams destroy false expectations, such as the 'victorious' Christian life with no real struggle or failure. They help us discover true hope. We need the help of shattered dreams to put us in touch with what we must long for, to create a felt appetite for better dreams. And living for better dreams generates a new, unfamiliar feeling that we eventually recognize as joy."[2]

Read Noni Joy Tari's perspective on shattered dreams, recorded in Florence Littauer's book *Dare to Dream:*

Because God loves us so much, He uses only two alternatives in how He ministers to us regarding our dreams: He turns them into fertilizer or He brings them to fruition.

When people have broken dreams or dreams die, it is one of the most painful experiences in a person's life. But God never simply buries our dead and broken dreams because He'd be burying our hearts along with our dreams. Instead, He creatively turns our failures into fertilizer for an even more wonderful dream, a dream with even more potential to come to fruition.

In my own life I have learned that I never need to be afraid to wish and hope and desire and dream big. Because when I honestly tell the Lord about my dreams, one of two positive things will happen. Either the dream will become fertilizer for something even better, or the Lord will give me the gumption and oomph to bring my dream to fruition. I can't lose either way![3]

I have seen God time and time again use the very circumstances that bring us pain to make our dreams come true. In the Garden of Gethsemane on the lower slopes of the Mount of Olives, Jesus cried in such anguish that drops of blood beaded on His forehead. Physicians tell us that in times of intense anguish, the body faints as a defense mechanism to prevent capillaries from bursting. In His angst, Jesus did not faint; thus His capillaries broke and blood spilled from the pores of His brow. Did He want to go to the cross? No! Three times He cried out to God in prayer: "My Father, if it is possible, may this cup be taken from me. Yet not as I will, but as you will" (Matthew 26:39).

Yet God's answer was *no.* Jesus accepted God's will and obediently went to the cross. He didn't like the pain, as none of us do, but He endured the pain, and His obedience changed all of eternity for those who believe. Amazingly, the place where the victory was won, in the garden where He committed to obey, is the same place where Jesus ascended into heaven to sit at the right hand of God the Father. Could it be that the obedience that causes us the most pain will be the very thing God uses to cause us to ascend above the pain and bring glory to Him?

God's greatest desire is for us to be conformed to the image of His Son.

Like Michelangelo, who chipped and chiseled the block of stone to reveal the magnificent statue of David, God uses the chisel of life's circumstances to remove the unnecessary or excess in our lives to reveal the image of Christ. Trials and pain are inevitable, but the lessons learned are a matter of our will.

Let's look at a few verses that reveal pain with a purpose:

Trials test our faith. "In this you greatly rejoice, though now for a little while you may have had to suffer grief in all kinds of trials. These have come so that your faith—of greater worth than gold, which perishes even though refined by fire—may be proved genuine and may result in praise, glory and honor when Jesus Christ is revealed" (1 Peter 1:6-7).

Trials mature our character. "Consider it pure joy, my brothers, whenever you face trials of many kinds, because you know that the testing of your faith develops perseverance. Perseverance must finish its work so that you may be mature and complete, not lacking anything" (James 1:2-4).

Trials purify our souls. "But he knows the way that I take; when he has tested me, I will come forth as gold" (Job 23:10).

Trials bring eternal glory. "For our light and momentary troubles are achieving for us an eternal glory that far outweighs them all. So we fix our eyes not on what is seen, but on what is unseen. For what is seen is temporary, but what is unseen is eternal" (2 Corinthians 4:17-18).

Trials keep us dependent on God. "To keep me from becoming conceited because of these surpassingly great revelations, there was given me a thorn in my flesh, a messenger of Satan, to torment me. Three times I pleaded with the Lord to take it away from me. But he said to me, 'My grace is sufficient for you, for my power is made perfect in weakness.' Therefore I will boast all the more gladly about my weaknesses, so that Christ's power may rest on me. That is why, for Christ's sake, I delight in weaknesses, in insults, in hardships, in persecutions, in difficulties. For when I am weak, then I am strong" (2 Corinthians 12:7-10).

Trials conform us to the image of Christ. "I consider that our present sufferings are not worth comparing with the glory that will be revealed in us" (Romans 8:18). "And we know that in all things God works for the good of those who love him, who have been called according to his purpose. For those God foreknew he also predestined to be conformed to the likeness of his Son, that he might be the firstborn among many brothers. And those he predestined, he also called; those he called, he also justified; those he justified, he also glorified" (Romans 8:28-30).

Yes, there is great purpose in the pain. I pray we won't miss it!

Safe in the Storm

Several years ago, my family went to Disney World. We were spun, splashed, and spit out on various fantasy rides. On one such ride, the Star Wars adventure, we were strapped into metal seats with 30 or so other vacationers. Then we watched a screen as our seats were tossed from side to side and jerked back and forth. From all appearances, we were flying through the galaxy in an intergalactic battle, caught between the cross fire of laser guns and asteroids. It sure felt like we were in danger and coming within a few micrometers of losing our lives. In reality, we were just being jostled about in our seats.

On another ride, we piled into a boat and meandered down a watery path as a narrator told the story of Jaws and how the giant shark instilled terror in the town of Amity. At various intervals of our cruise, you guessed it, Jaws lunged from the water and attacked our boat. Women screamed, babies cried, and one overall-clad, hefty man in the back burst out laughing. Soon his contagious laughter caused an avalanche of laughter and giggles throughout the boat. Each time Jaws appeared, the laughing man had the same effect.

In both cases, we were totally safe; we just had the appearance of being in danger. I was reminded of the time I was teaching a group of four-year-olds about Jesus and His disciples caught in the storm on the Sea of

Galilee. After describing the thunder and lightning and the giant waves that rocked the tiny boat, I asked the group if they would be afraid if they were caught in a storm like this. Undaunted by the entire scenario, one little girl shrugged and replied, "Not if Jesus was in the boat with me."

During the storms of our lives when our dreams are seemingly lost, we must remember that Jesus is in the boat with us. We are in no more danger of being separated from Him or deserted by Him than we are in danger on the fantasy rides at an amusement park. What we see with our eyes may appear life-threatening, but the reality is that nothing can separate us from the love of God. If we are going through a painful time, we must find its purpose and let the trial have its perfect work.

Just as a seed needs the darkness of the earth to sprout, many times we need the darkness of pain to cultivate a new and deeper walk with God. But oh, the flowers that bloom and the fragrance that emerges from a person who can embrace the Gardener and yield to His tender care.

Let Go and Let God

One day my son was turning flips on the monkey bars on the playground and got a piece of bark in his eye. "Get it out! Get it out!" he cried. While he was in pain and desperately wanted me to remove the bark, he wouldn't remove his hand from his eye to let me attend to it. He vacillated between "Get it out" and "Don't touch it." Finally the pain overcame his fear, and he decided to trust me. It took me 45 minutes to convince him to remove his hand and 30 seconds for me to remove the piece of bark in his eye.

What a lesson: Let go and let God.

Along the same lines, I heard a story about a little boy who had his hand caught in a valuable vase. His elders pushed and pulled, tugged and twisted, but nothing worked. After some time, they decided they would have to break the vase, valuable as it was, to free the boy's hand. But before the hammer came crashing down on the beautiful porcelain, the boy's father coaxed him one last time. "Son, I want you to open your fingers and spread them apart, draw them together at the tips, and try one more time to slide your hand from the vase."

He replied, "I can't open my fingers like that, Daddy, because if I do, I'll drop my penny!"

The boy's hand was stuck because his tight fist clutched a penny. They were about to sacrifice something very valuable because he would not let go of something worthless.

How about you? Are you hanging on to a disappointment, an unfulfilled dream, or a shattered dream, not allowing yourself to be free to move where God wants you to move? Like the boy with his hand caught in the vase, are you held captive because you, too, refuse to let go? Oh, my friend, God has such great plans for us, His children. Let's let go of the past and be free to become all that He has created us to be.

Broken Dreams

Just as my child brings his broken toys
    with tears for me to mend,
I took my broken dreams to God
    because He was my friend.
But then instead of leaving Him
    in peace to work alone,
I hung around and tried to help
    with ways that were my own.
At last I snatched them back and cried,
    "How could You be so slow?"
"What could I do, My child," He said,
    "You never did let go."[4]

By Faith Mitchner

10

Restored Dreams

In 2002 my family visited one of the greatest artistic masterpieces in the history of man: the Sistine Chapel. Many artists contributed to the paintings, tapestries, and sculptures within its walls, but the most magnificent feat is the ceiling painted by Michelangelo. From 1508 to 1512, Michelangelo lay on his back and painstakingly painted one gigantic spiritual, historical, and biblical account of man. But almost as soon as the paintings were completed, they began to fade. After years of fading, ill-conceived attempts to cover the paintings with varnish, and layers of smoke and dirt, the original masterpiece was barely visible.

The proprietors of this historical and spiritual international treasure decided to test a new process for cleaning the murals that lined the walls and ceilings. In 1981, a special cleaning solution called AB-57 was developed. When years of filth and grime were gingerly removed inch by painstaking inch, the proprietors were surprised by the vibrant colors that emerged.

The process of cleaning the ceiling took eight years, twice as long as it had taken Michelangelo to paint. Artisans were amazed and awed at the beauty, the colors, and the intricate details as the paintings were brought back to life. For the first time in nearly 500 years, spectators saw the masterpiece the way it was originally intended.

But not everyone was pleased with the restoration. Some local people rebelled at the newly restored works of art. They had become accustomed to the dulling filth and grime left by years of pollution and cried, "We want our paintings back!"

"Since I am now a single mother who struggles to make ends meet and get it all done, it is definitely not the life of my childhood dreams. But through it all, I have seen the hand of God work and move in my life. I do not regret for a minute that I am now in the relationship I am in with the King of kings. I have a wonderful child, and we live in the presence of the Lord."—*Sue*

It was difficult for me to fathom anyone not appreciating the vivid colors that the original artists intended. Then God reminded me of His desire to restore our dreams: Some of His children are much more comfortable with the filth and grime that mar His original works of art. Yes, God has dreams for our lives, but many times years of disappointment and pain pollute and mask those dreams. God's desire is to wash us clean and restore the dreams that He had when He created His original work of art in the Garden of Eden. Can we bear the beauty? Are we ready for the vibrant colors of a fulfilling and exciting life in Christ?

Let's look now at God, the Restorer of Dreams, and prepare for a breath-taking view of the masterpiece—you, an original work of art. The veil is about to be lifted! "And we, who with unveiled faces all reflect the Lord's glory, are being transformed into his likeness with ever-increasing glory, which comes from the Lord, who is the Spirit" (2 Corinthians 3:18).

But God

One evening I had the opportunity to be the speaker at a fund-raiser banquet for a women's and children's homeless shelter. The afternoon before the event, I went to the shelter to visit with some of the ladies who temporarily lived there. I listened to their dreams and noticed that theirs had been no different from those of the women I knew who had husbands with six-figure incomes and lived in grand estates.

When Sherry was a little girl, she dreamed that she would live in a house painted blue with a white picket fence. Darla dreamed she would marry, have three children, and live in a small bungalow. Patty dreamed she would become a nurse and work in the local hospital. Betty dreamed she would be a veterinarian. Rose dreamed she would be an ice skater and teach other people how to skate. Not one of the women, in their wildest dreams, imagined they would be living in a homeless shelter, sharing a bathroom with seven to eight other women, addicted to alcohol, running from an abusive boyfriend, or unable to keep a job.

But here they were. How were they going to make it in the world again? They had to have their dreams restored. They had to learn how to dream again, and that night I heard from many who had. The counselors at Miracle Hill gave the women more than food stamps, a 10-step program, or a roof over their heads. They introduced them to Jesus Christ.

The Bible is filled with stories of seemingly hopeless situations that serve as a backdrop for God's miracles and His divine intervention and ultimate plan. The escaping Israelites were met with the Red Sea on one side and encroaching Egyptians on the other. Joseph was thrown into prison, falsely accused of assaulting Potiphar's wife, with no one to defend him. The Israeli army was held at bay by a giant named Goliath, with no one brave enough to challenge him. The Messiah was crucified and the disciples scattered and hid, and the list goes on. Just when dreams are seemingly shattered or going unfulfilled, God shows up and miraculously intervenes. That's who He is . . . the Restorer and Fulfiller of Dreams.

"God called Jesus Christ to what seemed absolute disaster. And Jesus Christ called His disciples to see Him put to death, leading every one of them to the place where their hearts were broken. His life was an absolute failure from every standpoint except God's. But what seemed to be failure from man's standpoint was a triumph from God's standpoint, because God's purpose is never the same as man's purpose."[1]

I've noticed that many times man's hopeless situation and God's divine intervention are connected by the small word *but*. Two words have become favorite words of mine in Scripture: *but God*.

In Luke 9, after Jesus, Peter, James, and John returned from the Mount of Transfiguration, they were met by a desperate father whose dreams were being destroyed one seizure at a time. For years, his only son had been gripped by demons and thrown into convulsions accompanied by foaming at the mouth and ear-piercing screams. "It scarcely ever leaves him and is destroying him," the father explained (Luke 9:39).

The nine disciples who had remained behind during Jesus' absence were unable to cast out the demon. They had been empowered to do so, but with their most positive influences absent (Jesus, John, Peter, and James) and their most negative influences present (the Pharisees and unbelievers), they lacked the faith. So Jesus asked the father to bring the boy to Him.

"Even while the boy was coming, the demon threw him to the ground in a convulsion. But Jesus rebuked the evil spirit, healed the boy and gave him back to his father" (Luke 9:42). In one verse, a son's health and a father's dream were restored. Hopeless desperation and joyful elation were bridged by the words *But Jesus.*

And what was the outcome of this miracle? "And they [those who were watching] were all amazed at the greatness of God" (Luke 9:43). That's always the outcome of a dream restored.

If you're like me, you may read the story of God's intervention and restoration in Luke 9 and think, *But could He do that for me? Could He intervene in my hopeless situation, lift the fog and give me clear direction, and restore the years that the locusts have eaten?*

Mark 9 gives some insight into the father's heart that Doctor Luke omitted. Again, it involves the word *but.*

"Jesus asked the boy's father, 'How long has he been like this?' "

"'From childhood,' he answered. 'It has often thrown him into fire or water to kill him. But if you can do anything, take pity on us and help us.'"

"'If you can?' said Jesus. 'Everything is possible for him who believes.'"

"Immediately the boy's father exclaimed, 'I do believe; help me overcome my unbelief!' " (Mark 9:21-24).

"I was told when I was 12 that I could not be an actress or author because I wasn't good enough or smart enough. I was 40 before my husband convinced me that I had enough talent and drive to see my dreams become a reality."—*Eva Marie Everson, author*

Oh my. "But if you can." I cringe at the father's words, and yet those thoughts are too often the underlying current of my own prayers. I remember when I was 14 years old and a brand-new Christian, praying for my unsaved daddy. It went something like this: "God, I'm praying for my daddy. Now Lord, he's a bad man. He drinks, chases women, gambles,

. . . " I continued to enumerate his more colorful and less honorable activities so God would realize the gravity and bleakness of the situation. "And Lord, I know You saved Saul of Tarsus and spoke to him through a blinding light on his way to Damascus, but my daddy is probably worse than Saul. So, if You can, will You save my daddy, too?"

And praise God, He did. I didn't have a very strong faith at the time, but like the boy's father in Mark 9, I had enough.

Remember what the angels said to Abraham when they overheard his 90-year-old wife, Sarah, laughing at the angels' prophecy of her having a baby: "Is anything too hard for the LORD?" (with eyebrows raised, I'm sure!). Never doubt that, my friend. The boy's father said, "If you can do anything," and Jesus assured him God could do everything.

Restoring Sight to the Blind

Just as the prefix *de* means "to reduce," the prefix *re* means "to go back again" or "to return to the starting place." Hallelujah! God sent Jesus to restore our dreams. In Him we are redeemed, refreshed, renewed, reunited, revived, restored, and reborn. He resurrects our dreams by unearthing the gifts and talents long forgotten or hidden under mounds of pain.

One day Jesus was traveling down the road leaving Jericho when two blind men began to call out, "Lord, Son of David, have mercy on us!" (Matthew 20:30). Many blind men and women had traveled to Jericho with the hopes of obtaining the plentiful balsam used for eye defects.[2] However, the dream of regaining their sight went unfulfilled, and they continued to stumble in darkness.

When these two men cried out to Jesus, the crowd rebuked them and warned them to be quiet, but the men continued to call out, "Lord, Son of David, have mercy on us!"

Jesus stopped and called to the two, "What do you want me to do for you?" (Matthew 20:32).

I have to stop right here. Can you just imagine Jesus showing up at your door and asking, "What do you want Me to do for you?" Think about that for just a moment.

"When I met my husband, he drove a BMW, owned his own business, and was the picture of success and security. Through a business downturn and a number of poor decisions, we lost everything but our Suburban and each other. We're now in a rental house, but because the Lord finally turned me to surrender it all to Him, our marriage is better than ever and our family is strong."—*Dorothy*

The two men didn't have to think. "'Lord,' they answered, 'we want our sight'" (Matthew 20:33).

"Moved with compassion, Jesus touched their eyes; and immediately they regained their sight and followed Him" (Matthew 20:34, NASB). The *New International Version* says they "received" their sight, but the *New American Standard Bible* better translates the word "regained," meaning they saw again. They had not been born blind, but once had seen the sparkle in a child's smile, the deep blue of a loved one's eyes, the vibrant yellow of a desert flower, and the incandescent hues of a sunset. At some point, the two men had vision, but because of illness or circumstance they had lost that vision. With one touch from Jesus, their dreams of seeing again were restored.

Have you lost your sight? Jesus is asking, "What do you want Me to do for you?" Oh Lord, help us to see again.

God's Unrelenting Love

The heartbeat of Christianity is God's relentless pursuit of our hearts. That's what He longs for more than anything—our hearts. Whether or not we realize the nature of the longing within our breasts, it is our longing as well. We desire to be loved—wholly, completely, unabashedly—despite the warts and wrinkles, oddities and idiosyncrasies, faults and failures. But somewhere along the way, we settle for something less, human love that is incapable of satisfying our desire for love in its purest form. We long for a love unadulterated by sin, but settle for human love that must pass through the filter of fallen man's inability to really love.

I am in no way belittling my husband's precious and treasured love for me, nor mine for him. I had no idea that depth of love was possible until I met him. As wonder-filled as our love may be, it still cannot satisfy the depth of longing in my soul for the unconditional, agape love of God. I suspect this is a great tension in marriages, because many wives and husbands expect the love of God to be met in their spouse. In reality, a spouse is not capable of supplying, and was never intended to satisfy, the longing God has placed in every human heart to be loved by Him and to love Him in return.

Many, I dare say most, of us settle for earthly love and forget the longing, the dreams of Cinderella, Snow White, and the like. With quiet resignation we decide that they were fairy tales after all.

One reason we don't believe God has dreams for our lives is because we don't truly believe He loves us. Then, even if we are convinced that He does, we don't think that He likes us. This is also a feeling that many of us have about our earthly parents: *They love me because they are my parents, but I don't think they like me very much.* Unfortunately, the feelings we have toward our earthly parents are too often projected onto God. This is one of them.

At one particular speaking engagement, I met with the events prayer team before I approached the podium. As we held hands in a circle of intercession, one of the women said, "This morning as I was sitting in the church praying for the event, God showed me that Sharon is very valuable to Him."

"I wanted to be a career woman and not be someone who stayed home and cleaned the house. Now I am so pleased that I am able to stay at home, take care of my family, and clean my house!"—*Kristi*

At that moment I began to weep. I, in my speaker suit and makeup, began to cry like a baby. I travel all around the country telling people about God's love for them, but you know what? I had forgotten that He loves me too. I know how rotten I am. I know the ugliness that escapes my mouth, the thoughts that run across the pleasant plains of my mind, and the wickedness that pops up unexpectedly in my heart. *Why would He love me, much less like me?* I wonder. There is no earthly reason. There is only a heavenly one. When He looks at me, God sees His Son who dwells in me. That's all the reason He needs.

In the Bible, each time the words *unfailing love* are used, they refer to the love God has for His children. "Unfailing love" is never attributed to human affection. We love as we can, but our emotions must pass through a filter of sin, selfish desire, and imperfect humanness. However, God's love doesn't have to sift through a filter at all. He is love, and that love never fails. "'Though the mountains be shaken and the hills be removed, yet my unfailing love for you will not be shaken nor my covenant of peace be removed,' says the LORD, who has compassion on you" (Isaiah 54:10).

When we stray away from our Father, He draws us back with cords of kindness: "When Israel was a child, I loved him, and out of Egypt I called my son. It was I who taught Ephraim to walk, taking them by the arms; but they did not realize it was I who healed them. I led them with cords of human kindness, with ties of love; I lifted the yoke from their neck and bent down to feed them" (Hosea 11:1, 3-4). What a beautiful picture of a Father who loves us.

From the Pit to the Palace

Some dreams are shattered by what has happened to us and some dreams are shattered because of what has happened through us—the choices we have made. Let's take a look at both and see how God is the Restorer of Dreams regardless of the origin of the circumstance.

First let's look at a dream that was nearly shattered because of something done to Joseph. The story is recorded in Genesis 37–50. Joseph was the second youngest and the favorite of Jacob's 12 sons. Perhaps he's most well-known for his coat of many colors, which his father made for him. His brothers were very jealous of this tattletale and daddy's boy and couldn't speak a kind word to him.

When Joseph was about 17 years old, he had a literal dream—a vision—about his future. In this vision, he saw himself and his brothers binding bundles or sheaves of wheat in a field. Suddenly Joseph's sheaf stood upright, while the brothers' sheaves gathered around his and bowed down. Unfortunately, the young Joseph did not keep this morsel to himself, but shared it with his brothers. They didn't like him before he shared his dream; now their hatred was cemented securely in place.

Then Joseph had another vision of 11 stars (representing his 11 brothers) and the moon (representing his father) all bowing down to him. Again, this was something the lad should have "treasured in his heart," but instead, he told his brothers about the dream.

Sometime later, Joseph's brothers plotted to kill him and rid themselves of him altogether. "'Here comes that dreamer!' they said to each other. 'Come now, let's kill him and throw him into one of these cisterns [wells] and say that a ferocious animal devoured him. Then we'll see what comes of his dreams'" (Genesis 37:19-20).

One of his brothers, Reuben, talked the others out of killing Joseph, but threw him in a cistern alive instead. Then they noticed a caravan traveling along the way and decided to sell their baby brother to the Midianite merchants for 20 shekels of silver. They killed a goat, spread its blood on Joseph's coat, and told their father he had been killed by a ferocious animal. His demise had been by ferocious animals indeed—10 of them. (His younger brother, Benjamin, was not with them.)

"My biggest dream developed out of the fact that I was the only one in my family who went to church and had any interest in God. In my teen years, I always felt like an outsider at church because I was always alone. Everyone was gracious and included me, but it wasn't my family. I remember falling on my knees at age 15 and asking God if I could just be on the inside sometime in my life. I married a pastor who planted a church that has grown from 17 people in 1971 to 2,400 in 2002. God answered!"—*Gayle*

But God had a dream for Joseph, and 10 jealous boys could not thwart it. Things did not go well for Joseph for quite some time. He became a servant in Potiphar's house, but was falsely accused of attempted rape by Potiphar's wife and thrown into prison. But years later, Joseph became known as an interpreter of dreams. He interpreted the pharaoh's dream, which predicted an approaching famine. His interpretation gave the pharaoh the foresight to prepare for the coming drought by storing up enough grain to feed the Egyptians as well as those in the surrounding countries. As a reward, the pharaoh made Joseph the governor of Egypt.

During the famine, guess who showed up to buy some grain. You know the story—Joseph's brothers. Of course they didn't recognize him at first, but I wonder if visions of 11 sheaves of wheat bowing down to one standing upright danced in their heads.

God had a dream for Joseph. Yes, en route he traveled from the pit to the prison before reaching the palace, but he accomplished what God had purposed nonetheless. When I read the story of Joseph, I'm always struck with one thread throughout. He always did the best he could in every circumstance and did not let bitterness or resentment stymie his activity or love for God. When he was a servant, he was the best servant he could be. When he was a prisoner, he was the best prisoner he could be. And when he was governor, he was the best governor he could be. Unlike most of us, Joseph had a very clear picture of what God had planned for his life. God had revealed it in an actual dream. And yet, he never once did anything to try and make that dream come to fruition on his own. He simply did his best at each step along the way and waited on God to direct his path. And what of his attitude toward his brothers when they came begging for help?

Once they realized that the governor was their "long lost brother," they fell down in terror and cried, "Behold, we are your servants."

"But Joseph said to them, 'Do not be afraid, for am I in God's place? And as for you, you meant evil against me, but God meant it for good in order to bring about this present result, to preserve many people alive'" (Genesis 50:18-20, NASB).

While many were at work to destroy the plan that God had for this young boy, God, the Restorer of Dreams, fitted each piece of the puzzle together to create a magnificent masterpiece of hope, forgiveness, and the overriding power of God to fulfill the plans.

Dear friends, Satan, the destroyer of dreams, wants us to give up when times get tough. He wants us to remain in the pit of despair or in the prison of fear and shame. But God, the Restorer of Dreams, wants us to live as the children of the King, in the palace of His heart.

"Every little girl has dreams; and, if she trusts Christ with all her heart, nothing can disable God from surpassing a childhood reach with a divine reality. The suicide of her husband could not keep God from surpassing Kay Arthur's dreams. Her sudden paralysis could not keep God from surpassing Joni Eareckson Tada's dreams. Her horrifying stay in a Nazi concentration camp could not keep God from surpassing Corrie Ten Boom's dreams. Her world of poverty and suffering could not keep God from surpassing Mother Teresa's dreams.

"God surpasses our dreams when we reach past our personal plans and agendas to grab the hand of Christ and walk the path He chose for us. He is obligated to keep us dissatisfied until we come to Him and His plan for complete satisfaction."[3]

Perhaps your life has not turned out as you had planned. Perhaps you are at a place you did not expect to be. If you bloom where you are planted, there's no telling where your seeds will blow and into what vase you will be placed.

From the Penthouse to the Pigpen

Now let's turn our attention to a dream shattered because of someone's own choices: the prodigal son.

You may be thinking of the many times you let God down, denied, disobeyed, or dishonored Him. Many times I've cried out, "Oh God, how could You love me? I'm not worthy of being called Your daughter! I'm not worthy to fulfill the dreams You have for my life. I've strayed. I've taken control of my own life and made a mess."

God knows all about prodigals and wayward children who think they know what's best for their lives. To help us understand His unrelenting love, Jesus told us the story of the prodigal son in Luke 15:11-24.

There was a man who had two sons. The younger one said to his father, "Father, give me my share of the estate." So he divided his property between them.

Not long after that, the younger son got together all he had, set off for a distant country and there squandered his wealth in wild living. After he had spent everything, there was a severe famine in that whole country, and he began to be in need. So he went and hired himself out to a citizen of that country, who sent him to his fields to feed pigs. He longed to fill his stomach with the pods that the pigs were eating, but no one gave him anything.

When he came to his senses, he said, "How many of my father's hired men have food to spare, and here I am starving to death! I will set out and go back to my father and say to him: Father, I have sinned against heaven and against you. I am no longer worthy to be called your son; make me like one of your hired men." So he got up and went to his father.

But while he was still a long way off, his father saw him and was filled with compassion for him; he ran to his son, threw his arms around him and kissed him.

The son said to him, "Father, I have sinned against heaven and against you. I am no longer worthy to be called your son."

But the father said to his servants, "Quick! Bring the best robe and put it on him. Put a ring on his finger and sandals on his feet. Bring the fattened calf and kill it. Let's have a feast and celebrate. For this son of mine was dead and is alive again; he was lost and is found." So they began to celebrate.

In my Bible, this parable is titled "The Parable of the Lost Son," but for me it is the parable of "A Father's Unrelenting Love and a Son's Restored Dream." When the younger son asked for his share of the inheritance, it was like saying to the father, "I wish you were dead." The father could have refused and tried to protect the boy from making a bad decision, but instead he chose to let his son learn from his mistakes. As a parent of a grown son, I understand that this is the more difficult choice of the two, and yet it is the one that brings about the necessary trials for maturity and growth.

The prodigal was living it up in the penthouse with his new friends, but it wasn't too long before a drought hit the land. He lost all of his money, his so-called friends, and his dreams. When the young man rebelled, he stepped out from under God's protective umbrella and into the scorching heat of sin. And here comes the turning point in the young man's life. Luke 15:14 says, "And he began to be in need."

Ah, need has a predictable way of turning us back to God. He ended up tending pigs and even eating their food to stay alive. This was the lowest of the low for a Jewish boy who had been taught all his life that pigs were unclean. Another one of my favorite verses says, "When he came to his senses. . . ." *What am I, crazy? Even my father's hired servants get better treatment and have food to spare. I'm going home to ask for his forgiveness and a job!*

What do you think the father was doing all this time? I believe he was praying. I know he was expectantly watching. Here comes my favorite part in the story: "But while he was still a long way off, his father saw him and was filled with compassion for him; he ran to his son, threw his arms around him and kissed him."

"While the boy was still a long way off . . ." I can just picture the father scanning the horizon day after day, praying for his son to return. Then one day it happened. When he caught a glimpse of his son coming across the field, the father didn't stand stoically waiting for an appropriate apology or the chance to say, "I told you so." Instead, when he saw his boy, he was filled with compassion. He pulled up his robe, ran shamelessly toward his son, and covered him with kisses! He placed the robe meant for an honored guest on his shoulders, slipped a ring signifying authority on his finger, and fitted sandals of a freed man on his dusty bare feet.

Even though the son did not deserve forgiveness; even though he had squandered his inheritance; even though he had rejected his family, the father restored the son and his squandered dreams. Whether you are the son in this parable or the parent who is praying for a prodigal to return, Jesus gives us this picture of God's unrelenting love and His desire to restore shattered dreams.

Prodigal Patty

Perhaps you know a prodigal. Perhaps you are the prodigal. Let me share a story of a prodigal who is dear to my heart. We'll call her Prodigal Patty. Patty and I will tell you her story together.

When Patty was a little girl, all she wanted to be when she grew up was a mommy and a wife. Like me, she pretended on many occasions to be a bride and played dress-up to prepare for the big day. Patty's father was a preacher, and her upbringing was very strict: no television, no radio, no swimming with people outside of her immediate family, no wearing of pants, and even dark-colored clothes were considered too manly. While the family was very religious, Patty knew her parents fought a lot and she sensed the tension in their home.

When she was 15, she woke up one morning and her father was gone. It was then she discovered that this man she adored was having an affair. "My mother lost a husband, and my sister and brother lost a father, but I lost the one person in the world who loved me more than any other," she said. "I was a daddy's girl and I lost the most important person in my life."

Patty's family went from being incredibly close to each other, to each man for himself. They were in survival mode, fighting a similar battle but on individual battlefields in their own hearts and minds. Of course her father left the pastorate, and she rarely saw him after that. Patty does recall him leaving a birthday present on the porch for her 16th birthday. "I caught a glimpse of his taillights as he drove away. I was encouraged that he remembered my birthday, but when his lights were out of sight, I felt the light in my own life go dim."

"God has confirmed that my life has purpose, that I am important to His kingdom whether or not I'm married. He has helped me shift my self-identity from being 'not married' to being a servant in His kingdom. Consequently, once I shifted my focus, I was more open to some incredible ministry opportunities God had in store for me. One of those was a trip this past summer to the Czech Republic to teach English and share Christ at a summer camp. God helped me shift my focus from 'I want to be married' to 'I want to serve God.'"—*Mariana*

Patty's father married the woman with whom he had the affair, and her mother remarried six weeks after the divorce was final. Both parents divorced their second spouses and married a third some years later. Patty never shed a tear during this incredible time of loss, but bled internally as each arrow struck the tender chambers of her heart. She turned to anyone who would love her, accept her, and make her feel important. Unfortunately, she turned to other women. Patty joined the homosexual lifestyle.

"For 10 years, I lived a life of homosexuality, not only as a mere participant, but as a vocal and large supporter for the coalition for gay and lesbian rights. I volunteered at a gay and lesbian help-line center and counseled gays on issues they were dealing with at the time. I was the sick and hurting leading the sick and hurting. I later became in charge of a newsletter for the gay and lesbian coalition.

"It was a life of absolute immorality, and yet I continued to pray and ask God to not let go of me and turn me over to my own way of thinking. I hurt my parents very badly, and even demanded that if my mom wanted to see me, she would have to let me bring whomever I was with at the time with me, which included holidays.

"Oh how my mother must have loved me, and the complete heartbreak this must have been for her. Being in that lifestyle is so all-consuming and such a mind wash; unless you have been there it is hard to explain. Satan twists your thinking to where you honestly, wholeheartedly believe that your friends are your true family. "

Patty knew she was a prodigal. She knew what she was doing was wrong. But she did not have the strength or willpower to set herself free. Satan took one step of desperation taken by a hurting young girl and turned it into a life of bondage. But God . . . here come my favorite words again . . . but God didn't let go of Patty. Just as the prodigal son's father scanned the horizon day after day searching for his son, Patty's mother continued to pray that God would bring her daughter back.

Patty says, "I went from one relationship to another searching for true love to mend whatever hurts I was feeling instead of looking to God. I was feeding off of others who were searching as well. The change-of-address stickers on my mail started mounting up until they covered the envelopes. As odd as it seems, I attended a church for gays, hoping God would approve of what I was doing, even though I knew it was an abomination to Him. Oh, how faithful He was to me."

Just like the prodigal son in Luke 15, God allowed Patty to continue in her rebellion until she hit rock bottom. And just like the prodigal son, she began to be in need and came to her senses.

Patty moved to another state with one of the leaders of the gay movement in the area. During one of their "retreats," her entire group of "friends" turned against her and accused her of lying about a certain matter. Each one turned her back on Patty and asked her to leave their circle. This was the final rejection. Crying uncontrollably, Patty left and headed back to her hometown. She doesn't remember how she got there. Amazingly, when she arrived home, she had a small spare tire on her wheel, but didn't remember having a flat or anyone changing it along the way. (I suspect an angel took care of Patty.)

When she arrived, Patty was unable to speak, but simply rocked back and forth or lay in a fetal position. She was admitted to a counseling facility called Rapha to undergo intense treatment. When she arrived, like the prodigal son, she had not showered, eaten, slept, or combed her hair in days. She was unresponsive to therapy, and the staff suspected Patty would die.

After a week of no change, someone came into her room and placed the book *Search for Significance* on her nightstand. She picked it up and began reading about her life on every page. God began to whisper His loving words into Patty's heart, and even though she wasn't listening to the counselors, her heavenly Father, who had scanned the horizon for her, began calling out her name. With tears streaming down her cheeks, she responded to His voice and ran into His arms. When she turned toward Him, God began to run toward her as well.

"I was on my way back," Patty said. "The Lord had to strip me of my home, my job, and all my friends in order to save me from myself. What Satan meant for evil, God is using for good. Oh what mercy . . . oh what grace. I am amazed that God chose to save me, bless me, and now use me in His kingdom."

Patty's life is a portrait of restoration, and her dreams of being a wife and mother have come true. She is a beautiful young woman with a very masculine, handsome husband and two lovely children. God is using Patty to help families with prodigals living in the gay lifestyle and encouraging them to not lose hope. Patty came back to the Father, and He came running to meet her. He placed a royal robe of righteousness around her shoulders and proclaimed, "Let's have a feast and celebrate. For this daughter of mine was dead and is alive again; she was lost and is found." And God, with all the angels, began to celebrate!

Patty knows God, the Restorer of Dreams.

No matter what has been done to you or what has been done by or through you, God can take the pieces of your shattered dreams and make a beautiful mosaic of your life. When looking at the four women listed in the lineage of Jesus in Matthew 1, I noticed that one was involved in an incestuous relationship (Tamar), one had been a prostitute (Rahab), one had an affair with King David (Bathsheba), and one was from a cursed land (Ruth). And yet, God allowed these four women to be in the lineage of our Savior. What a wonderful picture of God's grace. There is no place so far from God that His mercy cannot save and use you for His glory. He is the Restorer of Dreams

"What You Was Made For"

I sat in a darkened theater watching the movie *The Legend of Bagger Vance*. Now I know the theology wasn't correct, but one scene caused tears to stream down my cheeks. It was during a time when I was struggling with my "call" in ministry.

As a young man, Randolph Junuh was an incredible golfer who showed great promise. But right in his prime, he was called away to war. During one particular battle, his entire company was killed. Junuh was the lone survivor, but he did not survive very well. When he returned home, Junuh lost his dream of becoming a professional golfer and lived in an abandoned old house in seclusion from the rest of the world.

Through a series of events, he was challenged to play in a golf tournament and represent the state of Georgia. Along with the challenge came a certain fellow, Bagger Vance, who would be his caddy. Bagger, as it turned out, was supposed to be a type of "angel" sent to help Junuh rediscover his dreams. In one final scene, Junuh is trying to recover after a bad shot by hitting a ball out of the woods. Standing among the trees, the horrors of war return, and Junuh cannot go any further. He hears the gunfire and sees the soldiers falling all around him. Then Bagger interrupts his vision of the past. Listen to this scene:

With shaking hands and a look of terror on his face, Junuh begins:

Junuh: I can't do this. You don't understand.

Bagger: I don't need to understand. Ain't no soul on this entire earth ain't got a burden to carry he didn't understand. You ain't alone in that. But you been carrying this one long enough. Time to go on an' lay it down.

Junuh: I don't know how.

Bagger: You've got a choice. You can stop or you can start.

Junuh: Start?

Bagger: Walkin'. Right back to where you always been and then stand there. Still . . . real still . . . and remember.

Junuh: It was long ago.

Bagger: No sir. It was just a moment ago. Time for you to come on out of the shadow, Mr. Junuh. Time for you to choose.

Junuh: I can't.

Bagger: Yes, you can. But you ain't alone. I'm right here wich ya. I've been here all along. Play the game. The one that only you was meant to play. The one that was given to you when you came into this world.

(Junuh takes his stance and places his hands on the club.)

Bagger: Ready? Take your stance. Strike the ball, Junuh, and don't hold nothin' back. Give it everything. Let yourself remember . . . remember your swing. That's right. Settle yourself. Now is the time, Junuh.

Randolph Junuh took his stance, clutched the club, and knocked the ball out of the woods and onto the green. He also came out of the darkness and remembered who he was and what he "was made to do."

I'm not a golfer, but I was standing right there in the woods with Junuh. With sweaty palms and racing heart . . . remembering the pains of the past . . . remembering past failures . . . remembering past defeats . . . remembering the battles lost and the wounded left behind. Then God came and whispered in my ear, "Sharon, take your stance. It's time for you to come out of the shadows. Don't be afraid. You do what I have created you to do, the plan that I set in place for you before you came into this world. Don't let the memories of the past hold you captive. I'm right here with you. I've been here all along."

Are you ready to come out of the shadows? Are you ready to tackle that thing God has placed in your heart to do? Settle yourself. Now's the time. Come now, and let's discover God's dreams for our lives. But first, let's take a brief intermission.

11

Interrupted Dreams

Most of us have had shattered dreams. Most of us have had restored dreams. But I dare say there are many of us in between, waiting for God to move or tell us where to move. Oh, I've been there, my friend. Like a long intermission before the final act of a play, I've sat in the dark waiting for the curtain to rise and for God to show me the ending. At times, I've felt as though life has come to a halt, interrupted by some invisible force.

I tried to steer away from men in this book, as it is specifically for us girls and the dreams we have for our lives. However, I can't leave this subject of dreams without talking about my dear friend Moses. He was a man whose dreams were interrupted by God.

When God began to whisper His dreams for my life into my ear—the ones He had for my future as well as the ones He had already fulfilled in Christ—He knew I would have the tendency to follow in Moses' stubborn footsteps. But I'm getting ahead of myself. Let me start at the beginning.

Moses was born during a time when the Israelites were slaves in Egypt. All day long they were under the whip of taskmasters who forced them to make bricks from mud and straw. Instead of breaking them, the work made them stronger. The pharaoh became concerned that the Israelites were becoming too numerous and would potentially try to take over the country. He made a decree that all the Hebrew boy babies had to be thrown into the Nile. But Moses' mother, Jochebed, had a dream for her son. It was very simple, really. She had a dream that her son would live.

"Mommy, what will we do if the baby you are carrying is a boy?" her seven-year-old daughter pleadingly asked.

"We will remain calm and pray that God will show us what we are to do," she replied. "I have a strange feeling about this child. I do not believe God will allow him to die."

At the proper time, Moses was born, and his mother hid him for three months. During that time, I believe Jochebed prayed and sought the Lord for what to do. Soon God began to weave a plan in her mind, and she began to weave a wicker basket for the baby. With nimble fingers, she wove reeds into a basket and covered it with pitch to make it watertight.

Then she obeyed the pharaoh's command and threw the baby into the crocodile-infested Nile River. However, Moses was set afloat in his personal ark. While he floated along on the water, his mother prayed that someone, anyone, would come by and save her precious child. Meanwhile, Moses' sister, Miriam, hid in the bulrushes by the river to see what would happen.

As God would have it, someone did come along. Well, not just someone, but the only one in the entire kingdom who could do whatever she wanted—the pharaoh's daughter. Once again, God answered exceedingly abundantly more than Jochebed could have ever asked or imagined.

"Oh, this must be one of the Hebrew babies," the princess remarked as they drew him out of the water. "Look how beautiful he is."

Miriam appeared out of the reeds and said, "Shall I go and get one of the Hebrew women to nurse the baby for you?" (Exodus 2:7)

"Yes, go," she answered. "And I will pay her."

Talk about a dream come true! Jochebed was ecstatic! She was going to nurse her baby and get paid to do it!

After Moses had been weaned, Jochebed delivered him to the pharaoh's daughter where he grew up as the pharaoh's grandson. We don't know how, but sometime before age 40, Moses discovered that he was not an Egyptian after all, but a Hebrew. (We know Charleton Heston discovered this when he found his baby blanket!) At that point, Moses devised a dream for his life. He decided that he was going to be the deliverer of the Hebrew nation.

Now this is crucial: Moses decided what to do. Moses decided when. Moses decided how. He planned a work and then set out to work the plan. It was all his doing.

One day, Moses saw a Hebrew and an Egyptian fighting. *This will be a good day to begin my dream of freeing the Hebrews from bondage,* he may have thought to himself. So Moses killed the Egyptian and hid him in the sand. One down, several million to go.

The next day, Moses saw two Hebrews fighting. "Why are you hitting your fellow Hebrew?" Moses asked the one in the wrong.

"The man said, 'Who made you ruler and judge over us? [That was a good question. Who had made him ruler and judge over them? Certainly not God.] Are you thinking of killing me as you killed the Egyptian?'" (Exodus 2:13-14).

Then Moses became afraid as he knew his act of murder must be widely known. Indeed, when the pharaoh heard about the murder, he tried to have Moses killed. So he ran away, fleeing to Midian. His dream was interrupted. Moses went from riches to rags in one day. In Midian, he married a woman named Zipporah and spent the next 40 years tending her father's sheep.

Moses had a dream. It was a good and noble dream. It was a dream to save the Hebrew nation from slavery and bondage. However, he ran ahead of God and tried to make his dream a reality in his own way, in his own time, and in his own strength. The result was disastrous, and God had to interrupt his life to stop him. After a while, Moses forgot his dream altogether. But remember, God is a God who restores our dreams.

The Moses we see 40 years after he fled from Egypt is not the same ostentatious Moses we saw earlier. In the beginning, he was a man "educated in all the wisdom of the Egyptians and was powerful in speech and action" (Acts 7:22). After 40 years of tending sheep, Moses had become so insecure that he had developed a speech impediment. No longer was he powerful in speech and actions. No resources. No self-confidence. No drive. No dreams.

Moses' mother had placed him in the river to save his life. God had placed him in the desert to save his soul. Now God had him right where He wanted him—at the end of himself. A. W. Tozer said, "The reason why many are still troubled, still seeking, still making little forward progress, is because they have not yet come to the end of themselves. We are still giving some of the orders, and we are still interfering with God's working within us." Moses came to the end of himself, and when he did, God was waiting there to embrace him.

One day while he was tending his sheep on Mount Horeb, he saw a bush that was burning but not being consumed. The Lord saw that Moses had gone over to see the bush, and when he had turned aside, God spoke to him.

"Moses! Moses!" God said.

And Moses replied, "Here I am."

Then, from the midst of the burning bush, God told Moses that He had a dream for his life. He had heard the cry of the Hebrews in Egypt and He was going to use Moses to deliver them.

But Moses argued with the Lord. "Who am I that I should go to the pharaoh? Who am I going to say sent me? What if they don't believe me?"

With each point of Moses' argument, God's answer was the same: "I will be with you."

In one last plea of desperation, Moses reminded God that he had a speech impediment and was not exactly eloquent. "O Lord, please send someone else to do it," he begged.

God grew angry with Moses and allowed him to take his brother, Aaron, along as a mouthpiece. But oh, the problems his brother caused.

I hope you'll go back and read the rest of the story beginning in Exodus 4:18. I want to stop right here and make a few observations. Did you notice that God's dream for Moses was the same dream Moses had for his life 40 years earlier? Yet, Moses had forgotten the flame that burned in his heart so many years before—to free the Hebrew people. He had forgotten his passion, his purpose, and his preordained preparation for the task. However, God had not forgotten. He was simply waiting for Moses to get ready.

Where did Moses go wrong? He went ahead of God. Anabel Gillham writes, "Moses wasn't wrong in his vision or in his goal. He was wrong in his method. His perception of how God worked and of God's ways was wrong. Moses didn't really know what God wanted him to be, and it took another 40 long years for God to build new patterns into Moses and bring him to that understanding. God wanted a man who was aware of his inadequacies; a man who, of necessity, would draw from God's strength, wisdom, and power; a man who would recognize God's ability through his own weakness."[1]

So many times, when we think we are ready, we aren't. Then when we think we aren't ready, we are. So what does it mean to be ready to fulfill God's dreams for our lives? We are ready when:

• We are willing to pray for God to accomplish His dreams for our lives rather than our own.

- We realize that we can accomplish nothing on our own strength, talents, and abilities, but are totally dependent on Him to work in and though us.
- We understand that God wants to accomplish God-sized dreams in our lives.
- We are willing to accomplish God's dreams in God's ways and by His leading.

Saint Augustine once said that our soul is restless until it finds rest in Him. That's where the only dreams that matter will take place. Unfortunately, we tend to believe (as Eve believed) that when we fulfill a certain desire, achieve a specific goal, or satisfy a felt longing, we will find happiness and live happily ever after. But just as with Eve when she took matters into her own hands, when we take matters into our own hands, we find out it is anything but a happily-ever-after ending.

God interrupted Moses' dreams and waited for him to learn a new method for success. God spoke. Moses obeyed. God accomplished what He purposed to do. Moses went from being a self-appointed "hit man" to a God-appointed "yes man."

Time in the Desert

Many times when we experience what we think is a shattered dream, God is in reality interrupting our plans to lead us into the desert for a period of time. His purpose is to develop our character or our understanding of who He is in order to prepare us for what He has in store. Moses spent most of his life in the desert. The Israelites spent 40 years in the desert. Jesus spent 40 days in the desert being tempted by Satan before He started His ministry.

The desert is not always welcomed, but it is always profitable. He doesn't take us into the wilderness to see if we have what it takes. He leads us into the wilderness to reveal to us what is truly in our hearts.

Think of how we train our own children. Babies don't necessarily like the fact that the world has a schedule, and they may balk at the inconvenience of having to sleep during the night and be awake during the day. But eventually they must learn to sleep through the night so their parents can rest.

I can still remember sitting on the edge of my bed, with tears streaming down my cheeks, hearing my son cry at night. I imagined he was thinking, *Where is she? Doesn't she care about me? Isn't someone going to come and get me out of this crib?*

But that wasn't it at all. I did love that little bundle of joy—every single ounce of him. But I had to let him cry a few nights so he could learn when to sleep. It wasn't selfishness on my part; I was awake during his entire struggle. It would have been easier to let him have his way. But that wouldn't have helped him learn. What made it more difficult was that I couldn't explain the process to him. He was too young to understand.

Likewise, when we are struggling, I think many times God has tears streaming down His cheeks. He has to let us cry to learn our lessons. And more often than not, if He tried to explain, we wouldn't understand. "I am the LORD your God, who teaches you what is best for you, who directs you in the way you should go" (Isaiah 48:17).

Broken dreams can be God's way of leading us into the desert for a time of intermission. The day my son was born, a dream came true. There he was with his shock of bushy black hair, record-breaking-length eyelashes, and cherub lips looking for something to suckle. He was seven pounds and six ounces of pure unadulterated love wrapped up in one tiny package. Over the years, God used that little man to shape me, mold me, and break me. While I loved every moment of being his mother, every day was not a "Kodak moment."

I still remember the pain of sitting in the principal's office when my son was in 10th grade thinking, *Where did I go wrong?* Of course, God reminded me that His kids made a few mistakes too, and He was a perfect parent.

But today, as I sit here in a silent house with only the sound of my fingers clicking over the computer keys, I miss my son. This is his second year away at college. My heart still wants to call him every day, just to hear his voice. My mind tells me to cut the apron strings and let him have his space.

My mind is winning the battle. I am so proud of him for going to college and making his way in the world. That was the goal when he made his first cry entering the world. But I am having a famine of hugs and smiles. And God is telling me to fill that new void with more of Himself.

In the Bible, when God wanted to get someone's attention, many times He sent them into the desert. In our own lives, when He wants to get our attention, He may send us into the desert as well. It may even come in the form of a shattered dream or an interrupted dream. Don't waste the dry times, but allow them to draw you to the Living Water that will refresh and satisfy your soul.

Suzi's Interruption

Suzi was a gifted speaker. Her bubbly personality and quick wit kept her audiences entertained, encouraged, and enlightened. After a few speaking engagements, Suzi began to feel very comfortable in her calling as a conference speaker. At the conclusion of her events, crowds came up to her and showered her with accolades: "Suzi, you were great today!" "Wonderful job tonight, Suzi. You are hilarious." "Suzi, you really blessed me with your words tonight. I hope you'll come back another time."

Pretty soon, Suzi began to believe her own press. *I am pretty good,* she thought to herself. *This isn't going to be as hard as I thought. I love being in front of people and I guess I inherited my father's quick wit because I can sure make them laugh. This must be God's will for me.*

Suzi became very confident in her new calling—too confident. One particular church enjoyed her so much at their retreat that they invited her back again for the next year's event. Suzi spent very little time in prayer, preparation, planning, or asking for God to fill her, use her, strengthen her, or guide her. Instead, she went into the battle alone.

The women laughed on cue, smiled, and seemed to enjoy themselves, but there was an emptiness to the weekend. There was no substance, no moving of the Holy Spirit, no anointing. The women's director felt it, the women in attendance felt it, and Suzi felt it.On the way home, Suzi turned to her friend who had attended with her and said, "I blew it, didn't I."

"Yes," she answered, "you did."

God interrupted Suzi's plans, and she stopped cold in her tracks. Like Moses, Suzi cringed at her failure and ran away to the desert. No, she didn't run to an actual desert, but she vowed never to speak again. She felt shame at her utter lack of dependence on her heavenly Father and attempt to do ministry in her own power. "I'm done," she said. "I'm not going to do this anymore."

But God (there are those words again) wasn't finished with Suzi. Now He had her where He wanted her. She spent two years in the desert, and then God came to her and called her back into ministry. She was reluctant at first, but like Moses, had learned the secret to effective ministry: total dependence on Christ. Let me clarify a bit: Suzi did not become a speaker again. She allowed God to speak through her again.

Belinda's Interruption

Suzi's interruption came as a result of her own decisions. However, sometimes our interruptions come because of decisions made by others that inevitably affect our lives. Here's Belinda's story.

As far back as I can remember, I really wanted only two things in life: to make a loving, warm, nurturing home for my family and others that crossed our paths in life, and to be used by God. I always thought I, as a woman, was called to be the "heart" of Jesus to others; that to be a wife and mother was to be called to the best work for the kingdom. I would make our home inviting, safe, and fun for my husband and family, and share it with the cold, cruel world.

When I met my husband, it was with this idea that I wanted to embrace his life in my sanctuary. He had come through incredible circumstances of life and had never known true love. God and I would love him and multiply that love to our home and our world. For 20 years I battled for that home, love, and God's purpose for me. We had three children and were active in our church. We were a "committed" Christian family. I played the piano for worship services and led a middle-school choir. My husband was a leader in Boys' Brigade, sang in the choir with me, and became a deacon. It was a dream come true.

For most of that time, however, there were "troubles" at home. I did everything I could to keep our Christian family afloat. Of course, it was what God wanted me to do. My husband didn't understand God's love or mine. There was a cancer growing in our marriage: My husband was a sex addict and had lived a double life since he was a teenager. To be a sex addict is to be a chronic liar, and I believed many, many lies. I watched my dreams sink to the depths of hell.

Months of anguish and wrestling before God opened my heart to the reality of God and my life. My dream seemed so godly, so biblical, so right. But I had made a Christian marriage and home my idol. It was my dream even though it was not a godly marriage and home in reality. It was a pretense, and I kept holding it together with all my strength. Gradually, God held my heart in His loving hands and said, "Trust me enough to let go of your dream and let Me show you the dream that I have for you. It is nothing like what you have made."

My dream died. My warm, loving, nurturing, sheltering home had not been enough for my husband. Detaching from the "rescue" effort was excruciating for me. Now, when I am tempted each day to grasp my life, I stretch out my hand and hold it open toward heaven: "God, may I not grasp anything in my life, but hold it up to You. Place in my life what You choose. Remove from my life what You choose." Christ has taught me that He is all I need, that to spend my life "dancing with Him" is enough.

As my dreams have been reduced to a pile of ashes, I've let go of them. I sift through the dust to gather any precious remains. Even in two years of brokenness and loss, God has used my home and kitchen to nurture many people both physically and spiritually. As I write this, I am thrilled and amazed that a friend of my son is going to church with us tomorrow morning. He came to Christ last weekend and wants to know more about God. What joy in the midst of sorrow. How like my Lord to use broken, struggling beggars to show another one where to find bread, to bring life even in death. What a dream come true!

Unforgiveness—Stumbling Block or Road Block?

After I had gone to college for two years, I returned to my hometown to work as a dental hygienist. But the following spring, I felt an urge to continue my education. I prayed, looked into various programs, but did not receive a clear direction from God. To not decide is to decide, and I did not return to college. The following spring, I began to feel the same promptings and the same cloud of confusion. At the same time, I began to have flashbacks of violent childhood memories.

One night, I went to visit one of my mentors and asked him to pray with me about what I was to do with my life. In the course of the conversation, I also mentioned the flashbacks. After listening to my dilemma, Mr. Thorp began our prayer time by turning to various scriptures. First he read Matthew 6:8-15:

For your Father knows what you need before you ask him. This, then, is how you should pray: "Our Father in heaven, hallowed be your name, your kingdom come, your will be done on earth as it is in heaven. Give us today our daily bread. Forgive us our debts, as we also have forgiven our debtors. And lead us not into temptation, but deliver us from the evil one." For if you forgive men when they sin against you, your heavenly Father will also forgive you. But if you do not forgive men their sins, your Father will not forgive your sins.

Then he turned to Matthew 18:19-22:

"Again, I tell you that if two of you on earth agree about anything you ask for, it will be done for you by my Father in heaven. For where two or three come together in my name, there am I with them."

Then Peter came to Jesus and asked, "Lord, how many times shall I forgive my brother when he sins against me? Up to seven times?"

Jesus answered, "I tell you, not seven times, but seventy-seven times."

Each time Mr. Thorp turned to a passage about God answering prayer, there was a verse about forgiveness embracing it either before or after. "Sharon," he said, "I sense God is telling you that you have unforgiveness toward your father. It that true?"

I wanted to say, "Wait a minute. I came here to pray about my future, not about my past." But God was showing me that unforgiveness in my past was impeding His work in my future. At that time in my life, I had been a Christian for seven years and my dad had become a Christian just the year before. I did not even realize that I had not forgiven him for the pain he had caused in my childhood. Now, when he made a mistake, all those old feelings I had toward him resurfaced like hot lava lying beneath a dormant volcano.

God was showing me that in order to get out of this intermission stage of my life, I needed to forgive my dad. Until I obeyed, my dreams were going to continue to be interrupted by His hand. That night, I forgave my father for everything he had ever done. When I did, God set me free, and my life moved to a new and deeper level with Him.

Interestingly, the next day the cloud of confusion lifted. I applied to college in late spring, even though the head of the department told me it was too late and the program I desired to enroll in was full. They told me the only way I could get in was if someone were to drop out, which was very unlikely. Confident that this was God's plan for me, I resigned from my job and looked for an apartment near the college campus. Ten days before the start of the fall semester, the head of the department called and said, "You won't believe this; this never happens, but someone dropped out of the program. We'd like you to come in the fall if you can make the arrangements."

I could believe it, and the arrangements were already made. I enrolled in the fall and met my husband four weeks later. Nine months later, I became his wife.

I am not saying that when you forgive, you'll strike it rich, find the man of your dreams, or live happily ever after. However, I do believe that unforgiveness can be a roadblock to God's power in our lives and cause us to stumble and miss out on a storehouse of blessings.

The Greek word for forgiveness, *aphiemi,* means "to let go from one's power, possession; to let go free, let escape."[2] Beth Moore explains, "In essence, the intent of biblical forgiveness is to cut someone loose. The word picture drawn by the Greek term for unforgiveness is one in which the unforgiven is roped to the back of the unforgiving. How ironic. Unforgiveness is the means by which we securely bind ourselves to that which we hate most. Therefore, the Greek meaning of forgiveness might best be demonstrated as the practice of cutting loose the person roped to your back."[3]

Unforgiveness is a snare, a trap, a stumbling block, and a roadblock to fulfilled dreams. Paul warns that when we don't forgive, Satan has outwitted us and a root of bitterness begins to grow (2 Corinthians 2:10-11, Hebrews 12:15). Amazingly, every time I type the word *unforgiveness* into my computer, my spell checker underlines it in red, implying that it is not a word. How like Satan to tell us that unforgiveness is not a problem! It is, my friends. Oh, it is.

Forgiveness has nothing to do with whether or not the person deserves to be forgiven. Most of the time he or she does not. But I have also observed that the person we hold a grudge against usually doesn't even know of our ill feelings and doesn't care. The only person being hurt is the person not forgiving.

I must always remind myself of how much Jesus has forgiven me. My offenses have been many. How can I not forgive others? When we cut someone loose, take that person off our hook, and place him or her on God's hook, we are setting ourselves free. It is a gift we give ourselves!

Forgiveness is not easy. When Jesus told Peter to forgive his offenders seventy times seven, Peter immediately said, "Increase our faith!" (Luke 17:5). But friends, the price for not forgiving those who have hurt us is very costly. If someone has hurt you once, don't allow him or her to continue to affect your dreams. Cut that person loose.

Intermission over. Let's get on with discovering God's dreams for our lives.

12

Discovering God's Dreams

How do you discover God's dreams for your life? How do you know His will? That is an age-old question men and women have asked for thousands of years. While I am not going to pretend to be an expert on discerning God's will, I do want to share some helpful steps I've learned along the way.

First and foremost, I want to emphasize what Henry Blackaby says in *Experiencing God Day by Day.* God's will for your life is to follow Christ. Jesus said, "I am the way and the truth and the life" (John 14:6). He does more than show you the way. He is the way! The New Testament can be summed up in two words: Follow Christ. "Delight yourself in the LORD and he will give you the desires of your heart" (Psalm 37:4).

With that said, let's take a look at how to discover God's dreams for your life. I've outlined some steps in a way you can remember them: D-R-E-A-M-S.

D—Dare to Dream God's Dreams for Your Life

God chooses to do extraordinary work through ordinary men and women who trust in Him. In *Experiencing God Day by Day,* Henry Blackaby writes, "Would you dare to believe that God, who called you to Himself and equipped you with His Spirit, could work mightily through you? Have you made the connection between the time and place in which you live and God's call upon you? World events never catch God by surprise. He placed you precisely where you are for a purpose."[1]

> "If I had to do it all over again, I would have pursued my dreams sooner, rather than making them chase after me."
> —*Eva Marie*

Blackaby goes on to say, "There will be times when obeying God will lead you to impossible situations. If you look at your own skills, knowledge, and resources, you will become discouraged. However, when you became a Christian, God placed His Spirit within you. You now have the resources of heaven at your disposal. The success of your endeavors will not depend on the way you use your own resources but on how you obey the Spirit of God."[2] " 'Not by might nor by power, but by my Spirit' says the LORD Almighty" (Zechariah 4:6).

Jesus didn't choose us just to make our simple dreams come true. Our dreams, like the disciples' dreams, are always too small. We are to fulfill God's dreams, and when we do, we will experience the abundant life that brings glory to God. That's how we produce fruit that remains for all eternity and discover personal fulfillment on this side of heaven.

As you begin to pray about your dreams, consider these questions:

- What interests are you most afraid to admit to others?
- What would you do if you knew you couldn't fail?
- What would you do if financial constraints were not an issue?
- What stirs your heart and makes you excited to get out of bed in the morning?
- What would you regret not having done if you knew your life was ending tomorrow?

When we are praying for God to show us the dreams for our lives and merely think on the small scale of what we can accomplish in our own strength, it is like going to the ocean with a teaspoon. We at least need to go with a pitcher! Then when He reveals what we are to do in His strength, we will be able to dip into His vast resources and pour His blessings onto those around us.

God has a plan and is looking for men and women who are willing to put their meager dreams aside and enter into a dream world of His making. "No eye has seen, no ear has heard, no mind has conceived what God has prepared for those who love Him" (1 Corinthians 2:9).

R—Remember Who God Is and Who You Are

Once God has revealed His dreams or purposes for your life, what you do next will reveal what you believe about His ability to accomplish what He has called you to do and whether or not you will experience His mighty power working in you. Remember, when He calls us to a task that is God-sized and beyond our abilities, He gets all the glory! If you can do the work in your own strength, you'll be less likely to depend on Him and give Him all the glory when the task is completed. The key is remembering who God is and who you are.

When we believe that nothing significant can happen through us, we are saying more about what we think about God than what we think about ourselves. " 'Not that we are sufficient of ourselves,' wrote Paul, 'to think of anything as being from ourselves, but our sufficiency is from God, who also made us sufficient as ministers of the new covenant' " (2 Corinthians 3:5-6, NKJV). He is able if we are obedient.

Who God Is

If you want to review just a few attributes of God, go back to chapter five and look over how Jesus is our Friend. Scripture tells us that Jesus is an exact representation of God (Hebrews 1:3) and if you know the Son, you know the Father (John 14:9). Perhaps the greatest name for God is I AM. He just is!

What was the difference between the cowardly Moses who said, "Pick someone else" and the courageous David who said, "Let me at that ugly giant"? David understood what God could do. Moses did not. David confidently said, "The LORD who delivered me from the paw of the lion and the paw of the bear will deliver me from the hand of this Philistine" (1 Samuel 17:37). David knew he would sling the stone, but God would kill the giant.

"I guess my dreams were unrealistic. They have not come true. I don't feel disappointed that these dreams were not realized. They were just dreams . . . how could they come true?"—*Yvonne*

In my den, I have a wooden box with five smooth stones. I keep them on my bookshelf to remind me that it is always God who goes before me—and He is able! "Now to him who is able to do immeasurably more than all we ask or imagine, according to his power that is at work within us, to him be glory in the church and in Christ Jesus throughout all generations, for ever and ever! Amen" (Ephesians 3:20-21).

Who You Are

When God called me to speak and write to encourage and equip women, we had quite some discussion. "Lord, there are some things about my life that You seem to have forgotten. There are aspects of my personality You seem to have overlooked. My family background isn't suitable for one who can teach others how to build godly homes. I know who other people think I am, but God, You know who I really am deep down. There's a lot of muck and mire."

But while I resisted, God persisted. He reminded me that He chose a prostitute to rescue the spies in Jericho, a woman with an immoral past to be the first person He appeared to after His resurrection, another with a sordid past to bring an entire Samaritan village to Himself, a seamstress to start the first church in Ephesus, a bankrupt widow to care for the prophet Elijah, and a teenage virgin to bear His only Son.

He enjoys using nobodies! The very fact that we are aware of our inadequacies makes us prime candidates for effective ministry. We might start out as nobodies, but once we are in Christ, we inherit many new attributes. Here are just a few:

- Salt of the earth (Matthew 5:13)
- Light of the world (Matthew 5:14)
- Child of God (John 1:12)
- Chosen by God (John 15:16)
- Joint heir with Christ (Romans 8:17)
- Temple of God (1 Corinthians 3:16)
- A new creation (2 Corinthians 5:17)
- A saint (Ephesians 1:1)
- Blessed with every spiritual blessing (Ephesians 1:3)
- Righteous and holy (Ephesians 4:24)
- Dearly loved by God (Colossians 3:12)

In order to accomplish God-sized dreams, we must move past who we think we are and start believing what the Bible says about our new identity as children of God. You have a daddy who loves you, a groom who adores you, spiritual children who look up to you, a best friend who's always available for you, and beauty that makes God's heart skip a beat.

"He chose the lowly things of this world and the despised things—and the things that are not—to nullify the things that are, so that no one may boast before him. It is because of him that you are in Christ Jesus, who has become for us wisdom from God—that is, our righteousness, holiness and redemption. Therefore, as it is written: 'Let him who boasts boast in the Lord'" (1 Corinthians 1:28-31).

E—Examine God's Word to Learn His Character and His Ways

How do you know if the ideas in your mind are from God, Satan, or of your own making? That is a very valid and common question among believers today. One way is to know the truth. Every thought, every idea must be filtered through the sieve of God's Word. Is what you are hearing consistent with God's character? Is it consistent with God's ways? Is it consistent with His Word?

Bank tellers are trained to detect counterfeit bills by studying the real ones. They learn about the markings, the ink, and the feel of authentic bills. Then when the counterfeit comes their way, they can recognize it as fake. We learn to recognize what is not true the same way, by learning what is true.

God has written us a wonderful love letter in which are hidden wisdom and knowledge. David wrote, "I have hidden your word in my heart that I might not sin against you" (Psalm 119:11). He took the word, meditated upon it, and moved it from his head to his heart. To meditate means to think deeply and continuously about something. Webster's defines meditate as "to reflect deeply, to spend time in spiritual exercise of thinking about some religious theme, to contemplate." It's not reading the Bible for information, but for transformation, and this takes time.

I don't know about you, but God hasn't spoken to me through a burning bush lately or guided me by a moving star in the east. God hasn't written a warning on my wall with His finger or spoken to me through a donkey the last time I visited the zoo. But it sure would make life easier, wouldn't it? We like visible signs!

> "I dream of serving God with my husband and children.
> I have dreams of making a significant impact in the lives of
> countless women for God through speaking, writing, and just
> being available. I dream of seeing God do more than I could
> ever imagine or fulfill on my own."—*Vickey*

The people wanted the same from Jesus: "Then some of the Pharisees and teachers of the law said to him, 'Teacher, we want to see a miraculous sign from you.'

"He answered, 'A wicked and adulterous generation asks for a miraculous sign! But none will be given it except the sign of the prophet Jonah. For as Jonah was three days and three nights in the belly of a huge fish, so the Son of Man will be three days and three nights in the heart of the earth'" (Matthew 12:38-40).

Yes, there were signs to confirm God's dreams for certain biblical individuals. However, they did not have the Bible as we do and they did not have the Holy Spirit living in them. "All Scripture is God-breathed and is useful for teaching, rebuking, correcting and training in righteousness, so that the man of God may be thoroughly equipped for every good work" (2 Timothy 3:16-17).

A—Ask God to Reveal His Dreams for Your Life

There is nothing that brings me greater joy than for my son to ask me for something I want to give him. I think our heavenly Father must feel the same.

> Ask and it will be give to you; seek and you will find; knock and the door will be opened to you. For everyone who asks receives; he who seeks finds; and to him who knocks, the door will be opened. Which of you, if his son asks for bread, will give him a stone? Or if he asks for a fish, will give him a snake? If you, then, though you are evil, know how to give good gifts to your children, how much more will your Father in heaven give good gifts to those who ask him! (Matthew 7:7-11)

When we pray and ask God to reveal His plans for our lives, we are saying that we want nothing more and nothing less than what God desires for us. We are placing our lives in the palm of His hand for Him to accomplish His purposes in His power with His provisions. His bountiful resources are limited only by our willingness to receive them.

In 2000, Bruce Wilkinson's little book *The Prayer of Jabez* took the world by storm. It was based on the prayer of a man in the Bible whose name meant "pain." "Jabez cried out to the God of Israel, 'Oh, that you would bless me and enlarge my territory! Let your hand be with me, and keep me from harm so that I will be free from pain.' And so God granted his request" (1 Chronicles 4:10).

I believe part of the success of this book was that many saw this as an invitation to bring their hopes and dreams to God in prayer. But the prayer of Jabez is not about getting what you want, and Dr. Wilkinson never intended it to be. He wrote:

Notice a radical aspect of Jabez's request for blessing: He left it entirely up to God to decide what the blessings would be and where, when, and how Jabez would receive them. This kind of radical trust in God's good intentions toward us has nothing in common with the popular gospel that you should ask God for a Cadillac, a six-figure income, or some other material sign that you have found a way to cash in on your connection with Him. Instead, the Jabez blessing focuses like a laser on our wanting for ourselves nothing more and nothing less than what God wants for us.

When we seek God's blessing as the ultimate value in life, we are throwing ourselves entirely into the river of His will and power and purposes for us. All our other needs become secondary to what we really want—which is to become wholly immersed in what God is trying to do in us, through us, and around us for His glory.[3]

After Jesus' resurrection, the early church experienced phenomenal growth. Luke wrote, "The Lord's hand was with them, and a great number of people believed and turned to the Lord" (Acts 11:21). Did you notice this passage didn't say, "They did a great job . . . They preached a good sermon . . . Their outlines were impeccable . . . Their PowerPoint was perfect . . . " No, the hand of the Lord was with them. Sure, it was their mouths that did the speaking, their feet that did the walking, their hands that did the touching, but it was God's hand that quickened their hearts and brought about the desired result.

Jesus clearly tells us to ask: "Ask and it will be given to you" (Matthew 7:7). "You do not have, because you do not ask God" (James 4:2). "You may ask me for anything in my name, and I will do it" (John 14:14). "If you remain in me and my words remain in you, ask whatever you wish, and it will be given you" (John 15:7).

So what are your dreams? Are you willing to let go of your smaller dreams and dream God-sized dreams, dreams that only He can accomplish in your life? He is looking for ordinary people through whom He can accomplish extraordinary feats. He's just waiting for you to accept the invitation.

Remember, we should never look for "typical dreams." This is not a multiple-choice answer to our prayer. Each one of us is fearfully and wonderfully made and God has uniquely designed dreams for each of our lives: "For we are God's workmanship, created in Christ Jesus to do good works, which God prepared in advance for us to do" (Ephesians 2:10). Have no doubt. He has a plan. "'You did not choose me," Jesus said, "but I chose you and appointed you to go and bear fruit—fruit that will last. Then the Father will give you whatever you ask in my name" (John 15:16).

God wants us to ask. "Nothing pleases God more than when we ask for what He wants to give. When we spend time with Him and allow His priorities, passions, and purposes to motivate us, we will ask for things that are closest to His heart."[4] If we read God's Word but do not pray, we end up being an intellectually barren believer. "Be still before the LORD and wait patiently for him" (Psalm 37:7).

M—Move When He Says Move

Once God has placed a dream in your heart and invites you to participate with Him in His dreams, you will have the opportunity to accept or reject the invitation. For most of us, that does not come in the form of actually rounding our lips and forming the word *no* but comes in the form of ignoring the call. We're good at pretending the nudge isn't there and letting our fears and doubts talk us out of moving forward.

At some point, God will call us to a God-sized assignment. Henry Blackaby noted, "When God invites you to join Him in His work, He has assigned a God-sized assignment for you. You will realize that you cannot do it on your own. If God doesn't help you, you will fail. This is the crisis point where many decide not to follow what they sense God is leading them to do. Then they wonder why they do not experience God's presence and activity the way other Christians do."[5]

We face the same crossroads that men and women in the Bible faced. Will we accept the invitation or deny the invitation? Will we believe that God can accomplish what He has purposed, or will we falsely assume that we must accomplish the assignment in our own power and with our own resources? Will we say, "I can't do that," or will we say as Paul said in Philippians 4:13, "I can do everything through him who gives me strength"?

"I would love to be involved in evangelistic ministry. I would love organizing large crusades or conferences, then possibly helping with the ministry part of those as well. It seems like a big dream and it's easy for me to doubt I could ever be involved in something like this." —*Geneva*

In the Bible we see miraculous events take place once someone obeyed. The Red Sea divided once the Israelites took the first steps of faith and placed their feet in the water. The walls of Jericho fell to the ground after they walked around it seven times. Naman was healed of leprosy after he dipped in the pool of water seven times. First they moved—then the miracle!

God's not going to force you to obey Him, but disobedience can be very costly. It cost the Israelites 40 years wandering in the desert. I don't know about you, but wandering around in the desert for 40 years doesn't sound too appealing. Unfortunately, I've had a few treks through the desert of disobedience myself. The oasis of obedience is better.

I'm not a great speller and had trouble with *dessert* and *desert*. My son finally told me, "Mom, remember, *dessert* has two *s*'s because you always want more." I don't want more deserts in my life; I want more desserts. "Taste and see that the LORD is good," David reminds us.

When God reveals what His dreams for our lives are, what we do next will determine what He does next. If we obey step one, He will most likely tell us step two. However, if we do not obey step one, He will most likely not tell us step two. If your spiritual life seems at a standstill, make sure you have done all that God has told you to do up to this point. It could be that He is waiting for you to complete what He has already called you to before He reveals more.

I have come to this crossroads many times in my life, but none so marked as when I was praying about whether or not to work with Proverbs 31 Ministries. In 1995, I began to feel God's call to minister to women in a different way than I was at the time. I had been teaching Bible studies and counseling women in crisis pregnancies, but I sensed a shifting of His will, a sense that He was about to do a new thing.

"I'm excited about what lies around the corner.
Taking our dreams and transforming them into
realities—that's the adventure of life in Him."—*Christie*

For years I had also been writing stories about listening to God in everyday life and tucking them away in a drawer. It made sense that perhaps God was calling me to write. I prayed, *God, You know I love to write and I sense that You may be calling me to a writing ministry. But God, just so you know, I will never stand up in front of anyone and say anything, so don't bother asking me to speak.*

(Isn't that comical. Me telling God what I would do and wouldn't do. I'm sure He got a big kick out of that one! Call me Ms. Moses.)

For one year I prayed about what God was calling me to do. I felt as though He had given me the introduction, but I had no idea what the coming chapters of my life would contain. Almost one year after I began praying for God to reveal His dreams for my life, I met Lysa TerKeurst of Proverbs 31 Ministries. She invited me to be a guest on the ministry's radio program to talk about infertility. After the recording session, she said, "Sharon, I've been praying for one year for a ministry partner. I think God is telling me that you are that person."

"I would like to go to India and work in an orphanage."
—*Annette*

I was very reluctant but did agree to pray about it. Now I have to tell you, I argued with the Lord just like Moses did. *God, you've got to be kidding. My voice is too Southern to do radio!* Then I thought about my friends Billy Graham, Charles Stanley, and Beth Moore. *Well Lord, my college degree is in dental hygiene, not public speaking!* Then I remembered His words to Moses: "I, even I, will be with your mouth, and teach you what you are to say" (Exodus 4:12, NASB).

But God, I don't know anything about radio! Then He reminded me of Bezalel and Oholiab whom He put in charge of working with gold and silver for the tabernacle. These guys had been making bricks with mud and straw as slaves for the Egyptians their entire lives, but God filled them with wisdom, understanding, and knowledge to do the task He called them to do (Exodus 31:1-6).

I told Him it didn't make sense. He reminded me it made no earthly sense for a man to build an ark to protect his family from a flood when it had never rained on the earth before. But when Noah obeyed, he and his family were saved. It made no earthly sense for an army commander to dip seven times in a common pond as a cure for a debilitating skin disease. But when he obeyed, his rotting flesh was restored anew. It made no sense for an army's battle plan to be walking around a fortified city seven times and then blowing horns. But when Joshua obeyed, the walls fell and victory was theirs.

So I agreed . . . to at least pray about it.

That summer my husband and I went to Bermuda for a romantic vacation. On one particular evening, Steve and I went on a dining adventure to a five-star restaurant filled with men and women dressed in their very finest evening apparel. In one corner of the dining area, an instrumental quartet filled the room with fluid sounds of music from the 1940s and 1950s. At one point, Steve urged, "Come on, Sharon. Let's go take a spin on the dance floor." We had taken just a few ballroom dance classes, and he wanted to see if we could remember the steps.

"No way," I replied. "Nobody else is out there. I'm not going to be the only one out there with everyone staring at me. And suppose we mess up. I'd be embarrassed. It's been a long time since we've danced, and I don't remember all the steps. Let's wait until there are some other people dancing. Then I'll go."

Finally the first couple approached the floor. They looked like professional dancers, moving as one and never missing a beat. This did not encourage me at all, but only strengthened my resolve that this was no lace for my feet to tread. Then a second couple, whose steps weren't quite erfect, joined the first. Reluctantly I agreed to go to a hidden spot on r where no one could see us.

a few minutes, I noticed a fourth couple approach the floor. mething very special about this couple; the husband was in a wheelchair. He was slightly balding with a neatly trimmed beard. On his left hand, he wore a white glove, I guessed to cover a skin disease. As the band played a peppy beat, the wife held her love's healthy right hand and danced with him. He spun her around as she stooped to conform to her husband's seated position. Lovingly, like a little fairy child, she danced around his chair. When the quartet slowed to a lazy romantic melody, she pulled a chair up beside her beloved, facing in the opposite direction, and they held each other in a dancer's embrace.

My heart was so moved by this love story unfolding before my eyes that I had to turn my head and bury my face on Steve's shoulder so no one would see the tears streaming down my cheeks. As I did, I saw every person in this rigid, formal dining room with the same tears trickling down their cheeks.

"When I was a little girl, I dreamed of being a preacher. I am from a small farm town and used to preach to the corn. I shook their hands (leaves) like a preacher."—*Joyce*

After watching this incredible display of love and courage, I realized that my inhibitions about not wanting others to watch me because my steps were not perfect were gone. The Lord spoke to my heart in a powerful way: *Sharon, I want you to notice: Who moved this crowd to tears? Was it couple number one, with their perfect steps? Or was it the last couple that not only did not have perfect steps, but had no steps at all? No, my child, it was the display of love, not perfection, that had an effect on the people watching.*

See, the Lord doesn't expect our steps to be perfect. He just expects us to be obedient, to take the first step, and to let Him do the rest. The man in the wheelchair never even moved his feet, but his wife did the moves for him. And we need to remember that the Lord will do it for us. We also need to remember it is not perfect steps the world is so desperately longing for. The world isn't impressed by supposedly perfect people who live in perfect houses with perfect children. They are impressed by love—genuine, God-inspired love. That's what moves a crowd.

That night in Bermuda, God sent a lame man to teach me how to dance. I came home from that trip and told Lysa that I would join her in ministry. No, my steps are not perfect, just obedient. And God does it for me.

God took two people who felt a call to obedience and brought them together to meet the needs of women all around the world. Amazingly, we had both been praying for one year. Why didn't He answer our prayers the first month we prayed? I believe it is because He was preparing us, molding us, and maturing us.

Sometimes I think about what my life would have been like had I said no to God; how many blessings I would have missed, how many opportunities I would have forfeited, how many dreams would have gone unfulfilled. A life of obedience is the most exciting life imaginable!

S—Stay Connected to the Vine

Jesus' last days with His disciples began as He rode into Jerusalem on a donkey's colt, just five days before Passover. Children sang "Hosanna to the King," women waved palm branches in adoration, and the Pharisees began to sweat at His unwelcome popularity. Yes, everything was going as the disciples had hoped. The kingdom of God was at hand.

But then it seemed to the Twelve that their dreams were going awry. There in the Upper Room as they shared their last supper together, Jesus began to talk about His eminent death, about the "prince of this world" coming (He wasn't talking about Himself), and about being a servant.

Their spirits drooped as Jesus removed His outer garment, assumed the posture of a servant, and stooped to wash their mud-caked feet.

Can you imagine what was going through their heads? *What do You mean, You are going away? Why are You stooping and acting like a servant when You are the King? What do You mean the prince is coming? I thought You were in charge.*

But then, amongst the disappointment, disillusionment, and despair, Jesus shared a family secret. It was not a secret in the sense that only a few could know it; it was a secret in the sense of being the key to having their dreams come true.

> I am the true vine, and my Father is the gardener. He cuts off every branch in me that bears no fruit, while every branch that does bear fruit he prunes so that it will be even more fruitful. . . . Remain in me, and I will remain in you. No branch can bear fruit by itself; it must remain in the vine. Neither can you bear fruit unless you remain in me. I am the vine; you are the branches. If a man remains in me and I in him, he will bear much fruit; apart from me you can do nothing. . . . If you remain in me and my words remain in you, ask whatever you wish, and it will be given you. This is to my Father's glory, that you bear much fruit, showing yourselves to be my disciples. (John 15:1-2, 4-5, 7-8)

This is the place where dreams are dreamt—in Christ. How do we discover God's dreams for our lives? Abide in Him and learn to hear His voice. How do we accomplish God's dreams for our lives? Stay connected to the Vine and draw our strength from Him. Why does God want us to accomplish His dreams for our lives? To bring Him glory. There you have it.

Jesus has a purpose. He is the Vine that provides support, nourishment, strength, and energy to the branches that sprout from its trunk.

God has a purpose. He is the Gardener or Vinedresser who does whatever is necessary to bring about the greatest yield of fruit from the branches.

We have a purpose. We must stay connected to the Vine, submit to the pruning of the Vinedresser, bear fruit, and glorify God.

"I know the Bible has dreams for my life, but it is hard for me to have faith because I've had so many disappointments."—*Janet*

What does it mean to remain? The *New American Standard Bible* translates the Greek word *meno* as "abide." It is a constant, conscious communion with God, not based on emotion or feelings, but a decision to think on God, to acknowledge His presence with you, His power in you, and His workings through you. John uses the word *abide* 40 times in his gospel, 10 of those times in John 15:1-6. Jesus said, "If you abide in me and my words abide in you, you will be my disciples and you shall know the truth and the truth shall set you free" (John 8:32, NKJV). This is not reading the Bible for information; it is meditating on the Bible for transformation.

To abide in the Word is to abide in Jesus because He is the Word: "The Word became flesh and dwelt among us" (John 1:14). When we are in the Word, we are in Christ. Jesus tells us to abide because He knows it doesn't come naturally. You don't have to tell a child to be selfish. That comes naturally. Abiding is an act of the will, a choice. When we abide, God tells us His secrets, and we begin to detect His still small voice: "Call to me and I will answer you and tell you great and unsearchable things you do not know" (Jeremiah 33:3).

But what is this fruit the Gardener cultivates us to bear? Fruit is accomplishing God's dreams for our lives, obeying His call to good works, bringing glory to Him in our everyday lives. In Galatians 5:22-23, Paul writes of the "fruit of the spirit" as being love, joy, peace, patience, kindness, goodness, faithfulness, gentleness, and self-control. This is "inner fruit." But then Paul also writes of another type of fruit I call "outer fruit," which is produced when we allow God to work through us and in us to accomplish His dreams. It could be leading a neighbor to Christ, becoming a missionary in India, taking a meal to a friend, writing books to encourage others, teaching Sunday school for four-year-olds, or learning to fly a plane. There is no list or limit.

Don't Miss It!

When I was born, my mother was put under general anesthetic and woke up to the news that her baby girl was resting peacefully in the nursery. On the contrary, when my son, Steven, was born, I refused to push (after 23-plus hours of labor) because the mirror needed adjusting for me to see his grand entrance into the world. I didn't want to miss it! Here are some points I've learned about God's dreams for our lives:

- God has dreams for you, right now, right where you are today.
- His dreams for you at one stage of your life will be different than His dreams for you at another stage of life.
- God has dreams for your life regardless of or in spite of the mistakes of your past. Often, those very mistakes are the springboards for ministry.
- God has dreams for your life regardless of your spiritual maturity. However, the task will always match your character.
- God's dreams for your life will be unique and specifically designed for you. We are not to compare His dreams for our lives to what He is doing in someone else's life.

• Accomplishing God's dreams is directly related to the depth of our relationship to Him, how in tune to His leading we have grown, and how dependent we are on the Holy Spirit to accomplish what He's called us to do.

God has many dreams to birth in our lives. They will not come without pain, agony, stretching, straining, and perhaps even some nausea along the way. But oh, the joy in the end! Discover God's dreams for your life and watch a beautiful bud unfold before your eyes.

13

Come Dream with Me

We're coming to the end of this journey of looking at our dreams together, but in reality, it is only the beginning. I believe when we realize that Jesus fulfills our childhood dreams to have a daddy who loves us, to be a bride, to be a mother, to be beautiful, and to have a best friend, we will be free to discover greater dreams for our lives than we ever imagined.

Your life is part of God's grand design. No matter how you came into the world, no matter what your past, God has known about you and has ordained an ever-unfolding plan for your life (Jeremiah 1:5). His ultimate design is for us to be conformed to the image of His Son. He uses the hammer and chisel of circumstances and shattered dreams to remove the unnecessary and superfluous parts to reveal the masterpiece within. Just as Michelangelo removed chunks and bits of marble to unveil the magnificent statue of David, so God removes anything that hinders or hides the beautiful creatures He created us to be.

But like all analogies, this one has a flaw. Michelangelo's block of marble had no choice but to submit to the artist's tools. We have a choice. God has invited us to join Him in the process of fulfilling His dreams for our lives. It is our choice whether to accept the invitation or not, whether to yield to His workings or resist, whether to be still and allow the artist to work or run from Him and remain a block of stone instead of a work of art.

"I would like to be an actress in the theater doing clean scripts, possibly in a children's theater."—*Kristie*

As women, we have girlish dreams. A few women have had the dreams mentioned in this book fulfilled this side of heaven. They may have an earthly father who loves, cherishes, and adores them; a photo album filled with pictures of their glorious wedding day; halls that echo the cacophony of children; a beautiful reflection in the mirror; and the security of a life-long friend.

And yet, such a woman who doesn't know Jesus Christ will still feel an incredible void in her life. Why? Because even though the well may be sweet, if she is drinking only from what this life affords, she will be drinking from the wrong well. Earthly relationships and circumstances may muffle the heart's cry, but it's still there. "It is only with the heart that one can see rightly, what is most important is invisible to the eye."[1] And that is a personal and on-growing relationship with Jesus Christ.

A Higher Dream

I hope you've caught a glimpse of God's dreams for our lives. Ours are temporary; God's are eternal. The highest dream we could ever dream, the wish that if granted would make us happier than any other blessing, is to know God and to actually experience His presence every day.

God's dreams are not cookie-cutter dreams. Just as we are fearfully and wonderfully made, so are His plans for our lives: " 'For I know the plans I have for you,' declares the Lord" (Jeremiah 29:11). To paraphrase Oswald Chambers, "Never try to forecast the way God is going to answer your prayers." What He calls someone else to do has nothing to do with what He is calling you to do.

After Jesus' resurrection, He told Peter what kind of death he would suffer. Peter turned and saw John following close behind. "Well, what about him? What's going to happen to him?" Peter asked. (Oh, how I love Peter.)

Basically, Jesus told Peter it was none of his business: "If I want him to remain alive until I return, what is that to you?" (John 21:22).

"I dream that I will be able to have the financial security
to homeschool my children."—*Susan*

God spoke through a burning bush—once (Exodus 3:1-4). He told a man to build an ark—once (Genesis 8). He spoke through a donkey to a wayward prophet—once (Numbers 22:21-35). He sent a man on an incredible journey in the belly of a fish—once (Jonah). He warned a rebellious king by writing on a wall with His finger—once (Daniel 5).

We can't look at how the Lord directs someone's life and make a 10-step plan for our life based on someone else's life. Chances are it won't work. The way to know God's dreams is to know God. Jesus said, "Follow me." That's the plan. It's a daily step-by-step pursuit following Jesus every day.

Make no mistake: God does have a plan. He told Jeremiah, "Before I formed you in the womb I knew you, before you were born I set you apart; I appointed you as a prophet to the nations" (Jeremiah 1:5).

A Big Dream

C. S. Lewis said the problem with Christians is that they don't want enough.[2] That is hard to imagine in our materialistic society. But Lewis wasn't referring to cars, houses, clothes, and the like. He was referring to heaven's riches: "We are half-hearted creatures, fooling about with drink and sex and ambition when infinite joy is offered us, like an ignorant child who wants to go on making mud pies in the slum because he cannot imagine what is meant by the offer of a holiday at the sea. We are far too easily pleased."[3]

"I would like to be able to trust myself to love again, knowing what it is really about this time. Not the fantasy of a young child, but the kind of love that keeps people together no matter what. I still have the same dreams as an adult that I had as a little girl. I think deep down inside, the same dreams linger in my heart."—Carol

---

I am calling us to dream again and dream God-sized dreams—to discover and do that thing He has placed in our hearts to do. We must continue to dream, but to dream God's dreams for our lives. Our desires are what God uses to draw us to Himself. Dreams make us fertile; without them we are barren. "Without vision, the people perish" King Solomon observed.

Florence Nightingale was a woman with a big dream. She was born in Florence, Italy, in 1820, the daughter of a wealthy landowner. Her father took responsibility for her education and taught her Greek, Latin, French, German, Italian, history, philosophy, and mathematics. Florence's mother's primary concern was finding her a suitable husband, but Florence had other ideas. She felt God had called her to some unnamed cause. When she was 25, after turning down many suitors, she discovered what that cause was: to be a nurse. Six years later, her father finally gave his permission for Florence to pursue her dream.

When she began working in hospitals, she was appalled at the unsanitary conditions. In military hospitals, only one in six died from battle wounds. The others died of diseases due to poor conditions in the hospital. Although she faced much opposition in a day when women in the workforce were looked down upon, Florence Nightingale fought and won a war of her own—to improve hospital sanitation and the quality of nursing care. Most modern nursing systems and techniques we know today can be traced back to this incredibly brave woman.

"Live your life while you have it," Florence said. "Life is a splendid gift. There is nothing small in it. For the greatest things grow by God's Law out of the smallest. But to live your life, you must discipline it. You must not fritter it away in fair purpose, erring act, inconstant will, but must make your thoughts, your acts, all work to the same end, and that end, not self but God."[4]

Have you ever heard of Agnes Bojzxhiu? Probably not. But you might know her as Nobel Prize winner Mother Teresa. She never drove a car, attended college, married, or raised a family. But God had a big dream for this little woman. She spent her life caring for the starving and sick of Calcutta and allowed them to face death with dignity. Her legacy lives on today as Missionaries of Charity continues to care for 500,000 hungry families and 90,000 lepers worldwide.

Someone asked her once if she was disappointed that she didn't see more success in her ministry. She replied, "God has not called me to a ministry of success. He has called me to a ministry of mercy." She also said, "We can do no great things; only small things with great love."[5] She was a small woman who served a big God.

A Childlike Dream

One thing I love about children is that you never have to remind them to dream. There is always more to discover, worlds to be explored, and conquests to be made. We never have to remind a child to want more. The doors of their hearts fling open to welcome all that life has to offer. And Jesus tells us that in order to receive the kingdom of God, we must come as a little child (Luke 18:17).

When we come as a child, we must remember it is into our Daddy's lap we crawl and on His loving arms that we lean. A. B. Simpson wrote, "Let us but feel that He has His heart set upon us, that He is watching us from those heavens with tender interest, that He is following us day by day as a mother follows her babe in his first attempt to walk alone, that He is working out for us His highest will and blessing, as far as we will let Him and then nothing can discourage us."

"I would like to set up a foundation to offer respite vacations to caregivers of those who are suffering from Huntington's Disease."—*Carmen*

It seems that all little children are born with a certain propensity to wild abandonment. A curly-haired girl twirls around with outstretched arms in a crowded airport singing, "Jesus loves me! This I know." She doesn't care who hears; it doesn't matter in the slightest. But somewhere along the line, she learns—we learn—to tame her wild abandon, become more "civilized," and keep her thoughts to herself.

My little friend Hope was eight years old when she led her Hindu neighbor through the sinner's prayer.

"Hope, what did you say to Ammon?" her mother asked.

"I would like to encourage other people who have MS, like myself."
—*Bunny*

"Mom, it's really very simple," she explained. "I just told him that Jesus came and died on a cross to save him from his sins. Either he prays the prayer or goes down there." (She pointed to where hell is supposed to be.) Then she added, "He prayed the prayer."

No one had explained to Hope that salvation was much more complicated than that. She knew nothing of sanctification, justification, glorification, redemption, propitiation, and so on. No one told her it is next to impossible for a Hindu to come to saving faith in Christ. Nope, she just took God at His word and believed what He said and did it.

Just as a child's initial response to the world at large is to live and love with reckless abandon, so are their dreams concocted without restrictions. When I ask children what they want to be when they grow up, they usually answer without a moment's hesitation. However, when I ask adults, they have to think about it for several minutes before they answer. Lysa wanted to be the next president of the United States until someone told her she couldn't. Barbara wanted to be an astronaut until someone told her that she wasn't smart enough. Susie wanted to discover a cure for cancer until someone told her it was impossible. Amy wanted to be an Olympic gymnast until someone told her she was too tall.

Shame on us for squashing a child's dreams. Shame on others for trying to squash ours.

Jesus tells us to become as little children. My hope is not necessarily that you will find the cure for cancer, be the first to live on the moon, or even write the next great American novel, although each of those may very well be within your reach! It is not the dream itself that I long to see fulfilled in you, but a heart opened to the Fulfiller of Dreams, a mind unlocked to welcome a life more fulfilling than you ever imagined, and a dissatisfaction with the earthly platitudes and idols we use to placate those childhood longings.

I long for you to come as a child and dream again.

Watch Out for the Border Bullies

God had great dreams for the children of Israel. He chose them from all the other nations, freed them from slavery under the Egyptians, parted the Red Sea to allow them to escape from their enemies, fed them daily with manna from heaven, gave them water from a rock, led them with a fire by night and a cloud by day, and kept their shoes and clothes from wearing out on their 40-plus years journey. When they neared the Promised Land, the land flowing with milk and honey that He had guaranteed would be theirs, they sent in 12 spies to "case the joint" and see what they were up against. Ten spies reported that the land was indeed filled with milk and honey, but it was also filled with giants so powerful that the Israelites appeared as grasshoppers in comparison. Two spies, Caleb and Joshua, silenced the other 10 by saying, "We should go up and take possession of the land, for we can certainly do it" (Numbers 13:30).

The 10 responded, "'We can't attack those people; they are stronger than we are.' And they spread among the Israelites a bad report. . . . 'The land we explored devours those living in it. All the people we saw there are of great size. . . . We seemed like grasshoppers in our own eyes, and we looked the same to them'" (Numbers 13:31-33).

Moses and Aaron begged the people not to believe the border bullies: "Do not rebel against the LORD," they pleaded. "And do not be afraid of the people of the land, because we will swallow them up. Their protection is gone, but the LORD is with us. Do not be afraid of them" (Numbers 14:9).

Guess who the people believed. They believed the 10 cowards rather than the two courageous men. See, Caleb and Joshua understood that God had already given them the land. All they had to do was obey and move forward. The 10 were afraid and became the border bullies, the naysayers, the joy stealers. Here are some common objections from border bullies:

- It's never been done.
- It's never been done that way before.
- You don't have the talent.
- You don't have the money.
- You aren't smart enough.
- Someone tried that and failed.
- That will never work.
- You don't know the right people.
- You don't have the right credentials.
- You don't have the right training.
- That's too risky.

As you begin to move forward to accomplish your dreams, don't be surprised if you encounter a few border bullies of your own. Jesus' own family looked down on Him when He began His ministry. And there will be those who don't understand your call or who can't fathom that you have been called to a God-sized task. The border bullies may be those who know you best. Perhaps they are well-acquainted with your strengths and weaknesses. But do not fear. Let me ask you, dear friend, whose report are you going to believe?

By the way, God was angry at the Israelites for believing the negative report, and that entire generation was not allowed to enter the Promised Land. Only Joshua and Caleb lived long enough to enjoy the fruit and live in the land. Unfortunately, they had to wait 40 more years until the entire rebellious and unbelieving generation passed away.

Will we continue wandering in the desert because of unbelief, or will we march into the Promised Land and take what God is anxious to give? Even though we may be certain of His call, we may still have to conquer a few giants along the way. Ruth had to leave her homeland and travel to a place where her race was despised. Esther had to put her life at risk by going before the king without being summoned. Rahab had to hide Jewish spies at the risk of being killed. Jochebed had to place her son in the crocodile-infested Nile. Sarah had to leave her comfortable home and travel to an unknown land. Mary had to face ridicule and gossip by being pregnant before her marriage to Joseph.

"I dream about writing a book about what God has taught me."

—*Karen*

Some of us have forgotten our dreams, perhaps because someone whose opinion we valued told us it couldn't be done. Paul's answer to the naysayers in our lives is this: "I can do all things through Christ who gives me strength" (Philippians 4:13). If He's placed a dream in your heart, He will also supply the power and resources to accomplish it. The dream may, or I should say will, require sacrifices on our part. "For reasons known only to Him, God has chosen to work through men and women who are willing to make sacrifices for the sake of the 'thing' He has placed in their hearts to do."[6] "The success of your endeavors will not depend on the way you use your own resources, but on how you obey the Spirit of God."[7] "'Not by might nor by power, but by my Spirit,' says the LORD Almighty" (Zechariah 4:6).

Here's a poem to fight the border bullies in your life.

It Couldn't Be Done

Somebody said that it couldn't be done,
But he with a chuckle replied
That "maybe it couldn't," but he would be one
Who wouldn't say so till he'd tried.
So he buckled right in with the trace of a grin
On his face. If he worried he hid it.
He started to sing as he tackled the thing
That couldn't be done, and he did it.

Somebody scoffed: "Oh, you'll never do that;
At least no one ever has done it;"
And the first thing we knew he'd begun it.
With a lift of his chin and a bit of a grin,
Without any doubting or quiddit,
He started to sing as he tackled the thing
That couldn't be done, and he did it.

There are thousands to tell you it cannot be done
There are thousands to prophesy failure;
There are thousands to point out to you, one by one
The dangers that wait to assail you.
But just buckle in with a bit of a grin,
Just take off your coat and go to it;

Just start to sing as you tackle the thing
That "cannot be done," and you'll do it![8]

Edgar A. Guest

Choose God's Best Over the World's Good

One of the pitfalls of a zealous Christian is saying yes to the good instead of waiting for God's best. As we begin to obey God, we must be certain that we are listening to the right voice and taking on responsibilities and challenges that God has called us to and not what others want us to do. I always tell women, "The need is not the call." Just as we pray about what God wants us to do, we need to pray that God will tell us what He does not want us to do.

Jesus gave us a good example in Mark 1. Early in His ministry, while in Galilee, He invited several men to follow Him and become His 12 closest friends. With Simon, Andrew, James, and John, Jesus traveled to Capernaum. While there, He taught in the synagogue, cast out demons, and healed many people. It was a very busy day!

The next morning, instead of sleeping in, Jesus rose while it was still dark and went to a place all by Himself and prayed. Sometime later, Simon and his companions interrupted Jesus' time with God and exclaimed, "Everyone is looking for you!"

They wanted Jesus to go back to Capernaum and continue to minister to the people. Would that have been a good thing to do? Yes, it would have been good, but it would not have been best. "Jesus replied, 'Let us go somewhere else—to the nearby villages—so I can preach there also. That is why I have come'" (Mark 1:38).

How did Jesus know to pick the best over the good? I believe when He spent time alone with His Father, Jesus received His "marching orders" for the day. Likewise, when we spend time with God each morning, we will be able to say yes and no with confidence and choose God's best over man's good. Satan knows that he may not be able to get you off course by tempting you with something blatantly evil, but he can easily get you distracted by making you busy doing something "good." When we get busy, leaving no time to carry out God's will, we sacrifice the best for the good.

Get Ready

While God will supply what we need, that doesn't mean that we do not prepare ourselves. Abraham Lincoln once said, "I will study and prepare myself and then someday my chance will come."[9] When his chance came to run for public office, he was ready for the challenge. Oswald Chambers said, "Be ready for the sudden surprise visits of God. A ready person never needs to get ready. Think of the time we waste trying to get ready when God has called."[10]

> "I would love to go back to college and get my English degree so I could teach."—*Rachel*

Let me give you an example. For many years I had a desire to write a book to encourage and equip mothers. In the meantime, I prepared material and spoke at women's conferences on how to be a great mom and raise great kids. Through the years, I added to my research, wrote down personal examples as they occurred, clipped out magazine articles, and listened to others talk about what they felt their mothers did well and where they fell short. I collected poems that would encourage and challenge mothers and stories that would spur them on to be the best mother possible. I even read about famous people in history and discovered what their mothers did to encourage them.

In my research, I noticed seven key ingredients that kept coming up time and time again. To help women remember those key ingredients, I ordered them to fit the acrostic BLESSED: Beacon, Listener, Encourager, Self-esteem builder, Seed-sower, Example-setter, and Diligent. Then through the years, as God revealed scriptures and situations that illustrated those seven essentials, I placed them in a folder.

In the fall of 1999, I received a call from a publisher. They had seen articles written by Proverbs 31 Ministries, knew of our radio program, and wanted to know if we had any book projects we'd like to write in the future. You guessed it. I didn't have to scramble to get ready; I was ready. Within weeks I was sitting in an office sharing my book proposal. *Being a Great Mom Raising Great Kids* was released in 2000.

My dream came true. It wasn't by the wave of a wand; I had to prepare. Oswald Chambers also wrote, "Dreaming about a thing in order to do it properly is right; but dreaming about it when we should be doing it is wrong."[11] But my preparation wasn't all it took. God prompted the publisher to call. I could prepare, but I could not make it happen. That is in God's hands.

Make Each Moment Count

When I was newly married, I attended a social club meeting of women whose husbands shared the same profession. There was absolutely nothing wrong with this gathering, but I left feeling empty and as though I had wasted a morning of my life.

The next month I opted not to attend. Instead, I went to a nursery to pick out some annuals to plant in my garden. While there, I spotted a woman whose husband was in the same profession as my husband. She and her two little girls were purchasing flowers for their garden. Carol had cancer and had been given only a few months to live. Suddenly, God whispered in my ear: *Sharon, if you knew you had only a few months to live, would you be at the social club or buying flowers with your children?* It was a poignant moment. I want to always live as if this might be the last day of my life.

Jonathan Edwards once said, "I resolve to live with all my might while I do live. I resolve never to lose one moment of time and to improve my use of time in the most profitable way I possibly can. I resolve never to do anything I wouldn't do if it were the last hour of my life."[12]

"I would like to learn how to drive a car."—*Christin*

Do you have dreams that you've put off? Consider this. If you knew you had only one more year to live, would you live your life differently? The truth is, we never know how much or how little time we have on this earth. The time to accomplish what God has called us to do is now.

I do have one word of caution for those in the process of raising a family. I know many mothers of young children who have great aspirations of accomplishing wonderful tasks for God. However, I believe that your family is your greatest mission field, and God has given you children as an investment opportunity greater than any other. As a mother, you have the great responsibility and privilege of raising the next generation for Christ! What a grand dream!

Theodore Roosevelt once said, "No other success in life—being President, or being wealthy, or going to college, or writing a book, or anything else—comes up to the success of the man or woman who can feel that they have done their duty and that their children and grandchildren rise up and call them blessed."[13]

President Roosevelt was quoting from Proverbs 31:28: "Her children arise and call her blessed." People often ask me if I think the Proverbs 31 woman was one woman or many women. I believe she was one woman. However, this was not a typical day in her life; it was a portrait of her entire life. We fall into a trap of exhaustion and frustration when we try to accomplish all our dreams when our children are small. So invest the short amount of time you have to raise godly children. That in itself is a God-sized dream! Later you can accomplish other dreams.

What Do You Want?

Suppose Jesus came to your door. Suppose upon answering the knock, you saw Him standing there and you were eye to eye with the Prince of Peace. Then what if He said, "What do you want?" Would you be stunned? Shocked? Speechless?

My eyes are filling with tears as I am trying to write these words. I know that I'd simply throw myself at His feet and say, "All I want is You." I imagine Jesus would reply, "I was hoping you'd say that. Now let Me show you what else I have in mind."

That's what happened to Andrew and John. They were enamored with Jesus' presence and began following Him from place to place. Finally, Jesus turned to the young men and asked, "What do you want?"

My goodness, they didn't know quite what to say. "Uh, where are you staying?"

"Come," Jesus replied, "and you will see."

The next day Jesus saw Phillip. "Follow me," Jesus told him. And he did.

Do you want to dream again? Follow Jesus. What does God have planned for your life? "Come and you will see." "For the eyes of the LORD range throughout the earth to strengthen those whose hearts are fully committed to him" (2 Chronicles 16:9).

Don't Give Up

Some of us have given up on our dreams because certain circumstances have seemingly placed them out of reach. Perhaps we've had an interruption. We have quit too soon and put a period where God put a comma. William James said, "Most people never run far enough on their first wind to find out they've got a second. Give your dreams all you've got and you'll be amazed at the energy that comes out of you."[14]

"I would like to write historical novels." Janet

Paul wrote, "I press on in order to take hold of that for which Christ Jesus took hold of me" (Philippians 3:12). William Barclay said this about Paul's fervor: "He was trying to grasp that for which he had been grasped by Christ. . . . Paul felt that when Christ stopped him on the Damascus Road, He had a vision and a purpose for Paul, and Paul felt that all his life he was bound to press on, lest he fail Jesus and frustrate His dream. . . . Every [person] is grasped by Christ for some purpose; and therefore every [person] should all his [or her] life press on so that he [or she] may grasp that purpose for which Christ grasped him."[15]

Some years ago, before I had my first book published, someone told me that the difference between a published author and an unpublished author is that the published author didn't give up on her dream. I've come to see much wisdom in that word of encouragement.

Paul encouraged the Philippians: "Brothers, I do not consider myself yet to have taken hold of it. But one thing I do: Forgetting what is behind and straining toward what is ahead, I press on toward the goal to win the prize for which God has called me heavenward in Christ Jesus"

(Philippians 3:13-14). The *New American Standard Bible* says, "reaching forward to what lies ahead." Paul compared his Christian life to a race, and in these verses he tells us to keep our eye on the goal. Press on! Don't give up!

Calvin Coolidge said, "Nothing in this world can take the place of persistence. Talent will not; nothing is more common than unsuccessful people with talent. Genius will not; unrewarded genius is almost a proverb. Education will not; the world is full of educated derelicts. Persistence and determination alone are omnipotent. The slogan 'press on' has solved and always will solve the problems of the human race."[16]

While this is a wonderful quote, I'd like to modify Mr. Coolidge's words of encouragement. God is the only One who is omnipotent, but persistence and determination while relying on His power are a holy combination that's hard to beat! Here are some fun facts to remember when we feel like quitting:

- After Fred Astaire's first screen test in 1933, the director noted, "Can't act! Slightly bald. Can dance a little."
- Louisa May Alcott, author of *Little Women,* was encouraged to find work as a servant or a seamstress.
- Beethoven's violin teacher once told him he was a "hopeless composer."
- Walt Disney was fired by a newspaper editor for lack of ideas.
- Thomas Edison's teacher said he was too stupid to learn anything.
- Albert Einstein didn't speak until he was four years old and didn't read until he was seven. His teachers described him as mentally slow.
- Isaac Newton did poorly in grade school.
- Henry Ford failed and went bankrupt five times before he finally succeeded.
- Babe Ruth, when he retired from baseball, set the home run record (714), but he also held the record for the most strikeouts (1,330).

- Winston Churchill failed sixth grade.[17]
- One basketball player missed 9,000 shots in his career. He lost more than 300 games. Twenty-six times he was trusted to take the game's winning shot and missed. His name is Michael Jordan. He said, "I've failed over and over again in my life. And that's why I succeed."[18]

There have been many days when I've wanted to quit working in ministry. Being a speaker carting three suitcases through an airport by myself, sleeping in strange beds, eating strange foods, missing my family, fighting spiritual battles for the souls of the ones I'm speaking to, traveling across the country alone, and spending endless hours at the computer alone grow old. Being in ministry is an honor, but it is not glamorous! Many days I wonder, *Is all this doing anyone any good?* That's when God reminds me of my piano story.

Once there was a little nine-year-old boy who wanted to give up. He desperately wanted to stop taking piano lessons. In hopes of encouraging her son to continue, his mother took him to hear the great concert pianist Ignacy Jan Paderewski. Before the concert began, the boy slipped away from his mother and made his way to the Steinway grand positioned on the stage under the spotlight.

He sat down on the piano bench, placed his chubby hands on the keys, and began to bang out the most annoying song known to humankind: "Chopsticks." The indignant crowd began to yell for someone to get the boy off the stage. Behind the curtain, Paderewski heard the commotion. He grabbed his coat, ran out on stage, and reached his arms around the boy to play a beautiful melody to enhance the boy's "Chopsticks." All the while, he whispered in the boy's ear, "Don't quit. Keep on playing. Don't stop. Don't quit."[19]

There are many days when my life seems just about as melodious as "Chopsticks." On those days, I imagine my heavenly Father placing His loving arms around me and playing a beautiful melody around my simple efforts. All the while, He whispers, "Don't quit. Don't stop. Never give up." It is the music of my dreams.

Once someone asked Michelangelo, "When is a painting finished?" He replied, "When it fulfills the intent of the artist."[20] When is our part of fulfilling God's dream complete? When He tells us it is time to move on and our work is done.

Jump In

I was sitting on the balcony of a condominium listening to the excited squeals and splashes as children played in the pool. One particular little girl caught my attention. She appeared to be about six years old and wore bright yellow water wings wrapped around her arms like blood pressure cuffs. As she stood on the side of the pool nervously flapping her arms, her daddy was poised in waist deep water with his arms outstretched.

"Come on, honey, you can do it," he coached. "Go ahead and jump. I'm right here."

"But I'm scared," she whined as she flapped her arms.

"Don't be afraid. I'm right here," he assured her.

This bantering went on for at least 15 minutes. I was amazed at the father's patience. Finally, she jumped! By the end of the morning, the little girl was making her way across the once seemingly treacherous waters.

God spoke to my heart through this scenario. Sometimes I'm that little girl standing on the side of the pool.

"Come on and jump in," my heavenly Father calls.

"But I'm scared," I cry.

"Don't be afraid, my child. I'm right here."

I've learned, like Peter, to jump in with both feet, but to never let go of His hand.

As women, we have dreams hidden in our hearts, and God, our heavenly Father, longs to fulfill them. "For no matter how many promises God has made, they are 'Yes' in Christ. And so through him the 'Amen' is spoken by us to the glory of God" (2 Corinthians 1:20). Jesus fulfills all our dreams when we will place our hand in His hand, our hopes in His keeping, and our dreams in His tender care.

Who needs a fairy godmother when our Father is a heavenly God. Who needs a yellow brick road when our final journey will take us down streets of gold. Who needs a knight in shining armor when we can walk hand-in hand with Jesus Christ, the Prince of Peace. Is God who fulfills our dreams a fairy tale? I think not. This, my friend, is a dream come true! "Things which eye has not seen and ear has not heard, and which have not entered the heart of man, all that God has prepared for those who love Him" (1 Corinthians 2:9, NASB).

Dreams I Dream for You

You taste the tears
You're lost in sorrow
You see your yesterdays
I see tomorrow
You see the darkness
I see the light
You know your failures
But I know your heart
The dreams I dream for you
Are deeper that the ones you're clinging to
More precious than the finest thing you knew
And truer than the treasures you pursue
Let the old dreams die
Like stars that fade from view
Then take the cup I offer

And drink deeply of
The dreams I dream for you
You see your shame
But I see your glory
You've read one page
I know the story
I hold a vision
That you'll become
As you grow into the truth
As you learn to walk in love
Let the old dreams die
Like stars that fade from view
Then take the cup I offer
And drink deeply of
The dreams I dream for you.[21]

$\mathscr{S}$tudy $\mathscr{Q}$uestions

Introduction

These questions are for those in a group setting who are having an introductory meeting before reading chapter one. If your group has already read the introduction and chapter one, you may skip them or answer them along with chapter one.

1. As a little girl, what did you dream about becoming when you grew up? What did you want to be or be doing one day?
2. What did those dreams look like in your imagination?
3. How have those dreams come true?
4. How have those dreams not come true?
5. What in your life would you like to be different than it is today?
6. What dreams do you have for your future?
7. If you could be assured of success, and money were no object, what would you like to accomplish in your life?

Chapter One

1. What is God's promise to you in 2 Corinthians 6:18?
2. Look up the following verses and note what you learn about the fatherhood of God.

   a. 1 Corinthians 8:6
   b. Ephesians 1:3-5
   c. Galatians 4:6-7
   d. James 1:17
3. Look up the following verses and note what you learn about the love of the Father.
   a. Ephesians 3:18-19
   b. Psalm 89:2
   c. Numbers 14:18
4. How do we know what God is like? (Hebrews 1:3, John 14:9)
5. Read the following and note what believers in Christ are called.
   a. John 12:1-2
   b. Philippians 2:15
   c. 2 Corinthians 6:18
6. Make a list of every characteristic of the perfect father. Now put a check by the ones you have experienced in God as His child.

Chapter Two

In chapter two, we learned that the bride-to-be had several months to prepare for her marriage while her groom was away building their home. Today, let's look at ways we can get ready for our groom's return.

1. Read Revelation 19:6-8. What has the bride done before the groom's arrival?
2. Read Matthew 25:1-13. What happened to the five virgins who were not prepared? Where were they when the groom arrived?
3. Let's look at some ways we can get ready for our groom! The next two exercises are fairly long. If you are doing this study in a group,

have half of the group look up one passage and the other half look up the other. Don't lose heart!

    a. Look up Ephesians 4:25–5:21 and list everything Paul tells us about purifying our character.

    b. Look up Colossians 3:1-17 and 4:1-6 and again, list everything Paul tells us about purifying our character.

Now, with those two lists, I think we've got plenty to work on until Jesus returns!

    4. In today's world, what does it mean to "wait for our groom"?

    5. One of the most important things we can do as we wait for our groom is to come to a deeper understanding of Jesus' love for us, His bride. Read Ephesians 3:14-21 and write out six points of Paul's prayer for each of us.

    6. What is the difference between a blind woman who has read all about and studied what a sunset looks like and a woman who has seen a sunset in all its glory? Think about that for a moment before you answer. How does that relate to Ephesians 3:14-21?

Chapter Three

Read 1 Samuel 1 and answer the following questions.

    1. Why was Hannah barren?

    2. What is Peninnah called in verse 6? What did she do and why?

    3. What signs of depression do you see in Hannah? What emotions are listed in chapter 1? Do you see a progression?

    4. Would you say Hannah's husband understood his wife's pain?

    5. Verse 16 says that Hannah was grieved. What do we usually associate with the word *grief*? Could this be the grieving of a lost dream?

    6. Where did Hannah take her grief?

    7. Describe the depth of her prayer.

8. How did her countenance change after Eli promised her a child?

9. What was the result of his prediction?

10. Hannah kept Samuel for three to four years and then gave him to God's service in the temple; she gave him back to the Lord. Suppose she had clung to her child and reneged on her promise. How would that have changed history?

11. What had Hannah learned about God during this trial in her life? (2:1-10)

12. Hannah had her dream fulfilled, but then gave that dream right back to God. Have you ever had a dream fulfilled and then realized that the ultimate fulfillment was a relationship with God Himself, and not what you originally longed for? Explain.

13. After Hannah gave her dream back to God, how did He continue to bless her? (2:18-21)

Chapter Four

1. According to Isaiah 43:7, why were we created?

2. Glory means to show one's self mighty. It is the way God makes Himself known or recognizable. With that in mind, what does Isaiah 43:7 mean to you?

3. What do the following verses tell you about God's glory?
   a. John 2:11
   b. Hebrews 1:3
   c. Isaiah 6:3
   d. Psalm 19:1

4. So far we've seen God's glory manifested in four ways. List them. Example: heavens

5. The glory of created things, including man, is what they are meant

by God to be, though not yet perfectly attained. Can man, apart from Christ, show God's glory? Why or why not? (Romans 3:23)

6. What happens when we accept Christ, according to Galatians 2:20 and 3:26?

7. What does 2 Corinthians 3:18 say about our continual transformation?

8. Read Exodus 34:28-35 and answer the following questions:

   a. Where had Moses been for 40 days and 40 nights?

   b. What effect did this extended time in God's presence have on his face?

   c. What happened over time after he left God's presence? (2 Corinthians 3:7)

   d. How can that scenario relate to our time spent in God's presence?

   e. How can we get the glow back? (James 4:8)

9. Read Job 23:10. List several characteristics of highly polished silver or gold.

10. What does God say about how trials polish us? What is His ultimate goal in our trials? (Isaiah 48:10, 2 Corinthians 4:16-18)

11. Describe a time when a specific trial brought you closer to God, removed "dross" from your life, and made you more spiritually beautiful in the end.

Chapter Five

1. How did Solomon describe God in Proverbs 18:24?

2. How did Jeremiah describe God in Jeremiah 3:4?

3. Read the following verses and note what you learn about the faithfulness of God.

   a. Deuteronomy 7:9

   b. 1 Thessalonians 5:24

    c. James 1:17

    d. Psalm 102:25-27

4. Faithfulness is a necessary quality of a friend. It means to be loyal to one's promises, trustworthy, firm, certain, true to what you say, predictable. How does God fit that description?

5. Suppose we are faithless. How does that affect God's faithfulness toward us, according to 2 Timothy 2:13?

6. As mentioned in chapter five, betrayal is the most common cause of broken friendships. Read Psalm 55:12-13.

    a. Who was coming against David?

    b. How did it make him feel?

    c. Have you ever felt the way David described feeling in this psalm?

7. If you have ever felt betrayed by a friend, Jesus knows how you feel. (Hebrews 4:14-16)

    a. What did the disciples do after Jesus' arrest?

    b. What did Peter do when a servant girl questioned if he was one of Jesus' disciples? (Matthew 26:69-72)

    c. Did Jesus continue to love Peter even though he had betrayed Him? (John 21:15)

    d. What does Jesus tell us about forgiving those who hurt us? (Luke 17:4, Matthew 18:21-22)

    e. Did the apostles think this was going to be difficult? What did they say to Jesus right after that command? (Luke 17:5) Amen to that!

    f. Is it enough just to say the words? (Matthew 18:35)

8. Read and record Jesus' promise to us found in Hebrews 13:5.

9. How did Jesus give us an example of being a friend in John 13:1-17? Note how that is emphasized in the following verses:

    a. 1 Peter 4:10

    b. Galatians 5:13

10. One of the best acts of friendship is to pray earnestly for someone. In closing, read Jesus' prayer for His disciples and for you, found in John 17:6-25.

Chapter Six

The first woman to interfere with God's dream was the first woman—Eve. That's a bit frightening to think about, isn't it? Let's look at Genesis 2 and 3 and see how she took control of her life and the devastating results that followed.

1. Read Genesis 2 for background and answer the following questions:
    a. What was the one restriction placed on Adam and Eve by God?
    b. How did Satan question God?
    c. How did Satan deny God?
    d. How did Satan question God's justice?
    e. What do you think appealed to Eve the most—the food or the ability to be like God and be in control?
    f. What was the result of her disobedience? (3:16)
    g. What has been the result of Adam and Eve's disobedience on all the generations that followed? (Romans 5:12)
    h. Give an example of how disobedience or sin can affect many generations.
2. Adam and Eve took control of their lives and thus shattered their perfect existence in the Garden of Eden. But as soon as Eve placed her lips on the forbidden fruit, God started the wheels in motion to restore fallen mankind. Read the following verses and note how He did that.
    a. Romans 3:23
    b. Romans 6:23
    c. Romans 5:8

   d. Romans 10:9

   e. John 3:16

   f. 2 Corinthians 5:21

   g. Romans 8:1

3. Satan is still on the prowl desiring to make us take our dreams and our lives into our own hands. Read Matthew 4:3-9 and note the following in contrast to Eve's response to temptation.

   a. How were the three temptations similar emotionally, physically, and spiritually?

   b. How did Jesus resist? What was His weapon?

   c. What does this passage say about when Satan would return to tempt Jesus again?

4. Satan works the same way today that he worked in the garden with Eve and in the desert with Jesus. Thinking about your own life, write out a scenario of how Satan might tempt you in a similar manner.

Chapter Seven

1. Today, let's look at two women in the Old Testament who forgot their dreams and see how God restored their dreams. Read 1 Kings 17 and answer the following questions:

   a. Who cared for Elijah during the drought?

   b. Why did God send Elijah to Zarephath?

   c. Note the similar words in 17:5 and 17:10. So he_____. So he _____.

   d. What was the widow doing when Elijah arrived?

   e. Would you say she was hopeful or hopeless?

   f. What was Elijah's promise to her and what was the outcome?

    g. Suppose she had not trusted God and cooked her last meal for herself and her son as she had planned. What do you think the outcome would have been?

    h. Did God need the widow's help to take care of Elijah?

    i. Why do you think God sent him to her?

    j. The widow was blessed because of her obedience. As a result, who else was blessed?

2. Sometimes, the best way to get beyond a seemingly desperate situation is to help someone else. Have you ever experienced that in your own life?

3. How does Luke 6:38 teach the principle of giving and receiving?

4. Now let's look at another prophet and another woman who was just about to forget her dream. Read 2 Kings 4:1-7 and answer the following questions:

    a. What were the widow's circumstances?

    b. What did Elisha ask her?

    c. How many jars did he tell her to collect and what did he tell her to do with the jars?

    d. How many jars do you think God would have filled?

    e. The woman told Elisha she had "nothing" except a little oil. How much does God need to restore a dream?

5. Interestingly, both of the women were widows. How does this support Deuteronomy 10:18 and Psalm 68:5?

Chapter Eight

1. In chapter seven, we looked at two women in the Old Testament who were financially challenged. Today, let's look at one who was financially blessed. Read 2 Kings 4:8-37 and answer the following:

    a. How did the Shunemite woman extend kindness to Elisha?

    b. What did she ask for in return?

    c. While she wanted nothing in return, Elisha wanted to bless her in some way. What did his astute servant, Gehazi, suggest?

    d. God sought to fulfill the Shunemite woman's dream that she dared not even conceive. Has God ever blessed you in an area where you did not have the courage to even ask?

    e. Like the widow in 1 Kings 17, this woman's dream child also died. What was her reaction to this shattered dream? (4:23-26)

    f. Compare her response to the widow's in 1 Kings 17.

    g. Who was the first person she actually told what had happened?

    h. When you are having a difficult time, to whom do you go first? What can we learn from this gracious woman?

    i. How was her dream restored?

2. Where does Jesus say to take our burdens and troubles? (Matthew 11:28-30)

3. You've read about Sarah who interfered with God's dream. Contrast her actions and reactions to Mary, the mother of Jesus. What was her response to Gabriel's news that she was going to have a child while still a virgin? (Luke 1:38)

Chapter Nine

Sometimes it is easy to feel God has forgotten us when our dreams are shattered. But the Bible assures us that God sees, God hears, and God understands.

1. Read the following verses and note what you learn about our God who sees.

    a. Proverbs 15:3

    b. Psalm 11:4

   c. Proverbs 34:15

2. Hagar was a woman who felt that God had forgotten her. But the angel of the Lord appeared to Hagar and assured her He had not. What did Hagar say about God, and what name did she give Him? (Genesis 16:13)

3. Read the following verses and note what you learn about our God who hears.

   a. Exodus 2:24

   b. Genesis 21:17

   c. Exodus 16:6-9

4. Read the following verses and note what you learn about our God who cares.

   a. Hosea 11:8

   b. Isaiah 63:9

   c. 2 Kings 13:23

   d. Nehemiah 9:27

5. Like Father, like Son. Read the following and note how Jesus had compassion on those with shattered dreams.

   a. Matthew 14:14

   b. Matthew 20:34

   c. Mark 1:41

   d. Luke 7:12-13

6. Let's take one final look at a man with a shattered dream and what He learned about God. Read Psalm 73:21-26 and answer the following questions:

   a. How did Asaph describe himself during this difficult time?

   b. What characteristics of God did Asaph cling to?

   c. What was Asaph's praise to God?

   d. If you are dealing with a shattered or unfulfilled dream today, consider writing a psalm to the Lord.

Chapter Ten

1. Job was a man who lost just about everything except a nagging wife and a few critical friends. Read Job 42 and answer the following questions:
   a. At the end of his struggle, what had he learned about God? (42:1-5)
   b. How did God restore Job's dreams? (42:10-17)
   c. Did Job praise God before or after He restored his dreams?
   d. What lesson can we learn from Job?
2. What are the promises found in Psalm 34:15-19?
3. Read the following and note how God restored each person's dream.
   a. Hagar (Genesis 21:18)
   b. Joseph (Genesis 41:39)
   c. Naomi (Ruth 4:13-15)
   d. Bathsheba (2 Samuel 12:15-25)
4. Let's turn our attention to the New Testament and see how Jesus restored several women's dreams. Also note whether or not each woman's faith was mentioned.
   a. Matthew 9:20-22
   b. Matthew 15:21-28
   c. Luke 7:11-16
   d. Luke 13:10-13
   e. John 8:1-11

It is always important that we do not put God in a box. He does what He pleases. As you see here, some of the women had great faith. On the other hand, the woman with the dead son didn't ask for Jesus' help, probably didn't even know He was there, and there was no mention of her faith. Sometimes He blesses us in ways we would never even think to ask!

5. As you are thinking about your shattered or unfulfilled dreams, consider Jeremiah 32:17!

Chapter Eleven

As we turn our attention to interrupted dreams, let's look at Miriam, Moses' older sister.

1. How did God use Miriam as part of His dream to free the Israelites from slavery? (Exodus 2:1-10)
2. Read Numbers 12:1-15 and answer the following:
   a. What did Miriam and Aaron begin to do?
   b. How did they attempt to exalt themselves?
   c. What did God say to Miriam and Aaron?
   d. What was Miriam's punishment?
   e. Who prayed for Miriam to be healed?
   f. What did the Israelites do while she was in "time out"?
   g. Sometimes, when God has to interrupt our dreams to teach us a lesson or bring us to repentance, others suffer as well. When Moses was 40 years old and took control of God's plan, the entire Israelite nation had to wait 40 more years for deliverance. Can you think of a time in your own life when you were experiencing an "interrupted dream" and others were affected?
3. What do the following verses teach us about pride and humility?
   a. 2 Chronicles 7:14
   b. Proverbs 11:2
   c. Proverbs 16:18
4. Daniel 4 is a dramatic story of a shattered dream, an interrupted dream, and a restored dream. Read 4:28-37 and describe each of the three. (For a clearer picture, begin at verse 1.)

5. Read and record James 4:10. Has God shown you an area where you are prideful? Name some specific ways you can be humble this week.

Chapter Twelve

Nehemiah was a man who dreamed a God-sized dream. Today, let's look at how the fulfillment of that dream follows the DREAMS model in chapter 12. We'll be reading in the book of Nehemiah.

1. What news did Nehemiah receive about his homeland? (1:1-3)
2. I'd like for us to read straight through the progression of the dream come true. But first, turn to 2:5 and record Nehemiah's God-sized dream.
3. Now let's look at how Nehemiah remembered who God is. Read 1:4-11.
   a. List his words of remembrance.
   b. What evidence in Nehemiah's prayer do we have that he had examined the Scripture?
4. What did he ask of God? (1:11)
5. What did he ask of the king? (2:5–8) How does this show that Nehemiah was a man who prayed and also a man who prepared? What a winning combination!
6. To what did Nehemiah attribute his success? (2:8)
7. Next, Nehemiah moved into action. How did he motivate others to move with him? (2:17-18)
8. The walls had been broken down for approximately 150 years. How long did it take this man who prayed and prepared to fulfill his God-sized dream? (7:15)
9. All the while, Nehemiah stayed connected to the Vine. Read and note how he did that. (4:9, 8:1-3, and 9:5)

10. What did the enemies surmise after the completion of Nehemiah's God-sized dream? (6:16)

11. Wow! What is our ultimate goal in the completion of any God-sized dream?

Chapter Thirteen

1. As you begin to dream God-sized dreams for your life, remember the resources that are at the fingertips of your hands folded prayer.
   a. Ephesians 1:18-21
   b. Ephesians 3:14-21
   c. Philippians 4:19

2. While you may not feel qualified to do what God has called you to do, remember, He doesn't need much and yet He wants it all.
   a. What did Jesus use to feed the 5,000? (Mark 6:30-44)
   b. What did Jesus use to make wine? (John 2:7)
   c. What did God use to bless the widow in 2 Kings 4:2?
   d. How much education did the disciples who changed the world possess? (Acts 4:13)

3. Acts 4:13 is key. Write out the last part of that verse: "and they took note _____ ."

4. What did Jesus say about reaching His goal? (Luke 13:32) From memory, recall as many people as you can who tried to stop Him.

5. What do the following verses say about God's plans?
   a. Isaiah 41:2-7
   b. Isaiah 46:11
   c. Isaiah 14:24

6. God has given us many gifts (1 Corinthians 12), much power (Acts 1:8), and magnificent treasures of wisdom and knowledge (Colossians 2:3). Let's turn our attention to Jesus' parable of the

landowner who gave talents to his servants, and think about what we will do with all God has entrusted to us. Read Matthew 25:14-30 and answer the following questions:

    a. Why was the landowner pleased with the servants to whom he gave five and two talents?

    b. Why was he angry with the servant to whom he gave one talent?

    c. Why did the servant with one talent hide his instead of invest it?

    d. Have you ever considered your past life experiences and spiritual gifts as "talents" that God wants you to invest in the lives of others? How could you invest what God has entrusted to you?

    e. Read 2 Corinthians 1:3-5 and record the verse in your own words.

I wish I were there with you, so I'm going to take this opportunity to share my answer to this question. God doesn't comfort us to make us comfortable. He comforts us to make us able to comfort others. That's investing in other people, which will bring great dividends!

7. Let's step into the future for a moment. Suppose you were going to write your own eulogy. What would you like it to say? In writing it, answer these five questions:

    a. Who were you?

    b. What did you accomplish on earth?

    c. What did you leave behind?

    d. Whose life did you impact?

    e. What lasting impact will your life have on generations yet to come?

8. In closing, go back to the introductory lesson and review your answers. How have you learned that God is the Fulfiller of all your dreams?

Notes

Introduction

1. "I Dreamed a Dream" from the musical *Les Miserables* by Alain Boublil and Claude-Michel Schonberg, music by Claude-Michel Schonberg, lyrics by Alain Boublil, Herbert Kretzmer, and Jean-Marc Natel. Used by permission.
2. Beth Moore, *Breaking Free: Making Liberty in Christ a Reality in Life* (Nashville, Tenn.: Lifeway, 1999), 194.

Chapter One

1. Thank you, Gayle Montgomery, for sharing this story.
2. Bob Carlisle, *Butterfly Kisses: Tender Thoughts Shared Between Fathers and Daughters* (Nashville, Tenn.: Countryman Books, 1997), iii.
3. David Blankenhorn, *Fatherless America: Confronting Our Most Urgent Social Problem* (New York: Harper Collins Books, 1995), 1.
4. Bridget Maher, editor, *The Family Portrait: A Compilation of Data, Research and Public Opinion of the Family* (Washington, D. C.: Family Research Council, 2002), 113.
5. Edwards, Tamala M., "Flying Solo," *Time,* August 28, 2000, 37-43.

6. J. I. Packer, *Knowing God* (Downers Grove, Ill.: InterVarsity Press, 1973), 183.

7. Ibid., 182.

8. John MacArthur, *The MacArthur New Testament Commentary: Romans 1–8* (Chicago: Moody Press, 1991), 436-7.

9. Packer, *Knowing God,* 195.

10. Mary A. Kassian, *In My Father's House: Women Relating to God as Father* (Nashville, Tenn.: Lifeway, 1993), 13.

11. Packer, *Knowing God,* 187-8.

12. Anabel Gillham, *The Confident Woman: Knowing Who You Are in Christ* (Eugene, Ore.: Harvest House Publishers, 1993), 27.

13. Ibid., 29.

14. W. E. Vine, Merrill F. Unger, William White, Jr., *Vine's Complete Expository Dictionary of Old and New Testament Words* (Nashville, Tenn.: Thomas Nelson Publishers, 1985), 379-80.

15. Beth Moore, *Breaking Free: Making Liberty in Christ a Reality in Life* (Nashville, Tenn.: Lifeway, 1999), 160.

16. Jack Cranfield, Mark Victor Hansen, Jennifer Hawthorne, and Marci Shimoff, comps., *Chicken Soup for the Woman's Soul* (Deerfield Beach, Fla.: Health Communications, 1996), 163.

17. Vine, Unger, White, Jr., *Vine's Dictionary,* 143.

Chapter Two

1. Brent Curtis and John Eldredge, *The Sacred Romance: Drawing Closer to the Heart of God* (Nashville, Tenn.: Thomas Nelson Publishers, 1997), 109.

2. Lyrics by Judie Lawson. Copyright © 1995, Pyewacket Frog (ASCAP). Used by permission.

Chapter Three

1. "Trust His Heart," Eddie Carswell/Babbie Mason, Causing Change Music (Admin. by Dayspring Music, Inc.), Dayspring Music, Inc., May Sun Music (Admin. by Word Music, Inc.), Word Music, Inc. All rights reserved. Used by Permission.
2. U. S. Department of Health and Human Services, Centers for Disease Control and Prevention, National Center for Health Statistics, Division of Data Services, Hyattsville, MD 20782 (301) 458-4636.
3. www.ukbabyonline.co.uk
4. Brothers, Joyce. "When a Dream Doesn't Come True," *Parade,* March 24, 2002.
5. Pamela Reeve, *Parables of the Forest* (Sisters, Ore.: Multnomah, 1989).
6. Ken Gire, *The Reflective Life* (Colorado Springs, Colo.: Chariot Victor Publishing, 1998), 137-8.
7. Emily Pearl Kingley, from an October 1992 "Dear Abby" column ("Letting Go of Disappointments").

Chapter Four

1. Sharon Jaynes, *Ultimate Makeover: Becoming Spiritually Beautiful in Christ* (Chicago, Ill.: Moody Press, 2003), 11-12.
2. John Eldredge, *Wild at Heart* (Nashville, Tenn.: Thomas Nelson Publishers, 2001), 16-7.
3. Pulfer, Laura. "What Really Sent Barbie to the Body Shop," *The Cincinnati Enquirer*, November 23, 1997.
4. Robert J. Morgan, *Nelson's Complete Book of Stories, Illustrations and Quotes* (Nashville, Tenn.: Thomas Nelson Publishers, 2000), 52.

5. Plastic Surgery Information Service, www.plasticsurgery.org/mediactr2000release.htm

6. Nancy Leigh DeMoss, *Biblical Womanhood in the Home* (Wheaton, Ill.: Crossway Books, 2002), 33.

7. Avins, Mimi. *The Press Democrat,* Santa Rosa, Calif., July 3, 2001, D1.

8. Maragolis, Mac, and others. "Reshaping the World," *Newsweek International* (Atlantic Edition), August 16, 1999, 38.

9. Carla Muir, "Beauty Contest." Used by permission.

10. Nancy Stafford, *Beauty by the Book* (Sisters, Ore.: Multnomah Publishers, 2002), 118.

11. Jaynes, *Ultimate Makeover,* 23-4.

12. Thomas Watson, *Gleanings from Thomas Watson* (Morgan, Penn.: Soli Deo Gloria Publications, 1995), 49.

13. Stafford, *Beauty by the Book*, 31.

14. Willard Harley, *His Needs, Her Needs* (Grand Rapids, Mich.: Flemming H. Revell, 1986), p. 100.

15. Jan Meyers, *The Allure of Hope* (Colorado Springs, Colo.: NavPress, 2001), 64.

16. Written by Harry Reeder. Used by permission.

Chapter Five

1. L. M. Montgomery, *Anne of Green Gables* (Pleasantville, N.Y.: The Reader's Digest Association, Inc., 1992), 48-50.

2. Lever, Janet. "Sex Differences in the Games Children Play," *Social Problems,* 23, 1976, 478-87.

3. Engel, Elliot. "Of Male Bondage," *Newsweek*, June 21, 1982, 13.

4. Andrews, Lori. "How Women Think" *Parents,* April 1986, 74.

5. Kruger, Pam. "Can You Be Too Close to a Friend?" *Good House-keeping,* September 1997, 76.

6. Ibid.

7. Taylor, S. E. and others. "Female Responses to Stress: Tend-and-Befriend, Not Fight-or-Flight," *Psychological Review 2000*, 107 (3), 411-29.

8. Dee Brestin, *The Friendships of Women* (Wheaton, Ill.: Victor Books, 1988), 37.

9. Beth Moore, *Jesus the One and Only* (Nashville: Lifeway Press, 2000), 137.

10. Parlee, Mary Brown. "The Friendship Bond," *Psychology Today*, October 1979, 43.

11. Montgomery, *Anne of Green Gables*, 73.

Chapter Six

1. Kathy Collard Miller, *Women of the Bible* (Lancaster, Penn.: Starburst Publishers, 1999), 37.

2. Billy Graham, *How to Be Born Again* (Waco, Texas: Word, 1977), 129-30.

Chapter Seven

1. Jill Briscoe, as quoted by Kathy Collard Miller, *Women of the Bible* (Lancaster, Penn.: Starburst Publishers, 1999), 195.

2. Bruce Wilkinson, *Secrets of the Vine* (Sisters, Ore.: Multnomah Publishers, 2002), 33.

3. Ibid., 73.

4. Ibid., 74-5.

5. Kathy Collard Miller, *Women of the Bible* (Lancaster, Penn.: Starburst Publishers, 1999), 149.

Chapter Eight

1. William M. Taylor, "Ruth the Gleaner" and "Esther the Queen," *Bible Biographies,* as quoted in *Women of the Bible* by Kathy Collard Miller and Larry Richards, eds. (Lancaster, Penn.: Starburst Publishing, 1999), 137.
2. Judith Couchman, *Esther—Becoming a Woman God Can Use* (Grand Rapids, Mich.: Zondervan Publishing House, 1999), 43.
3. Gustav Niebuhr and Laurie Goldstein, "Who Will Take Graham's Place on the World Stage?" *The Charlotte Observer,* January 2, 1999, 15A.
4. Robert J. Morgan, *Nelson's Complete Book of Stories, Illustrations, and Quotes* (Nashville, Tenn.: Thomas Nelson, 2000), 151.

Chapter Nine

1. Neil Anderson, *The Bondage Breaker* (Eugene, Ore.: Harvest House, 1990), 23.
2. Larry Crabb, *Shattered Dreams* (Colorado Springs, Colo.: WaterBrook Press, 2001), 35.
3. Florence Littaeur, *Dare to Dream* (Dallas: Word Publishing, 1991), 260.
4. As quoted by Anabel Gillham in *The Confident Woman* (Eugene, Ore.: Harvest House Publishers, 1993), 131.

Chapter Ten

1. Oswald Chambers, *My Utmost for His Highest* (Grand Rapids, Mich.: Discovery House, 1992), August 5.
2. Kenneth L. Barker and John R. Kohlenberger, *Zondervan NIV Bible Commentary* (Grand Rapids, Mich.: Zondervan Publishing House, 1994), 93.

3. Beth Moore, *Breaking Free: Making Liberty in Christ a Reality in Life* (Nashville, Tenn.: Lifeway, 1999), 132.

Chapter Eleven

1. Anabel Gillham, *The Confident Woman* (Eugene, Ore.: Harvest House Publishers, 1993), 117.
2. Spiros Zodhiates and others, eds., *The Complete Word Study Dictionary: New Testament* (Chattanooga, Tenn.: AMG Publishers, 1992), 229.
3. Beth Moore, *Breaking Free: Making Liberty in Christ a Reality in Life* (Nashville, Tenn.: Lifeway, 1999), 120.

Chapter Twelve

1. Henry T. Blackaby and Richard Blackaby, *Experiencing God Day by Day* (Nashville, Tenn.: Broadman and Holman Publishers, 1997), 3.
2. Ibid., 344.
3. Bruce Wilkinson, *The Prayer of Jabez* (Sisters, Ore.: Multnomah Publishers, 2000), 24.
4. Bruce Wilkinson, *Secrets of the Vine* (Sisters, Ore.: Multnomah Publishers, 2002), 115.
5. Blackaby, *Experiencing God Day by Day,* 109.

Chapter Thirteen

1. Antoine de Saint-Exupery, trans. Katherine Woods, *The Little Prince* (San Diego: Harcourt Brace Jovanovich, 1993), 87.
2. Jan Meyers, *The Allure of Hope* (Colorado Springs, Colo.: NavPress, 2001), 84.

3. C. S. Lewis, *The Weight of Glory and Other Addresses* (New York: Touchstone, 1975), 27.
4. www.livinglifefully.com/character.html
5. Wilkinson, *The Prayer of Jabez Devotional,* 23.
6. Andy Stanley, as quoted by Bruce Wilkinson in *The Prayer of Jabez Devotional* (Sisters, Ore.: Multnomah Publishers, 2001), 36.
7. Henry Blackaby, *Experiencing God Day by Day* (Nashville, Tenn.: Broadman and Holman Publishers, 1997), 344.
8. Quoted by Florence Littauer in *Dare to Dream* (Dallas: Word Publishing, 1991), 261.
9. Ibid., 70.
10. Ibid., 111.
11. Ibid., 242.
12. Wilkinson, *The Prayer of Jabez Devotional,* 83.
13. Linda Webber, *Mom, You're Incredible* (Colorado Springs, Colo.: Focus on the Family, 1994), 101.
14. Wilkinson, *The Prayer of Jabez Devotional,* 39.
15. William Barclay, *The Letter to the Philippians, Colossians, and Thessalonians,* rev. ed. (Philadelphia: The Westminster Press, 1975), 66.
16. Rob Gilbert, ed., *Bits and Pieces,* Vol. N/4, 1, Fairfield, Conn.: Economic Press.
17. Jack Canfield and Mark Hansen, eds., *Chicken Soup for the Soul* (Deerfield Beach, Fla.: Health Communications, 1993), 228-30.
18. www.brainyquote.com
19. Alice Gray, ed., *Stories from the Heart* (Sisters, Ore.: Multnomah Publishers, 1996), 41.
20. Nell W. Mohney, *From Eve to Esther* (Nashville, Tenn.: Dimensions for Living, 2001), 43.
21. © Andi Beat Goes on Music/River Oaks Music Company/Sparrow Song. Writers Charlie Peacock/Douglas Kaine McKelvey. All rights reserved. Used by permission.

FOCUS ON THE FAMILY®

Welcome to the *Family!*

Whether you received this book as a gift, borrowed it, or purchased it yourself, we're glad you read it. It's just one of the many helpful, insightful, and encouraging resources produced by Focus on the Family.

In fact, that's what Focus on the Family is all about—providing inspiration, information, and biblically based advice to people in all stages of life.

It began in 1977 with the vision of one man, Dr. James Dobson, a licensed psychologist and author of 18 best-selling books on marriage, parenting, and family. Alarmed by the societal, political, and economic pressures that were threatening the existence of the American family, Dr. Dobson founded Focus on the Family with one employee and a once-a-week radio broadcast aired on only 36 stations.

Now an international organization, the ministry is dedicated to preserving Judeo-Christian values and strengthening and encouraging families through the life-changing message of Jesus Christ. Focus ministries reach families worldwide through 10 separate radio broadcasts, two television news features, 13 publications, 18 Web sites, and a steady series of books and award-winning films and videos for people of all ages and interests.

• • •

For more information about the ministry, or if we can be of help to your family, simply write to Focus on the Family, Colorado Springs, CO 80995 or call (800) A-FAMILY (232-6459). Friends in Canada may write Focus on the Family, P.O. Box 9800, Stn. Terminal, Vancouver, B.C .V6B 4G3 or call (800) 661-9800. Visit our Web site—www.family.org—to learn more about Focus on the Family or to find out if there is an associate office in your country.

We'd love to hear from you!

Transformation Tools

from Focus on the Family

Live The Only Life That Counts

You can be the busiest person at your church, office or home—and still miss the deep fulfillment God desires you to have. In **Passion on Purpose**, psychologist Deborah Newman beckons women to readjust their priorities by identifying their God-given passions. As you begin walking out what God has called you to do—rather than what you feel you should do—you'll experience the exhilaration of being exactly who you were created to be.

Is Your Heart "Off-Limits"?

Deep within many women lies a "secret place" of hidden thoughts, painful experiences and emotions most feel are better left untouched. But God has other plans. **Who Holds the Key to Your Heart** is a freeing journey into a woman's soul. As you identify your pain, you'll find hope and healing through Scripture, testimonials, study questions and more.

Gaze at What God Sees

Poor body image. It's the stumbling block of so many women, Christians included, who feel they never quite measure up to the world's standard of beauty. Dr. Deborah Newman's **Loving Your Body** sweeps away beauty myths to reveal the rock-solid truth about appearances. Start seeing yourself and your body the way God does!

• • •

Look for these special books in your Christian bookstore or request a copy by calling (800) A-FAMILY (232-6459). Friends in Canada may write Focus on the Family, PO Box 9800, Stn Terminal, Vancouver, BC V6B 4G3 or call (800) 661-9800.

Visit our Web site (www.family.org) to learn more about the ministry or find out if there is a Focus on the Family office in your country.